Between Empire
and Alliance

Between Empire and Alliance

America and Europe during the Cold War

Edited by
Marc Trachtenberg

ROWMAN & LITTLEFIELD PUBLISHERS, INC.
Lanham • Boulder • New York • Oxford

ROWMAN & LITTLEFIELD PUBLISHERS, INC.

Published in the United States of America
by Rowman & Littlefield Publishers, Inc.
A Member of the Rowman & Littlefield Publishing Group
4501 Forbes Blvd., Suite 200, Lanham, Maryland 20706
www.rowmanlittlefield.com

PO Box 317
Oxford
OX2 9RU, UK

The introduction as well as chapters 1, 2, 5, 6, and 7 were previously published in
Liaison Committee of Historians (eds.), *Journal of European Integration History,*
volume 6, number 2 (2000). Verlagsgesellschaft NOMOS, Baden-Baden, 2000.

British Library Cataloguing in Publication Information Available

Library of Congress Cataloging-in-Publication Data

Between empire and alliance : America and Europe during the cold war /
edited by Marc Trachtenberg.
    p. cm.
Includes bibliographical references and index.
    ISBN 0-7425-2176-1 (cloth : alk. paper)—ISBN 0-7425-2177-X (pbk. :
alk. paper)
    1. Cold War. 2. United States—Foreign relations—Soviet Union. 3.
Soviet Union—Foreign relations—United States. 4. World
politics—1945– 5. North Atlantic Treaty Organization—History. 6.
Europe—Politics and government—1945– I. Trachtenberg, Marc, 1946–
    D843 .B4865 2003
    909.82'5—dc21   2002013054

Printed in the United States of America

⊗™ The paper used in this publication meets the minimum requirements of
American National Standard for Information Sciences—Permanence of Paper
for Printed Library Materials, ANSI/NISO Z39.48-1992.

Contents

Introduction

Marc Trachtenberg

This is a book about U.S.–European relations during the most intense phase of the Cold War, the quarter-century from about 1950 to 1974. For the Europeans at that time, their relationship with America was of fundamental importance. The "America factor" played a far-reaching role in shaping their policies, and indeed in shaping their relations with each other. The United States was the protector of Western Europe; the freedom of Europe, it was generally believed, depended on American military power. But a relationship of dependence was always a source of unease. How could Europe depend so heavily on a non-European power, no matter how well intentioned, for the defense of its most vital interests? Wouldn't it make sense for the European countries to come together as a political unit—for Europe to organize itself and become stronger, so that Europe would not be so dependent on America? This problem was of absolutely central importance. The "America factor" was thus bound to play a major role in European history in that period, and in particular in the history of European integration.

But the actual role it played depended on the specific policies the U.S. government pursued. Those policies, it turns out, had a profound effect on what was going on within Europe. The articles in this book were all written independently of each other. There was no overall agenda that laid out the themes the various authors were to develop. It is therefore striking that most of the contributors here stress the way dissatisfaction with America affected—one is tempted to say, lay at the heart of—the European integration process. Paul Pitman, for example, stresses the way dissatisfaction with the United States had been building up in many areas—political, economic and strategic—in the mid-1950s; he argues that those feelings played a key role in the process that led to the Treaties of Rome. Wolfram Kaiser notes the ambivalence of the

European Christian Democrats toward America—their sense that although their interests overlapped, Europe and America were culturally distinct, and that Europe therefore had to pursue a policy of her own in world affairs, a policy that was rooted in her own distinctive values. Hubert Zimmermann and Georges-Henri Soutou both emphasize the impact of America's rather cavalier monetary policy during the Nixon period on the European integration process at that time. And the article Christopher Gehrz and I wrote discussed the way in which a bare-knuckled American policy in late 1950 led the French and the Germans to see that they had major interests in common, interests somewhat distinct from those of the United States; what this episode suggested was that by coming together, the Europeans might be able to provide something of a counterweight to American power within the Western alliance.

All of this is important because the basic argument here is at variance with a common view of the U.S.–European relationship during the Cold War period, and in particular with a common interpretation of the origins of European integration. This is the idea that the American security guarantee and the Cold War political system in general largely depoliticized relations among the major West European states: they no longer had to worry about providing for their own security and thus no longer had to worry about relative power in their dealings with each other, and that meant that they could now cooperate with each other much more easily in the economic sphere and in other areas. They could, in other words, get on with the business of European integration because the political stakes were no longer very high.[1] But the thrust of the argument in many of the articles here is that for the Europeans the political stakes *were* very high. The goal of building Europe was *not* rooted in an acceptance of the fact that the European states could no longer play a major political role and that they should therefore focus on economic cooperation. It was rooted instead in the sense that building Europe was a way for the Europeans to reclaim their political autonomy.

But as fundamental as that goal was, the alliance with America was also very important, so throughout this period, the Europeans needed to balance between those two aims: reaching for greater autonomy and maintaining the tie with the United States. How that balance was struck depended on circumstance, so as circumstances shifted, the U.S.–European relationship had to adjust to those changes. The relationship itself, that is, changed over time, and the story of how it developed is more complex and richly textured than one might suppose.

The basic structure of U.S.–European relations, in other words, was by no means set in concrete in the late 1940s. The important developments that

---

[1]See especially Kenneth Waltz, *Theory of International Politics* (New York: McGraw-Hill, 1979), pp. 70–71, and Josef Joffe, "Europe's American Pacifier," *Foreign Policy*, no. 54 (1984), pp. 67–68.

took place in the 1950s, the 1960s and early 1970s had a certain logic to them, a logic, as Leopoldo Nuti stresses in his article here, that can only be understood by looking at both the domestic and the foreign policy sides of the story and analyzing their connections with each other. And there *was* a real story here; things could have gone in all kinds of different directions. What emerges from this series of articles is a sense that even what we assume to be fundamental policies were not sacrosanct—that attitudes could shift dramatically, that far-reaching shifts in policy could rarely be ruled out. As Francis Gavin and Erin Mahan show, for example, the Kennedy administration was by no means committed to the Bretton Woods monetary regime as a fundamental element of a U.S.-dominated system, but was instead inclined to view Bretton Woods as a kind of albatross; it was far more open to fundamental change in this key area than people have generally recognized. They also show how, during the Kennedy period, the French government (or at least the French minister of finance) was not out to destroy this dollar-based monetary system, the supposed symbol of American hegemony, but was instead quite interested in shoring up the system and pursuing a policy of monetary cooperation with the United States. And Soutou, in an article drawing on some new and quite extraordinary French and American archival sources, shows how different both the Pompidou and the Nixon–Kissinger policies were from the policies that had preceded them. Perhaps the most remarkable finding here was how far things had moved during the Pompidou–Nixon period in the area of nuclear weapons cooperation—a very important development that reflected fundamental shifts in basic political thinking in both countries.

One might think, given the many books and articles that have been published on U.S.–European relations during the Cold War period, that not much remains to be said on the subject. But taken as a whole, what these articles show is how misleading that sort of assumption can be. Archival research, even on the early Cold War, can still yield important new insights; and work on the later period, especially the early 1970s, can profoundly reshape our understanding of what was going on. And with the opening in recent years of important new archival sources on both sides of the Atlantic, one can safely predict that we will be learning a good deal more about the subject in the near future.

Most of the contributions here were originally published in the *Journal of European Integration History*, vol. 6, number 2 (2000); some of them are republished here in slightly revised form. I would like to thank the *Journal* and its editors and publisher for allowing us to republish those articles here, and I am particularly indebted to Professor Charles Barthel for all the help he has given us with this project.

1

America, Europe, and German Rearmament, August–September 1950: A Critique of a Myth

Marc Trachtenberg and Christopher Gehrz

In September 1950, U.S. Secretary of State Dean Acheson met in New York with the British foreign secretary, Ernest Bevin, and the French foreign minister, Robert Schuman. Acheson had an important announcement to make. The United States, he declared, was prepared to "take a step never before taken in history." The American government was willing to send "substantial forces" to Europe. The American combat force would be part of a collective force with a unified command structure, a force that ultimately would be capable of defending Western Europe on the ground. But the Americans were willing to take that step only if the European allies, for their part, were prepared to do what was necessary to "make this defense of Europe a success." And his government, he said, had come to the conclusion that the whole effort could not succeed without a German military contribution. So if the NATO allies wanted the American troops, they would have to accept the idea of German rearmament—and they would have to accept it right away. The U.S. government, he insisted, needed to "have an answer now on the possible use of German forces" in the defense of Western Europe.[1]

The position Acheson took at the New York conference was of quite extraordinary historical importance. The American government was finally committing itself to building an effective defense of Western Europe and to playing a central role in the military system that was to be set up. But the Americans were also trying to lay down the law to their European allies: the U.S. government wanted to force them to go along with a policy that made them very uneasy.

It was not, of course, that the Europeans disliked the whole package Acheson was now proposing. They knew that an effective defense of Western Europe would have to be based on American power, and therefore welcomed

1

much of the American plan. The offer of a major American troop presence in Europe, the proposal to set up a strong NATO military system, the suggestion that an American general would be sent over as NATO commander—all of this was, in itself, music to their ears. The problem lay with the final part of Acheson's proposal, the part relating to German rearmament, and even here the issue had more to do with timing than with ultimate objectives.

The allied governments were not against the very idea of German rearmament. Of all the NATO allies, the French were the most reluctant at this point to accede to Acheson's demands. But Schuman was not dead set against German rearmament as a matter of principle.[2] He in fact now admitted that it was "illogical for us to defend Western Europe, including Germany, without contributions from Germany."[3] The French government, he told Acheson, was "not irrevocably opposed to German participation" in the NATO army. Indeed, he thought it was likely that "some day" Germany would join the Western defense force.[4]

The problem from Schuman's point of view was that Acheson wanted to move too quickly. The Americans were insisting on immediate and open acceptance of the principle of German rearmament. But Schuman could go along with the U.S. plan, he said, only if this were kept secret. It was politically impossible for him to accept the plan publicly at that point.[5] Only a minority in France, he pointed out, appreciated "the importance of Germany in Western defense."[6] The French public could probably be brought along and would ultimately accept the idea of a German defense contribution, but only if the West moved ahead more cautiously—only if a strong European defense system had been built up first.

Domestic politics was not the only reason why Schuman took this line. The East-West military balance was perhaps an even more fundamental factor. In late 1950 the Western powers were just beginning to rearm. In military terms, they felt they could scarcely hold their own in a war with Russia. General Omar Bradley, chairman of the U.S. Joint Chiefs of Staff (JCS), for example, thought in November 1950 that if war broke out, the United States might well lose. The Soviets, on the other hand, seemed to be getting ready for a war: the sense was that they were poised on the brink and might be tempted to strike before the West built up its power. In such circumstances, people like Schuman asked if it was wise to move ahead with the rearmament of Germany, something the Russians were bound to find highly provocative. Rather than risk war now, at a time of Western weakness, didn't it make sense to put off the decision until after the West had rearmed itself and would thus be better able to withstand the shock?[7]

These were perfectly reasonable arguments, and were in fact supported by the U.S. government's own assessments of the risk of war with Russia at the time. The U.S. high commissioner in Germany, John McCloy, thought, for example, in June 1950 that "the rearmament of Germany would undoubtedly speed up any Soviet schedule for any possible future action in Germany and would, no doubt, be regarded by [the Soviets] as sufficiently provocative to warrant extreme countermeasures."[8] In December, the CIA concluded that the USSR would "seriously consider going to war whenever it becomes convinced that progress toward complete Western German rearmament," along with the rearmament of NATO as a whole, had reached the point where it could not be "arrested by other methods."[9] It was, of course, possible that the Soviets might choose to live with a rearmed Germany, especially if there continued to be major limits on German power, but certain groups within the U.S. government—army intelligence, for example—believed that if the West moved ahead in this area, it was more likely "that the Soviets would decide on resort to military action rather than make the required adjustment."[10]

So if even American officials were worried about what a decision to rearm Germany might lead to, it is not hard to understand why the Europeans, and especially the French, were so disturbed by the U.S. proposal. The NATO allies would have to accept the whole package, Acheson told them. They would have to agree, publicly and immediately, to the rearmament of Germany. They would have to go along with what they honestly viewed as a very provocative policy vis-à-vis Russia and risk war at a time when no effective defense was in place—either that, Acheson said, or the Americans would simply not defend them.

The fact that the U.S. government had chosen to deal so roughly with its allies had one very important effect: it helped bring France and Germany together. It helped bring about a certain change in perspective—a change in the way the Europeans viewed America and thus in the way they viewed each other. Up to this point, the French, for example, had tended to think of the policy of "building Europe" in essentially manipulative and instrumental terms. It was, to use Raymond Poidevin's phrase, a way "to seduce and to control" Germany.[11] But now the idea was beginning to take hold that the Europeans—that is, the continental West Europeans—were all in the same boat in strategic terms. The Europeans had interests of their own—interests that overlapped with, but which were in important ways distinct from, those of the United States. The fact that the Americans could adopt a highly provocative policy toward Russia, with scant regard for European interests, meant that the Europeans could not afford to be too dependent on the United States. Yes, there had to be a strong counterweight to Soviet power in Europe, and yes, that counterweight had to rest largely on American power. The American presence in Europe was obviously essential and an American combat force would have to be the heart of an effective NATO defense system. But there needed to be some counterweight to American power within the Atlantic alliance. And given the fact that Britain held itself aloof from Europe, that counterweight had to be built on a real understanding between France and Germany.

We do not want to overstate the argument here. This sort of thinking was just beginning to take shape in 1950 and things obviously had a long way to go.[12] But the importance of what was going on at the time should not be underestimated either. The line Acheson took at the New York conference was quite extraordinary, and what was at stake was of enormous importance. The events of late 1950, therefore, were bound to make a profound impression. They were bound to lead many Europeans to begin thinking more seriously about the importance of coming together as a unit in order to give Europe more of a voice in setting the policy of the West as a whole.

Consider, for example, the reaction of the German chancellor, Konrad Adenauer, to the American plan. Shortly after the New York conference, Adenauer had his top advisor, Herbert Blankenhorn, tell Armand Bérard, the French deputy high commissioner in Germany, that he did not want Germany to simply provide forces for an American army—that is, an army in which the Americans would have all of the power. The two men soon met again and Blankenhorn returned to the charge. "With great emphasis," Bérard wrote, Blankenhorn "repeated what he had already told me a couple of weeks ago, namely, how desirable it was that an initiative come from the French side. Germany did not want to take her place in an American army." "If France," Blankenhorn continued, "proposed the creation of a European army under allied command, an army whose supreme commander might even be a Frenchman," his government "would support that solution."[13]

Bérard's comment on this is worth quoting at length:

> The chancellor is being honest when he says he is worried that what the German [military] contribution will boil down to is simply German forces in an American army. He is afraid that his country will end up providing the foot soldiers and shock troops for an anti-Communist offensive force that the United States might build in Europe. People in our own country are worried about the same sort of thing. Adenauer is asking for a French initiative that would head off this American solution, which he fears. I think he is sincere in all this, just as sincere as he was, and still is, in his support for the Schuman Plan [for a coal and steel community in Western Europe]. He believes that the problems of Western Europe have be to resolved on a Franco-German basis, the military problem as well as the economic problems.[14]

The important point here was that France and Germany had major interests in common, not just vis-à-vis Russia, but vis-à-vis America as well. There was, Bérard noted, "a certain parallelism between the position of France and that of West Germany with regard to the defense of the West. Both of them are concerned above all with making sure that they are not invaded and that their territory does not serve as a battleground; they both feel very strongly that the West should hold back from provoking the Soviets, before a western force, worthy of the name, has been set up."[15] To go from that point to the conclusion that the Europeans had to act more as a strategic unit—that European integration had to be real, and not just a device to keep Germany from becoming a problem—did not require any great leap of the imagination.

Reading these and related documents, one thus has the sense of a new way of thinking beginning to take shape—of French leaders rubbing their eyes and waking up to the fact that they and the Germans had more in common than they had perhaps realized, of an important threshold being crossed, of France and Germany just starting to think of themselves as a strategic unit. And if this kind of thinking was beginning to emerge, it was, in large part, a reaction to the heavy-handed way in which U.S. government had chosen to deal with its European allies in September 1950.

But had the American government, in any real sense, actually *chosen* to deal with the allies in that way? It is commonly argued that the policy Acheson pursued in September 1950 is not to be understood as a choice freely made at the top political level, but rather is to be seen as the outcome of a bureaucratic dispute in which Acheson ultimately had to give way to pressure from the Pentagon.[16] The State Department, according to this argument, understood the need for an effective defense of Western Europe; now, following the outbreak of the Korean War in June, the need for action was obvious. It therefore wanted to begin building an effective defense by sending an American combat force over to Europe. But this gave the military authorities the leverage they needed to achieve their "long-standing objective of German rearmament."[17] They were willing, they now said, to go along with the plan to send over the U.S. combat divisions, but only as part of a "package": the JCS "wanted categorical assurances that they could count on German assistance in the shape they desired and that they would be able to make an immediate start on raising and equipping the German units"; they insisted that the offer to deploy the U.S. force "be made strictly conditional upon iron-clad commitments by the Europeans to their own contributions, and in particular, upon unequivocal acceptance of an immediate start on German rearmament in a form technically acceptable to American strategists."[18]

The State Department, the argument runs, resisted the Pentagon's efforts to bring the German rearmament question to a head in such a blunt and high-handed way. The two sides debated the issue for about two weeks in late August, but the "Pentagon stood united and unmovable." Acheson, according to his own widely-accepted account, "agreed with their strategic purpose," but "thought their tactics murderous."[19] At the end of August, however, Acheson had reluctantly decided that he had to give way. He had felt earlier that insisting on the inclusion of Germany at the outset "would delay and complicate the whole enterprise," and that a more flexible approach made more sense, but, by his own account, he was almost totally isolated within the government and therefore had no choice but to back off from that position. "I was right," he said, "but I was nearly alone."[20] Most of the State Department, and even the president himself, seemed to be on the other side. So somewhat against his better judgment, he accepted what he later recognized as a mistaken policy.[21] He accepted not only the "package" approach—that is, as one scholar put it, a formula that "tied German rearmament to the State Department package much more rigidly than the State Department had intended"[22]—but a plan that would allow Germany to rearm on a national basis, which was also very much at variance with what the State Department had originally wanted.[23] But this was the only way he could get the Pentagon to accept the rest of the plan.

If all of this is true—if the American government just stumbled into the policy it pursued in September 1950, if the policy, that is, is to be understood essentially as the outcome of a bureaucratic process—then the episode might not tell us much about how the American government, at the top political level, dealt with its European allies. But if that standard interpretation is not accurate, then the story might tell us something fundamental about the nature of America's European policy, and indeed about the nature of U.S.–European relations in general.

The goal here, therefore, is to examine this interpretation of what happened in August and September 1950 in the light of the evidence. But is there any point, one might wonder, to conducting an analysis of this sort? If so many scholars who looked into the issue all reached essentially the same conclusion, that conclusion, one might reasonably assume, is probably correct. There is, however, a basic problem with this assumption: the standard interpretation rests on a very narrow evidentiary base. It rests, to a quite extraordinary extent, on Acheson's own account and on scholarly accounts that depend heavily on Acheson's story.[24] A self-serving account, however, should never be taken at face value; given the importance of the issue, the standard interpretation really needs to be tested against the evidence. And a good deal of archival evidence has become available since Acheson's memoirs and the first scholarly accounts were published. But what light does this new material throw on the issue?

GERMAN REARMAMENT: ON WHAT BASIS?

The State and Defense departments did not see eye-to-eye on the German rearmament question in mid-1950. On that point, the standard interpretation is indeed correct. But the differences between the two departments were not nearly as great as they sometimes seemed, and the area of disagreement had virtually disappeared by the time the New York conference met in early September.

The military authorities had favored German rearmament since 1947. On May 2, 1950, they officially called for the "early rearming of Western Germany," and formally reiterated this call on June 8. But the State Department took a very different line and on July 3 flatly rejected the idea that the time had come to press for German rearmament.[25] It was not that top State Department officials felt that Germany could never be rearmed. Acheson himself had noted, even in 1949, that one could not "have any sort of security in western Europe without using German power."[26] But until mid-1950, it was thought for a variety of reasons that it would be unwise to press the issue.

In July 1950, however, a major shift took place in State Department thinking. Acheson told President Truman at the end of that month that the issue was not whether Germany should be "brought into the general defensive plan," but rather how this could be done without undermining America's other basic policy goals in Europe. He pointed out that the State Department was thinking in terms of a "European army or a North Atlantic army"; that force would include German troops, but the German units "would not be subject to the orders of Bonn."[27] A whole series of key State Department officials, both in Washington and in the major embassies abroad, had, in fact, come to the conclusion at about this time that some kind of international army that included German troops would have to be created, and Acheson's own thinking was fully in line with this emerging consensus.[28]

This shift in State Department thinking is not to be viewed in bureaucratic politics terms as an attempt by the State Department to reach some kind of compromise with the JCS on the German rearmament issue. It was instead a quite straightforward consequence of the outbreak of the Korean War in June. As Acheson later noted, after the North Korean attack:

we and everybody else in Europe and the United States took a new look at the German problem. It seemed to us that it was now clear that Germany had to take a part in the defense of Europe; it seemed clear that the idea that we had had before that this would work out through a process of evolution wasn't adequate—there wasn't time, the evolution had to be helped along by action. It was quite clear by this time, as a result of the staff talks in NATO, that the Western Union idea of defense on the Rhine was quite impractical and foolish, and that if you were going to have any defense at all, it had to be in the realm of forward strategy, which was as far east in Germany as possible. This made it absolutely clear that Germany had to be connected with defense, not merely through military formations, but emotionally and politically, because if the battle was going to be fought in Germany it meant that the German people had to be on our side, and enthusiastically so.

The U.S. government "immediately went to work" on "this German matter"—at least as soon as it could, given the need to deal, in July especially, with even more urgent problems relating to the Korean War.[29]

So there was now a certain sense of urgency: an effective defense of Western Europe had to be put in place and, indeed, put in place rather quickly.
It was obvious from the start that this would "require real contributions of
German resources and men." But the German contribution could not take
the form of a German national army; the Germans could not be allowed to
build a military force able to operate independently. The only way the Germans could make their defense contribution was thus to create some kind of
international army that included German forces—but forces not able to conduct military operations on their own.[30]

A key State Department official, Henry Byroade, worked out a plan based
on this fundamental concept at the beginning of August. Byroade, the director of the State Department's Bureau of German Affairs, discussed his ideas
with the army staff officers most directly concerned with these issues on August 3. (The army, for obvious reasons, took the lead in setting policy on this
issue for the military establishment as a whole.) Those officers were pleased
by the fact that the State Department now appeared "to be looking with favor toward the controlled rearmament of Western Germany"; they "felt that
great progress had been achieved on the question of German rearmament,
since both the State Department and the Department of Defense are now at-
tempting to work out a suitable plan which would make possible a German
contribution to the defense of Western Europe." These army officers had in
fact just come up with their own plan for a "controlled rearmament of Germany."[31]

There were, however, major differences between the two plans, or so it
seemed to both sides at the time. The Byroade plan called for the establishment of a highly integrated "European Army," which would include practically all Western military forces—American and German as well as West
European—stationed in Europe; it would have a "General Staff of truly international character," and a single commander, an American general, with
"complete jurisdiction" over the whole army. The force would have as much
of an international character as possible. The goal, Byroade said, was to apply the Schuman Plan concept to the military field; the aim was to enable the
Germans to contribute to the defense of the West, without at the same time
becoming too independent—that is, without getting a national army of their
own.[32]

The army, on the other hand, was not in favor of setting up a highly integrated "European Army." It did not explicitly call for a "German national
army," but key officers did seem to feel that any plan the U.S. government
came up with would need to "appeal to the nationalistic tendencies of the
German people." The army plan, moreover, called for "controlled rearmament," but the officers who drafted it were reluctant to state formally what
the "nature of the controls" would be. In short, the State Department called
for a truly international force, while the military authorities, it seemed,

wanted a less highly integrated force composed of national armies. The two plans, in Byroade's view, were "miles apart." Or, as the army staff put it, the State Department proposal would reduce the "military sovereignty status" of the European countries down "to the level of Germany in order to secure her contribution," while the army proposed "to raise Germany's status" to the level of the NATO allies.[33]

So there was clearly a major difference of opinion on this issue—at least at the level of rhetoric. But in practical terms, were the two sides really so far apart? The great goal of the State Department was to make sure that there was no new German national army—that is, an army capable of independent action, and thus able to support an independent foreign policy. The military authorities understood the point, and it was for this reason that they, from the start, favored the "controlled" rearmament of Germany. And when one examines the sorts of controls they had in mind and notes that certain key military controls in their plan would apply to Germany alone, it becomes obvious—the rhetoric notwithstanding—that military leaders had no intention of giving the Federal Republic the same "military sovereignty status" as the NATO allies. In the Byroade plan, not just allied headquarters, but also field army and corps headquarters were to be "international"; in the plan worked out by the officers in the Pentagon, "Army and Corps should be national," except that the Germans would be "allowed none." In both plans, the Germans would contribute only ground forces, not air or naval forces; there would be German divisions, but no larger, purely German units; the German forces would be under allied control; the Germans would not be allowed to manufacture certain kinds of weapons ("heavy ordnance, etc."); and, finally, both plans implied German participation in NATO.[34]

Thus, the real difference between the plans did not have to do with Germany, but with how the NATO forces were to be treated. Byroade was not too explicit about this part of the proposal, but his plan called for virtually all of the allied forces in Europe to be integrated into the proposed European defense force. There would be no distinct British, French, or even American army on the Continent, only an international army with a single commander served by an integrated international staff. The U.S. military authorities did not like this proposal at all, even though the whole force would have an American general as its commander. Byroade, it seemed to them, wanted to go too far in pushing the allies down to the German level; the Chiefs also felt that something that radical was not essential, and that instead of creating an entirely new institution, the "European Defense Force," it made more sense to build on the one basic institution that had already been created: the North Atlantic Treaty Organization. Both NATO and the Western Union military organization set up by the Brussels Treaty of 1948 were already in existence; to create a new international force would "tend to complicate an already confusing structure."[35] And there was no point in doing so, because NATO itself could provide the necessary degree of integration; a German force integrated into the NATO system—especially a strengthened NATO system—would be incapable of independent action.

This logic was quite compelling. It did not matter if the international force was called EDF or NATO. The name was not important. What really mattered was whether you had an international structure within which the Germans could make their contribution, but which at the same time would prevent them from becoming too independent. And if an institution that had already been created—that is, NATO—could achieve that result, then so much the better.[36]

Even Byroade himself, who by his own account was quite conservative on these issues in comparison with other State Department officials, was quick to see the point. His original plan, in any event, had not really been put forward as a practical proposal; his aim had been to sketch out a "theoretical solution from which one could work backwards" with an eye to working out a "compromise between the theoretical and what is already in existence." So when a top army officer explained to him on August 10 how NATO could do the trick, he at least temporarily dropped his objections and basically accepted their approach: he agreed that "German divisions, organized as such, might well be integrated into the NATO forces as now planned, provided only an American commander for these forces were set up in the near future." The differences between the two departments were clearly narrowing. Indeed, it turned out that Byroade's earlier objection to the army plan had "stemmed entirely from a misunderstanding of terms." Byroade had thought that when army officers referred to "controlled rearmament," they had only a "limitation on numbers and types of divisions" in mind. When he was told that the army "also contemplated as part of the control a very definite limit as to the types and quantities of materiel and equipment which Germany should manufacture, Byroade said he was in complete accord."[37]

By the end of the month, it seemed that a full consensus had been reached. For Acheson, far more than for Byroade, only the core issue was really important. For him, it was not a problem that the Germans would have a national army in an administrative sense—that is, that they would recruit their own troops, pay them, provide them with uniforms, and so on. The only important thing was to make sure that things did not go too far—that the "old German power," as Acheson put it, was not resurrected.[38] If an arrangement could guarantee that, he was prepared to be quite flexible on the secondary issues. Acheson was certainly not going to go to the wall to defend those parts of the Byroade concept that would tend to strip the NATO forces, including the American force in Europe, of their national character.

Acheson had an important meeting with JCS Chairman Bradley on August 30 to work things out, and he discussed that meeting with his principal advisors later that morning. He did not complain that the military wanted to go too far toward creating a German national army; his real complaint was that the JCS was "confused" and had somehow gotten the idea that the State Department position was more extreme than it really was. The Pentagon's own position, Acheson thought, was just not clear enough: "he did not know what was meant by 'national basis' and 'controlled status.'"[39]

But the military authorities were now willing to be more accommodating on this point and were prepared to state more explicitly what they meant by those terms. This represented a certain shift from the line they had taken at the beginning of the month. In early August, they had preferred not to outline formally the sorts of controls they had in mind.[40] But by the end of the month, the army leadership had concluded that it needed to be more forthcoming.

This was because President Truman had intervened in these discussions on August 26. On that day, he asked the two departments to come up with a common policy on the whole complex of issues relating to European defense and West German rearmament. Given the president's action, a simple rejection of the Byroade plan was no longer a viable option. Leading military officers now felt that they needed to come up with a more "positive approach" to the problem. A "Plan for the Development of West German Security Forces" was quickly worked out and approved by the army leadership at the beginning of September. This plan spelled out the controls the military had long favored: the NATO organization would be strengthened; Germany would not be allowed to have an air force or a navy; the largest German unit would be the division; there would be no German general staff; German industry would be permitted to provide only light weapons and equipment. The military authorities were thus not pressing for the creation of a German national force that would have the same status as the British army or the French army or the American army. Indeed, by the beginning of September, there was no fundamental difference between their position and that of Acheson on this issue.[41]

THE ORIGINS OF THE PACKAGE PLAN

So the State Department and the Pentagon had clashed in August 1950 on the question of German rearmament. That conflict had focused on the question of the extent to which the German force would be organized on a "national" basis—or, to look at the issue from the other side, the degree of military integration needed to keep Germany from having a capability for independent action. By the end of the month, however, that conflict had essentially been resolved. There would be a German military contribution, both departments agreed, but no German national army. The German force would be fully integrated into the NATO force; that is, the German force would not be able to operate independently. This was all Acheson required, and the JCS had never really asked for anything more by way of a German national force.

But even if the conflict had been sharper, even if the Pentagon had been intransigent on this issue, and even if the State Department had capitulated to the JCS on this question, all of this would in itself tell us very little about the most important issue we are concerned with here: the question of the origins of the "package plan." This was essentially a separate issue. The American government, at the New York conference in mid-September, demanded that the NATO allies agree, immediately and publicly, to the rearmament of West Germany; if they refused to accept that demand, the Americans would not send over the combat divisions or an American general as NATO commander. Everything was tied together into a single package, and it was presented to the allies on a "take it or leave it" basis. It was this policy, this tactic, which created the whole problem in September 1950.

How exactly did the issue of German rearmament get tied to the question of sending over American combat divisions and to appointing an American general as NATO commander? The standard view is that the JCS was responsible for the package plan. The military authorities, it is commonly argued, simply refused to accept the deployment of the American combat force unless the Europeans, for their part, agreed to the rearmament of West Germany. Acheson supposedly thought these tactics "murderous" and tried hard to get the Pentagon to change its mind. But the JCS was intransigent, this argument runs, and to get the troops sent, Acheson gave way in the end and reluctantly accepted the tactic the military leadership had insisted on.[42] But does this basic interpretation hold up in the light of the archival evidence now available?

First of all, did the military push throughout August for the package approach? The military leaders certainly felt that a German military contribution was essential. The West European NATO allies, in their view, could not generate enough military force by themselves to provide for an effective defense; German troops were obviously necessary for that purpose. German rearmament was therefore seen as a "vital element" of an effective defense policy.[43] The military authorities also supported the idea of beefing up the U.S. military presence in Europe and sending over an American general as NATO commander.[44] But the key point to note here is that these were treated as essentially separate issues. Military leaders did not say (at least not in any of the documents that we have seen) that U.S. troops should be sent only if the allies accepted German rearmament. They did not say that the way to press for German rearmament was to tell the allies that unless they went along with the American plan, the U.S. combat divisions would be kept at home.

Indeed, in the formal policy documents on the defense of Europe, the JCS did not make the German rearmament issue its top priority. The Chiefs instead tended to play it down. The basic JCS view in those documents was that NATO Europe—the "European signatories" of the North Atlantic Treaty—needed to "provide the balance of the forces required for the initial defense" over and above what the United States was prepared to supply.[45] West Germany, which at this time, of course, was not a member of NATO, was not even mentioned in this context. What this suggests is that the military leadership was not pounding its fist on the table on the German rearmament question. The German issue was important, of course, but the choice of this kind of phrasing suggests that the Chiefs were prepared to deal with it in a relatively reasonable, gradual, and businesslike way.

What about the State Department? How did it feel about the package approach? Did it agree to the inclusion of German rearmament in the package because this was the only way to get the Pentagon to go along with its plan to send additional troops to Europe? Some scholars suggest that this was the case, but the real picture is rather different.[46]

The outbreak of the Korean War was the key development here, and State Department officials understood from the start that if Europe was to be defended, a German force of some sort would be required. As McCloy wrote Acheson on August 3: "to defend Western Europe effectively will obviously require real contributions of German resources and men."[47] This simply was the conventional wisdom at the time: neither McCloy nor anyone else in the State Department needed the JCS to remind them that an effective defense meant a German military contribution. But they were also dead set against the idea of allowing the Germans to build up an army of their own—a national army, able to operate independently and thus capable of supporting an independent foreign policy. It followed that some kind of international force would have to be created: the Germans could make their contribution, an effective force could be built up, but there would be no risk of a German national army. The whole concept of a multinational force—of military integration, of a unified command structure, of a single supreme commander supported by an international staff—was thus rooted in an attempt to deal with the question of German rearmament. It was not as though the thinking about the defense of Western Europe and the shape of the NATO military system had developed on its own, and that it was only later that the German rearmament issue had been linked to it by the JCS for bargaining purposes.

The fundamental idea that the different elements in the equation—the U.S. divisions, the unified command structure, the forces provided by NATO Europe, and the German contribution—were all closely interrelated and needed to be dealt with as parts of a unified policy thus developed naturally and organically as the basic thinking about the defense of Europe took shape in mid-1950. This idea—in a sense, the basic idea behind the package concept—took hold quite early in August 1950, and it was the State Department that took the lead in pressing for this kind of approach. The Byroade plan, for example, explicitly tied all of these different elements together: in this plan, which in mid-August became a kind of official State Department plan, German units could be created if and only if they were integrated into an allied force with an American commander.[48]

The State Department was thus the driving force behind this kind of approach. For the entire month of August, its officials pressed for a unified policy. But the military authorities, because of their dislike for the Byroade plan, tended to drag their feet in this area.[49] The State Department, in frustration, and aware that a policy needed to be worked out before the NATO ministers met in mid-September, then got the president to intervene. On August 26 (as noted above), Truman asked the two departments, State and Defense, to come up with a common policy. He laid out a series of eight questions that the two departments were to answer by September 1, a deadline that was later extended to September 6.[50] The "Eight Questions" document was actually drafted in the State Department by two of Acheson's closest advisors. The State Department goal, in getting Truman to sign it, was to prod the Pentagon into accepting a common plan.[51]

The tactic worked. Military leaders understood that the Eight Questions document was based on the State Department plan.[52] Given the president's intervention (again, as noted above), they now felt they could no longer simply "disregard" that plan, but instead needed to take a more accommodating and "positive" line.[53]

The military authorities now drafted a document that, they felt, might serve as a basis for a joint reply to the president. That draft was given to the State Department on September 1; Acheson had been shown a preliminary version a couple of days earlier.[54] Events now moved quickly. In a few days of intensive talks, a joint reply acceptable to both departments was worked out. The final document was approved by the president and circulated to top officials as "NSC 82" on September 11, a day before the New York conference was due to begin.[55]

This period from August 26 through September 8—from the Eight Questions letter to the joint reply—is thus the most important phase of this whole episode, and the evidence relating to this period needs to be examined with particular care. Does it support the view that the military insisted on the package approach and that the State Department opposed it, but gave in reluctantly at the end?

By far the most important document bearing on these issues is the record of a meeting Acheson had on August 30 with his three top advisors in this area, the three officials who, in fact, were conducting the negotiations with the Defense Department: Byroade, Assistant Secretary for European Affairs Perkins, and Paul Nitze, head of the State Department's Policy Planning Staff. Acheson (as noted in the previous section) had just met with JCS Chairman Bradley earlier that morning. He had also just seen the draft reply the JCS had prepared to the president's Eight Questions letter. At the meeting with his advisors, Acheson discussed the JCS draft section by section and found most of it acceptable. The few small problems he had with it did not involve any issue of principle. At no point did Acheson complain about, or even comment on, any insistence on the part of the military that all of the elements in the program were to be tied together in a single package. The conclusion to be drawn from this is absolutely fundamental for the purposes of the analysis here: if the JCS had been insisting on the package concept, and if Acheson and the State Department had been opposed to that concept, it is scarcely conceivable that the issue would not have come up at this meeting.

Nor is it very likely that a conflict over the package issue developed suddenly over the next few days. Nitze's recollection (in 1953) was that, following the Acheson-Bradley meeting, things moved very quickly.[56] He says nothing about a dispute over the package question suddenly emerging at that point, and it is in fact highly unlikely that things could have moved so quickly if a serious dispute had developed. Indeed, Perkins and Nitze spoke in those 1953 discussions of the common policy document—the document that later became NSC 82—as though it essentially reflected their views, and which, through great efforts on their part, they had finally managed to get the military authorities to accept. "We had great difficulty," Perkins recalled, "in finally getting the Pentagon" to sign on to the common policy.[57] Nitze agreed: he remembered going over to the Pentagon after Acheson had worked "this thing" out with General Bradley on August 30, and "we trotted out the specific piece of paper which spelled out the package proposal with the Pentagon people and got their agreement to this document."[58] It was scarcely as though the State Department was going along with the package plan reluctantly or against its better judgment.

An analysis of the drafting history points to the same general conclusion. The passage in NSC 82 that served as the basis for the package policy—indeed, the only passage in the document that called for such a policy—was part of the answer to the sixth question: "We recommend that an American national be appointed now as Chief of Staff and eventually as a Supreme Commander for the European defense force but only upon the request of the European nations and upon their assurance that they will provide sufficient forces, including adequate German units, to constitute a command reasonably capable of fulfilling its responsibilities."[59] That final document was based on the draft the JCS had turned over on September 1; the key phrase "including adequate German units" did not appear in the original JCS draft.[60] It scarcely stands to reason that the military authorities, having decided to be cooperative, would harden their position in the course of their talks with State Department representatives, above all if State Department officials had argued strongly against an intransigent policy.

None of this means, of course, that the JCS was opposed to including a call for German rearmament in the package. In their view, this was a goal that the U.S. government obviously had to pursue. But this does not mean that the Chiefs were going to try to dictate negotiating tactics to the State Department—that they were going to insist on a diplomatic strategy that Acheson and his top advisors rejected.

State Department officials, in fact, did not really blame the JCS for what had happened at the New York conference. Nitze, for example, although he said in 1953 that the Chiefs would not agree to sending additional forces until they got assurances from the British and the French about a German military contribution, did not actually hold them primarily responsible for the confrontation with the Europeans in mid-September.[61] He pointed out at that time that the German rearmament issue could have been dealt with very differently. The issue, he said, could have been presented "to the British and French in a way which emphasized the supreme commander and the American commitment"; the "question of German participation" could have been "put in a lower category and kind of weaved in gradually."[62] Nitze did not blame the JCS for vetoing that approach. In his view, the real responsibility lay elsewhere. "We were fouled up on this," he said, by press leaks primarily coming from McCloy, "who agreed entirely with the tactical importance of doing it the other way"—that is, of dealing with the German rearmament issue head on.[63]

But Acheson was not fundamentally opposed to the blunt approach, and (contrary to his later disclaimers) he himself, on balance, thought that the U.S. government had chosen the right course of action at the time. Would it have been better, he asked in that same discussion, to have opted for quiet talks with the British and the French, when a plan had just been worked out, when a NATO foreign ministers' meeting was about to be held, and when the issue was being "talked about everywhere"? "It seemed to me then," he said, "and it seems to me now, that we did the right thing."[64]

And indeed, in his reports to Truman from the New York conference, Acheson gave no sign that he was pursuing the package plan strategy reluctantly or against his better judgment. He gave no sign that he was looking for a way to soften the general line and deal with the allies in a more conciliatory manner. He explained to the president on September 15 how he had laid out the American demands, how he had discussed the issue "with the gloves off," how he had "blown" some of the allies' objections to the American plan "out of the water," and how it might well be a question of "whose nerve lasts longer." He was clearly pleased with his own performance and was not at all unhappy about the line he had taken.[65]

As one of its top officials pointed out at the time, the State Department was conducting a "hard-hitting kind of operation" in this area—and was proud of it.[66]

DEAN ACHESON: THE MAN AND THE STATESMAN

There is a final set of considerations that needs to be taken into account in an assessment of U.S. policy in September 1950, and this has to do with what we know about Acheson in general—about the sort of person he was and the kind of policy he favored throughout his career. Was he the type of leader who believed in compromise, especially with America's most important allies, and was inclined to take a relatively moderate and cautious line? Or was he, as General Bradley later called him, an "uncompromising hawk," aggressive in terms of both his goals and his tactics?[67]

The great bulk of the evidence points in the latter direction.[68] In 1950 in particular, he tended to take a very hard line. He was in favor of a rollback policy at that time. This was the real meaning of NSC 68, an important policy document with which Acheson was closely associated.[69] American scholars generally tend to portray U.S. policy as essentially defensive and status quo-oriented, and NSC 68 is commonly interpreted as simply a "strategy of containment."[70] But the aggressive thrust of this document is clear from its own text: NSC 68 called explicitly for a "policy of calculated and gradual coercion"; the aim of that policy was to "check and roll back the Kremlin's drive for world domination." The whole goal at that time, as Nitze recalled in 1954, was to "lay the basis," through massive rearmament, for a policy of "taking increased risks of general war" in order to achieve "a satisfactory solution" of America's problems with Russia while the Soviet nuclear stockpile "was still small."[71]

This extraordinary aggressiveness was not out of character for Acheson, and its wellspring was not simply anti-Communism or extreme distrust of the Soviet Union. His general hawkishness can in fact be traced back to the summer of 1941, when, as a mid-level State Department official, he played a major role in shaping the policy that put the United States on a collision course with Japan. Acheson was one of a handful of officials who helped engineer the oil embargo in mid-1941—a development that led directly to a sharp crisis in U.S.–Japanese relations and ultimately to the attack on Pearl Harbor in December.[72]

His aggressiveness was also apparent in the early 1960s. During the Berlin and Cuban missile crises especially, he pushed for very tough policies. In 1963, he even called (in a talk to the Institute for Strategic Studies) for what amounted to a policy of armed intervention in East Germany.[73] When he was attacked for taking this line, he lashed out at his critics: "Call me anything you like, but don't call me a fool; everybody knows I'm not a fool." "I will not say that Mr. Acheson is a fool," one of his critics replied. "I will only say that he is completely and utterly reckless."[74]

Acheson often sneered at those he viewed as soft and indecisive. After Eisenhower took office in 1953, Acheson complained repeatedly to Truman about the "weakness" of the new administration.[75] After the Democrats returned to power in 1961, President Kennedy allowed Acheson to play a major role in the making of American policy, but Acheson viewed the young president with barely concealed contempt. The Kennedy administration, in his view, was weak, indecisive, and obsessed with appearances.[76] He even criticized the administration in public, going so far at one point that he was virtually forced to apologize.[77]

At another point, he practically told the president to his face that he was indecisive. Kennedy had asked Acheson to look into the balance of payments problem, and in early 1963 he presented his report to the president. It was a "very strong, vivid, Achesonian presentation. And the President thanked him and said, 'Well, we have to think about that.' Acheson said, 'There's nothing to think about, Mr. President. All you have to do is decide. Here it is, and why don't you decide?'" Kennedy turned red, and then broke up the meeting. He was furious. "It's a long time before Dean Acheson's going to be here again," he remarked to an aide.[78] As for Acheson, he continued to criticize Kennedy as weak and indecisive, even after Kennedy's death.[79]

Acheson treated President Johnson the same way he had treated President Kennedy. When he met with Johnson in 1965, he was so irritated by the president's whining and indecisiveness that he "blew [his] top" and told him to his face that all the trouble America was having in Europe "came about because under him and Kennedy there had been no American leadership at all. The idea that the Europeans could come to their own conclusion had led to an unchallenged de Gaulle."[80]

These stories reveal a lot about Acheson. A man who could deal with presidents that way was not the type of person who would allow himself to be pushed around by mere military officers on an issue of central political importance—above all at a time when he was at the height of his power and had the full confidence of President Truman. Nor was he the type who would be understanding if he thought allied leaders were reluctant to face up to fundamental problems and make the really tough decisions.

Acheson, in fact, did not believe in taking a soft line with the allies or in treating them as full partners. In 1961, he played the key role in shaping the new Kennedy administration's policy on NATO issues; the goal of that policy was to get the Europeans "out of the nuclear business" (as people said at the time)—that is, to concentrate power, and especially nuclear power, in American hands.[81]

Acheson, moreover, was not the sort of statesman who viewed consultation and compromise as ends in themselves. At one point during the Berlin crisis in 1961, he complained that the U.S. had been trying too hard to reach agreement with the Europeans. The U.S. government did not need to coordinate policy with the allies, he said, "*we need to tell them.*"[82] "We must not be too delicate," he said at another point, "about being vigorous in our leadership." It was America's job, practically America's duty, to lay down the law to the allies. The United States—and he actually used this phrase—was "the greatest imperial power the world has ever seen."[83] "In the final analysis," he told McGeorge Bundy, "the United States [is] the locomotive at the head of mankind, and the rest of the world is the caboose."[84]

American interests were fundamental; European concerns were of purely secondary importance. Paul Nitze, who was very close to Acheson throughout this period, made the point quite explicitly in 1954. The "primary goal," he said, was the "preservation of the United States and the continuation of a 'salutary' world environment"; the "avoidance of war" was of secondary importance. "Even if war were to destroy the world as we know it today, still the U.S. must win that war decisively." He then again stressed the point that "the preservation of the U.S." was "the overriding goal, not the fate of our allies."[85]

People like Nitze and Acheson were thus not inclined to take European interests too seriously or to deal with the Europeans on a basis of mutual respect. And Acheson himself was clearly not the kind of person who would have found it difficult to deal roughly with the allies in September 1950.

THE MEANING OF THE STORY

The goal here was to test a particular interpretation of what happened in the late summer of 1950. According to that interpretation, the military authorities had essentially forced the package plan on Acheson, who had accepted it reluctantly, and only after a struggle. The basic conclusion is that that interpretation simply does not stand up in the light of the evidence from late 1950 and in the light of what we know about Acheson in general. The policy the U.S. government pursued at the New York conference is not to be understood as a more or less accidental by-product of a bureaucratic dispute in Washington. The way Acheson dealt with the allies at the New York conference—the bare-knuckled tactics he pursued, the way he tried to lay down the law to the Europeans, the way he dismissed their most fundamental concerns out of hand—has to be seen as deliberate: he knew what he was doing, and he had not been forced by the Pentagon to proceed in that way. There is certainly no evidence that he thought those tactics were "murderous": he did not give way on this point after a long battle; he never complained at the time about the military's (alleged) insistence on this strategy; he never raised the issue with Truman or expressed misgivings about the policy as he was carrying it out.

Does this mean that the Acheson interpretation was a complete fabrication? The truth is probably not quite that simple. For Acheson, as for many people in public life, honesty was not the top priority, and he was fully capable of deliberately misleading the public on these issues.[86] But that in itself does not mean that the Acheson story about the package plan was manufactured out of whole cloth.

Indeed—in a certain sense at least—there was probably some basis to the story. After all, the military authorities were willing to send over the American troops only if the European allies agreed to provide the balance of the forces needed to make an effective defense possible, and the JCS did believe that German forces would be needed for that purpose. So in that sense, from the military point of view, German rearmament was certainly a vital part of the package. But this was at the level of fundamental objectives, not at the level of tactics, and the basic JCS view was consistent with a relatively soft negotiating strategy: if the State Department (to paraphrase Nitze) had called for emphasizing the U.S. troop commitment and only then gradually "weaving in" the question of a German defense contribution, it is hard to believe that the JCS would have objected. But an agreement on the part of the JCS that all of the elements of the problem were interconnected could be interpreted as a call for presenting the allies with a single package: the basic policy could be interpreted as translating directly into a particular negotiating strategy. The basic military point of view, in other words, could serve as cover—that is, as a kind of license for pursuing the sort of negotiating policy State Department officials considered essential at this point.[87] The fact that the military view could be interpreted (or misinterpreted) in this way—whether deliberately or not is not the issue here—made it easier for Acheson and his advisors to do what they probably really wanted to do in any case.

This is all quite speculative, of course, and there is not enough evidence to get to the bottom of this particular issue. But these uncertainties should not be allowed to obscure the facts that the documents are able to establish. And one thing, at least, is very clear: the State Department did not fight the military over the package plan. If Acheson actually thought the tactics the U.S. government adopted were "murderous," he certainly had a very odd way of showing it.

Why is this story important? Partly because it shows how easy it is for scholars to get taken in by self-serving memoir accounts, and thus how crucial it is to test claims against archival evidence; partly because of what it tells us about civil-military relations in the United States, about the willingness and ability of the military leadership to impose its views on issues of great political importance, and about the validity of the bureaucratic politics theory of policy-making in general; but mainly because of the light it throws on the political meaning of what happened in September 1950. The American government did not just stumble along and adopt a policy against its better judgment because of pressure from the military; the package policy was adopted quite deliberately, and this has a certain bearing on how American policy toward Europe during the early Cold War period is to be interpreted.

There has been a certain tendency in recent years to idealize U.S.–
European relations during the Cold War period. The argument is that the
NATO system worked because, no matter how lopsided power relations
were, the Americans did not simply insist on running the show. Instinc-
tively, the democratic countries dealt with the problems that arose in their
relations with each other the same way they dealt with domestic issues:
not through coercion, but through persuasion and compromise, "by cutting deals instead of imposing wills."[88] The democratic habit of compromise, of give and take, was the bedrock upon which the Atlantic Alliance
was built. The Americans treated their allies with respect, and this, it is
said, was one major reason why the Europeans were able to live with a
system that rested so heavily on American power.[89]

The story of how the U.S. government managed the German rearmament
issue in late 1950 suggests that things were not quite so simple. The Americans were capable of dealing rather roughly with their European allies, even
on issues of absolutely central political importance. If the package plan story
tells us nothing else, it certainly tells us that. And the fact that the Americans
were capable of treating their allies that way had a certain bearing on how
many people, especially in Europe, thought about core political issues.

In 1880, after a remarkable electoral campaign, William Gladstone was
swept back into office as prime minister of Great Britain. Gladstone, in that
campaign, had laid out a series of principles on which British foreign policy
was to be based; one fundamental aim was "to cultivate to the utmost the
concert of Europe." Five years later, Gladstone's policy lay in ruins. He had
managed to alienate every other major power in Europe—even France and
Germany had come together in 1884 in a short-lived anti-British entente—
and in 1885 his government fell from power. The Gladstone government had
achieved its "long desired 'Concert of Europe'" all right, Lord Salisbury noted
bitterly at the time. It had succeeded in "uniting the continent of Europe—
against England."[90]

The parallel with American policy during the early Cold War period is
striking. The U.S. government very much wanted the European countries to
come together as a political unit, and support for European unification was
one of the basic tenets of American foreign policy in this period.[91] But it was
not American preaching that led the Europeans to cooperate with each
other and begin to form themselves into a bloc. The United States played an
important role in the European integration process, but America had an impact mainly because of the kind of policy it pursued—a policy which, on
occasion, did not pay due regard to the most basic interests of the European
allies.

Acheson's policy in late 1950 is perhaps the most important case in point.
Acheson was pressing for a course of action that would have greatly increased
the risk of war at a time when Western Europe was particularly vulnerable.

The U.S. government could treat its allies like that—it could pursue a policy that might well have led to total disaster for Europe—only because the United States was so much stronger than any single European country. It followed that there had to be a counterweight to American power within the Western alliance, a counterweight based on the sense that the Europeans had major strategic interests in common and that those interests were distinct from those of the United States. The events of late 1950 helped push the Europeans—especially the French and the Germans—to that conclusion; it helped get them to see why they had to put their differences aside and come together as a kind of strategic unit. This episode thus plays an important role in the history of European integration, and indeed in the history of the Western alliance as a whole.

NOTES

Copies of the more important unpublished documents cited here are available on the Internet (www.polisci.ucla.edu/faculty/trachtenberg/acheson/1950.html); those documents are marked in the notes with an asterisk.

1. Minutes of foreign ministers' meetings, September 12–13, 1950, U.S. Department of State, *Foreign Relations of the United States* (FRUS), 1950, vol. 3 (Washington: GPO, 1977), pp. 1192, 1208. Henceforth references to this source will be cited in the following form: FRUS 1950, 3:1192, 1208.

2. This claim is somewhat at variance with the conventional wisdom on this point. See, for example, Laurence Martin, "The American Decision to Rearm Germany," in *American Civil-Military Decisions: A Book of Case Studies*, ed. Harold Stein (Birmingham: University of Alabama Press, 1963), 658: "To the end of the New York meetings, however, the French representative refused to accept even the principle of German rearmament." But the real story is not nearly that simple.

3. Foreign ministers' private meeting, September 12, 1950, FRUS 1950, 3:1200.

4. Acheson to Truman and Acting Secretary, September 16, 1950, ibid., 312–313.

5. Acheson-Schuman meeting, September 12, 1950, and meeting of British, French and American foreign ministers and high commissioners, September 14, 1950, ibid., 287, 299–300.

6. Acheson-Schuman meeting, September 12, 1950, ibid., 287–88.

7. Schuman and Bevin in a meeting of British, French, and American foreign ministers and high commissioners, September 14, 1950, ibid., 296–97. This fear of provoking a Soviet attack had been an important element in French policy since early 1948. The concern at that time was that the Russians would interpret movement toward the establishment of a West German state as a major step toward German rearmament, which, it was felt, might provoke preventive military action. See, for example, Chauvel to Bonnet, March 18 and May 19, 1948, Bonnet Papers, vol. 1, and Massigli to Foreign Ministry, May 3, 1948, Massigli Papers, vol. 67, both French Foreign Ministry Archives (FFMA), Paris. In 1950, this factor continued to play a fundamental role in French policy on the issue, even before the German rearmament question was pushed to the top of the agenda by the events in Korea in June. See, for example, a Quai d'Orsay mem-

orandum from April 1950, published in *Die Bundesrepublik Deutschland und Frank-reich: Dokumente 1949–1963*, ed. Horst Möller and Klaus Hildebrand (Munich: K.G. Saur, 1997), 1:376: "We can expect the Americans to bring up the question of an eventual German contribution to the rearmament of the Western powers. A program of that sort is acceptable to us only to the extent that it would not constitute a provocation vis-à-vis the USSR." On these issues in general, and for the Bradley quotation in particular, see the discussion in Marc Trachtenberg, *A Constructed Peace: The Making of the European Settlement, 1945–1963* (Princeton: Princeton University Press, 1999), 96–100, 111–12, and in Marc Trachtenberg, *History and Strategy* (Princeton: Princeton University Press, 1991), 118–127, 130–31.

8. McCloy to Acheson, June 13, 1950, President's Secretary's Files (PSF), box 178, Germany, folder 2, Harry S. Truman Library (HSTL), Independence, Missouri.

9. "Probable Soviet Reactions to a Remilitarization of Western Germany," NIE 17, December 27, 1950, PSF/253/HSTL.

10. "Soviet Courses of Action with Respect to Germany," NIE 4, January 29, 1951, PSF/253/HSTL.

11. Raymond Poidevin, *Robert Schuman, homme d'état: 1886–1963* (Paris: Imprimerie Nationale, 1986), 220.

12. For the best study of the subject, see Georges-Henri Soutou, *L'Alliance incertaine: Les rapports politico-stratégiques franco-allemands, 1954–1996* (Paris: Fayard, 1996). Soutou begins his story in 1954, which, as he points out (for example, on p. 22), is when a real bilateral Franco-German strategic relationship began. This is true enough; the point here is simply that the thinking had begun to take shape a number of years earlier.

13. *Bérard to Foreign Ministry, mid-October 1950, series "Europe 1949–55," subseries "Allemagne," volume 187 (formerly vol. 70), folio 7, FFMA.

14. Bérard's next sentence is also worth noting, because it shows how French officials were already thinking in terms of balancing between Germany and America within the Western alliance: "This is not to say that one has to think in terms of a Western army from which the Americans would be excluded, and within which the French and the Germans would provide the main forces. Such a solution might some day force us to fight, if not 'for the king of Prussia' [*pour le roi de Prusse*—a French expression implying that one is not getting anything for oneself in return], then at least for the reconquest of Prussia." *Bérard to Foreign Ministry, October 17, 1950, Europe 1949–55, Allemagne, vol. 187 (formerly vol. 70), ff. 16–17, FFMA. These documents shed light not only on the beginnings of European integration (and on the origins of the European Defense Community project in particular), but also on the evolution of Franco-German relations. Adenauer, for example, is often portrayed as pursuing a very pro-American policy at this point; the standard view is that his attitude toward France at this time was relatively cool. Note the tone, for example, of the discussion in Hans-Peter Schwarz, *Adenauer: Der Aufstieg, 1876–1952*, 3rd ed. (Stuttgart: Deutsche Verlags-Anstalt, 1986), 836. But it is clear from these French sources that the roots of his later policy were already in place in 1950.

15. *Bérard to Foreign Ministry, October 17, 1950 (as in n. 14).

16. See, for example, Martin, "American Decision to Rearm Germany," 656–657; Robert McGeehan, *The German Rearmament Question: American Diplomacy and European Defense after World War II* (Urbana: University of Illinois Press, 1971), 41, 47;

David McLellan, *Dean Acheson: The State Department Years* (New York: Dodd, Mead, 1976), 328–329; James Chace, *Acheson: The Secretary of State Who Created the American World* (New York: Simon and Schuster, 1998), 324; David Clay Large, *Germans to the Front: West German Rearmament in the Adenauer Era* (Chapel Hill: University of North Carolina Press, 1996), 84–85; Saki Dockrill, *Britain's Policy for West German Rearmament, 1950–1955* (Cambridge: Cambridge University Press, 1991), 32–33.

17. McLellan, *Acheson*, 328.

18. Martin, "American Decision to Rearm Germany," 656.

19. Dean Acheson, *Present at the Creation: My Years in the State Department* (New York: Norton, 1969), 438; McLellan, *Acheson*, 329; McGeehan, *German Rearmament Question*, 41.

20. Acheson, *Present at the Creation*, 438.

21. Ibid., 440; Dean Acheson, *Sketches from Life of Men I Have Known* (New York: Harper, 1961), 26, 41; McGeehan, *German Rearmament Question*, 41.

22. Martin, "American Decision to Rearm Germany," 657.

23. McGeehan, *German Rearmament Question*, 41. This aspect of the argument is emphasized in Thomas Schwartz, *America's Germany: John J. McCloy and the Federal Republic of Germany* (Cambridge: Harvard University Press, 1991), 134.

24. The two published accounts Acheson gave—*Present at the Creation*, 437–440, and *Sketches from Life*, 25–27, 41–43—are cited frequently in the historical literature relating to this issue. Scholars sometimes also relied on information Acheson provided in personal interviews. See Martin, "American Decision to Rearm Germany," 665, and McLellan, *Acheson*, viii. Other sources are sometimes cited, but upon examination this additional evidence turns out to be quite weak. McLellan, for example, cites a memorandum of a conversation between Acheson and JCS Chairman Bradley on August 30 from the Acheson Papers at the Truman Library as supporting his contention that Acheson had at this point "given in to the military point of view" (329). But according to the archivists at the Truman Library, no such document exists in that collection. The press accounts cited in n. 41 in the Martin article also do not prove the point they are meant to support. They are cited to back up the claim that the JCS was insisting on including German rearmament in the package, but the picture they give is that the German rearmament issue was a relatively minor issue ("only an incidental part of a much larger American program"), and that the U.S. government had not embraced the package concept ("Acheson has not definitely made it a condition without which the United States would refuse to send troops to Europe"). "Western Europe" (editorial), *Washington Post*, August 31, 1950, p. 8, and "Schuman Got Little Warning on U.S. Plans," *Washington Post*, September 17, 1950, p. 10.

25. "Extracts of Views of the Joint Chiefs of Staff with Respect to Western Policy toward Germany," NSC 71, June 8, 1950, and "Views of the Department of State on the Rearmament of Western Germany," NSC 71/1, July 3, 1950, in FRUS 1950, 4:686–687, 691–695.

26. Policy Planning Staff meeting, October 18, 1949, Records of the Policy Planning Staff, 1947–53, box 32, RG 59, U.S. National Archives (USNA), College Park, Maryland.

27. Acheson memo of meeting with Truman, July 31, 1950, FRUS 1950, 4:702–703. President Truman had earlier opposed the JCS call for German rearmament. See Truman to Acheson, June 16, 1950, ibid., 688–689.

28. Bruce to Acheson, July 28, 1950; Acheson-Truman meeting, July 31, 1950; McCloy to Acheson, August 3, 1950; Douglas to Acheson, August 8, 1950; Kirk to Acheson, August 9, 1950; in FRUS 1950, 3:157, 167–168, 181–182, 190–193.

29. Princeton Seminar, pp. 910–911, 921, Acheson Papers, HSTL. Soon after he left office, Acheson and some of his former collaborators got together at Princeton to discuss what had happened during the Truman administration; tapes were made of those discussions and a transcript was prepared. Microfilm copies of the transcript of this "Princeton Seminar," as it was called, are available at a number of university libraries in the United States. But the microfilm is often illegible and the best source is the original transcript at the Truman Library. All of the references from this source cited here come from the transcript of October 11, 1953 discussion.

30. See the sources cited in n. 28 above, esp. pp. 157, 181 (for the quotation), 190, 193.

31. The Byroade Plan, "An Approach to the Formation of a 'European Army,'" was drafted on August 3; the text is included in *Byroade to McCloy, August 3, 1950, 740.5/8–350, Department of State Central Files (DSCF), RG 59, USNA. For the record of Byroade's talks with the Army officers on August 3, see *Memorandum for General Schuyler, August 5, 1950, Army Operations General Decimal File 1950–51, box 21, file G-3 091 Germany TS, Sec. 1c, Case 12, Book II, RG 319, USNA. For the Army plan, see *"Staff Study: Rearmament of Western Germany," August 2, 1950, and *Bolté Memorandum for General Gruenther on Rearmament of Germany, August 10, 1950 (containing a systematic comparison of the State and Army plans), both in same file in RG 319.

32. Byroade meeting with Army staff officers, August 3, 1950, in *Memorandum for General Schuyler, August 5, 1950, and *Army "Staff Study: Rearmament of Western Germany," August 2, 1950, both in Army Operations General Decimal File 1950–51, box 21, file G-3 091 Germany TS, Sec. 1c, Case 12, Book II, RG 319, USNA. *"An Approach to the Formation of a 'European Army,'" in Byroade to McCloy, August 3, 1950, 740.5/8–350, DSCF, RG 59, USNA.

33. *Army "Staff Study: Rearmament of Western Germany," August 2, 1950; *Byroade meeting with Army staff officers, August 3, 1950 (document dated August 5); *Bolté to Gruenther, August 10, 1950 (with attached "Comparison of Plans"); all in Army Operations General Decimal File 1950–51, box 21, file G-3 091 Germany TS, Sec. 1c, Case 12, Book II, RG 319, USNA.

34. *Bolté to Gruenther, August 10, 1950 (with attached "Comparison of Plans"), Army Operations General Decimal File 1950–51, box 21, file G-3 091 Germany TS, Sec. 1c, Case 12, Book II, RG 319, USNA. See also Byroade meeting with Army staff officers, *August 3, 1950, Memorandum for General Schuyler, August 5, same file in RG 319, and, for the Byroade plan, see *Byroade to McCloy, August 3, 1950, 740.5/8–350, DSCF, RG 59, USNA.

35. Byroade meeting with Army staff officers, August 3, 1950, in *Memorandum for General Schuyler, August 5, 1950, and *Army "Staff Study: Rearmament of Western Germany," August 2, 1950, both in Army Operations General Decimal File 1950–51, box 21, file G-3 091 Germany TS, Sec. 1c, Case 12, Book II, RG 319, USNA.

36. The idea that NATO could do it—that one did not need to create a new institution but could rely on a strong NATO structure to solve this whole complex of problems—reemerged in 1954 as the European Defense Community project was

collapsing and people were looking for alternatives. The military authorities, especially the NATO commander, General Alfred Gruenther, played a key role at that point in pushing for the NATO solution; see Trachtenberg, *Constructed Peace*, 127. But they were drawing on basic thinking that had taken shape in 1950. At that time, both Gruenther—then Deputy Army Chief of Staff for Plans—and General Schuyler, another top Army officer who would end up as Gruenther's Chief of Staff in 1954, were already pressing for the NATO solution.

37. Byroade to McCloy, August 4, 1950, FRUS 1950, 3:183–184; *Bolté to Gruenther, July 25, 1950 (account of Byroade's meeting with Schuyler the previous day), and *memorandum of Byroade-Schuyler-Gerhardt meeting, August 10, 1950, in Army Operations General Decimal File 1950–51, box 21, file G-3 091 Germany TS, Sec. 1c, Case 12, Books I and II, RG 319, USNA.

38. *Acheson-Nitze-Byroade-Perkins meeting, August 30, 1950, *Official Conversations and Meetings of Dean Acheson (1949–1953)* (University Publications of America microfilm), reel 3.

39. *Ibid. The references are probably to various JCS documents from this period that contained these terms. See, for example, JCS 2124/18 of September 1, 1950, p. 162, in CCS 092 Germany (5-4-49), JCS Geographic File for 1948–50, RG 218, USNA.

40. See the *Army "Staff Study: Rearmament of Western Germany," August 2, 1950, paragraph 8, Army Operations General Decimal File 1950–51, box 21, file G-3 091 Germany TS, Sec. 1c, Case 12, Book II, RG 319, USNA.

41. *Gruenther to Davis, Duncan, and Edwards, September 1, 1950, enclosing the "Plan for the Development of West German Security Forces." The plan had been worked out "pursuant to verbal instructions" Gruenther had given General Schuyler on August 31; the feeling in military circles was that after the president's letter, the JCS needed to take a more accommodating line in their discussions with the State Department than they had taken thus far. Gruenther, Bolté, and Army Chief of Staff Collins were briefed on the plan on September 1, Collins approved it, and it was officially presented to the JCS that same day. *Miller memorandum for record, September 1, 1950, *Bolté to Collins on Rearmament of Western Germany, August 31, 1950, and *Ware to JCS Secretary, September 1, 1950. All in Army Operations General Decimal File 1950–51, box 21, file G-3 091 Germany TS, Sec. 1c, Case 12, Book II, RG 319, USNA. The old conventional argument—laid out, for example, in McGeehan, *German Rearmament Question*, 41—was that the U.S. government, by early September, had decided to press for a German national army "with no particular control arrangement other than that which would have resulted simply by virtue of the German troops being under NATO command and without their own general staff." But this, it turns out, was incorrect: the controls the Army was now calling for were quite far-reaching.

42. See especially McLellan, *Acheson*, 328–330; Martin, "American Decision to Rearm Germany," 656–657; and Acheson, *Present at the Creation*, 437–438, 440.

43. See, for example, Joint Strategic Survey Committee report on Rearmament of Western Germany, July 27, 1950, JCS 2124/11, JCS Geographic File for 1948–50, 092 Germany (5-4-49), RG 218, USNA.

44. *Bolté to Collins, August 28, 1950, Army Operations General Decimal File 1950–51, box 20, file G-3 091 Germany TS, Sec. 1, RG 319, USNA. Note also the initial draft that the military had prepared of a joint reply to the president's "Eight Ques-

tions" letter, given in JCS 2116/28 of September 6, 1950. The original draft, according to another document, was given to the State Department on September 1. See Bolté to Collins, September 2, 1950. Both documents are in Army Operations General Decimal File 1950–51, box 21, file G-3 091 Germany TS, Sec. 1c, Case 12, Books II and (for the September 6 document) III, RG 319, USNA.

45. This key phrase found its way into a whole series of major documents in early September. See appendix to memorandum for the Secretary of Defense, "United States Views on Measures for the Defense of Western Europe," JCS 2073/61, September 3, 1950, JCS Geographic File for 1948–50, Box 25, RG 218, USNA. The same document, after being approved by the Secretary of Defense, was forwarded to the State Department on September 12 and appears in FRUS 1950 3:291–293. A very similar phrase was included in NSC 82; see FRUS 1950 3:274.

46. See, for example, McLellan, *Acheson,* 328.

47. McCloy to Acheson, August 3, 1950, FRUS 1950, 3:181.

48. *Byroade-Schuyler-Gerhardt meeting, August 10, 1950, Army Operations General Decimal File 1950–51, box 21, file G-3 091 Germany TS, Sec. 1c, Case 12, Book II, RG 319, USNA. For the final Byroade plan, and for its adoption as the official State Department position, see Matthews to Burns, August 16, 1950, with enclosure, FRUS 1950, 3:211–219.

49. See, for example, Paul Nitze, with Ann Smith and Steven Rearden, *From Hiroshima to Glasnost: At the Center of Decision* (New York: Grove Weidenfeld, 1989), 123; and Princeton Seminar, p. 914. Note also the tone of Secretary of Defense Johnson's initial reply to State Department letter asking for comments on the August 16 Byroade plan: Johnson to Acheson, August 17, 1950, FRUS 1950, 3:226–227.

50. Truman to Acheson and Johnson, August 26, 1950, FRUS 1950, 3:250–251.

51. Draft memo by Nitze and Byroade, August 25, 1950, Records of the Policy Planning Staff, Country and Area File, Box 28, RG 59, USNA. Some scholars—Martin, for example, in "The American Decision to Rearm Germany," 659—portray the JCS as "prodding" the State Department to take "prompt diplomatic action." And Acheson, in *Present at the Creation* (428), also portrays himself as having been pushed forward, especially by pressure from the president, and actually cites the Eight Questions document in this context. But in reality—and not just at this point, but throughout this episode—it was the State Department that was pushing things forward, and it was Truman who followed Acheson's lead. The president, for example, had been against German rearmament when the JCS had pressed for it in June. But when Acheson told him on July 31 that it no longer was a question of whether Germany should be rearmed, that the real issue now was how it was to be done, and that the State Department was thinking in terms of creating "a European army or a North Atlantic army," Truman immediately "expressed his strong approval" of this whole line of thought. Truman to Acheson, June 16, 1950 (two documents), and Acheson-Truman meeting, July 31, 1950, FRUS 1950, 4:688, 702.

52. *Bolté to Collins, August 28, 1950: "The questions listed in the President's letter are apparently based upon the State Department's proposal for the establishment of a European defense force." Army Operations General Decimal File 1950–51, box 20, file G-3 091 Germany TS, Sec. 1, RG 319, USNA. The point was clear from the text of the letter. The two departments were not simply asked, for example, to consider what, if anything, should be done on the German rearmament question; they were

asked instead to consider whether the U.S. government was prepared to support "the concept of a European defense force, including German participation on other than a national basis"—which was not exactly a neutral way of putting the issue. Truman to Acheson and Johnson, August 26, 1950, FRUS 1950, 3:250.

53. Bolté to Collins, August 31, 1950, and *Gruenther to Davis, Duncan and Edwards, September 1, 1950, enclosing the "Plan for the Development of West German Security Forces," both in Army Operations General Decimal File 1950–51, box 21, file G-3 091 Germany TS, Sec. 1c, Case 12, Book II, RG 319, USNA.

54. Bolté to Collins, September 2, 1950, Army Operations General Decimal File 1950–51, box 21, file G-3 091 Germany TS, Sec. 1c, Case 12, Book II, RG 319, USNA; *Acheson-Nitze-Byroade-Perkins meeting, August 30, 1950, cited in n. 38 above.

55. Acheson and Johnson to Truman, September 8, 1950, FRUS 1950, 3:273–278.

56. Princeton Seminar, pp. 920–921.

57. Princeton Seminar, p. 914.

58. Princeton Seminar, p. 914.

59. NSC 82, FRUS 1950, 3:276.

60. See JCS 2116/28, September 6, 1950, which gives the final draft and shows changes from the earlier draft; Army Operations General Decimal File 1950–51, box 21, file G-3 091 Germany TS, Sec. 1c, Case 12, Book III, RG 319, USNA. For another copy, see JCS to Johnson, September 5, 1950, Records of the Administrative Secretary, Correspondence Control Section Decimal File: July to Dec 1950, CD 091.7 (Europe), box 175, RG 330, USNA.

61. Princeton Seminar, p. 915.

62. Princeton Seminar, p. 916.

63. Princeton Seminar, p. 916; see also p. 912. The archival evidence confirms the point that McCloy favored a very tough line at this time. See especially the handwritten letter from McCloy to Acheson, September 20, 1950, in the Acheson Papers, Memoranda of Conversations, September 1950, HSTL. A high French official, McCloy reported, had just "referred again to the delicacy of French opinion" on the German rearmament issue. "I think the time has come," he wrote, "to tell these people that there is other opinion to deal with and that U.S. opinion is getting damn delicate itself. If there should be an incursion in January and U.S. troops should get pushed around without German troops to help them because of a French reluctance to face facts, I shudder to think how indelicate U.S. opinion would suddenly become."

64. Princeton Seminar, p. 913.

65. Acheson to Truman, September 15, 1950, FRUS 1950, 3:1229–31. For more information relating to the part of the story from the New York conference on, see Christopher Gehrz, "Dean Acheson, the JCS and the 'Single Package': American Policy on German Rearmament, 1950," *Diplomacy and Statecraft* 12 (March 2001): 135–60.

66. Undersecretary Webb, in telephone conversation with Acheson, September 27, 1950, Acheson Papers (Lot File 53D 444), box 13, RG 59, USNA. Webb was comparing the State Department "operation" with the way the Defense Department under Marshall was handling the issue.

67. Omar Bradley and Clay Blair, *A General's Life* (New York: Simon and Schuster, 1983), 519.

68. The idea that Acheson was an exceptionally aggressive statesman is scarcely the consensus view. American writers tend to treat Acheson rather gently, but this, we think, is to be understood in essentially political terms. Acheson's reputation profited enormously from the fact that during his period in office he had been the target of a great deal of ill-informed criticism from right-wing Republicans; Richard Nixon's famous reference at the time to the "Acheson College of Cowardly Communist Containment" is a good case in point. And with enemies like that, it was not hard to find friends—among liberal academics, at any rate.

69. Trachtenberg, *History and Strategy*, 109–110.

70. See, for example, Ernest May, ed., *American Cold War Strategy: Interpreting NSC 68* (New York: St. Martin's, 1993), and John Lewis Gaddis, *Strategies of Containment: A Critical Appraisal of Postwar American National Security Policy* (Oxford and New York: Oxford University Press, 1982), chapter 4.

71. NSC 68, April 7, 1950, FRUS 1950, 1:253, 255, 284; Nitze quoted in Trachtenberg, *History and Strategy*, 112n. Nitze, the principal author of NSC 68, was quite close to Acheson throughout this period. See, for example, David Callahan, *Dangerous Capabilities: Paul Nitze and the Cold War* (New York: HarperCollins, 1990), 95–96, 155, and Strobe Talbott, *The Master of the Game: Paul Nitze and the Nuclear Peace* (New York: Knopf, 1988), 51.

72. See Jonathan Utley, "Upstairs, Downstairs at Foggy Bottom: Oil Exports and Japan, 1940–41," *Prologue* 8 (Spring 1976), 17–28; Jonathan Utley, *Going to War with Japan* (Knoxville: University of Tennessee Press, 1985), 153–156, 180; Irvine Anderson, "The 1941 *de facto* Embargo on Oil to Japan: A Bureaucratic Reflex," *Pacific Historical Review* 44 (1975), 201–231; and Irvine Anderson, *The Standard Vacuum Oil Company and United States East Asian Policy, 1933–1941* (Princeton: Princeton University Press, 1975).

73. Acheson speech at annual meeting of the Institute of Strategic Studies, September 1963, in Adelphi Paper No. 5, *The Evolution of NATO*. See also Douglas Brinkley, *Dean Acheson: The Cold War Years, 1953–71* (New Haven: Yale University Press), 153. Note also Acheson's comment in 1961 about the need for the sort of forces that would enable the Western powers to intervene in the event, for example, of a new uprising in Hungary: Acheson-de Gaulle meeting, April 20, 1961, *Documents diplomatiques français* 1961, 1:494.

74. Bernard Brodie, *War and Politics* (New York: Macmillan, 1973), 402. The critic in question was the former defence minister in the Macmillan government, Harold Watkinson.

75. See, for example, Acheson to Truman, May 28, 1953, box 30, folder 391, and Acheson memorandum of conversation, June 23, 1953, box 68, folder 172, in Acheson Papers, Sterling Library, Yale University, New Haven, Connecticut. Note also Nitze's complaint at the very end of the Truman period that the U.S. government had a purely defensive policy. America, he was afraid, was in danger of becoming "a sort of hedge-hog, unattractive to attack, but basically not very worrisome over a period of time beyond our immediate position." Nitze to Acheson, January 12, 1953, FRUS 1952–54, 2:59.

76. See especially Acheson to Truman, June 24, July 14, August 4, and September 21, 1961, Acheson Papers, Box 166, Acheson-Truman Correspondence, 1961, Sterling Library, Yale University; some extracts are quoted in Trachtenberg, *History and Strategy*,

230. See also Michael Beschloss, *The Crisis Years: Kennedy and Khrushchev, 1960–1963* (New York: Edward Burlingame, 1991), 410; and Honoré Catudal, *Kennedy and the Berlin Wall Crisis: A Study in U.S. Decision-Making* (Berlin: Berlin-Verlag, 1980), 182n.

77. Walter Isaacson and Evan Thomas, *The Wise Men: Six Friends and the World They Made* (New York: Simon and Schuster, 1986), 612–613; see also Brinkley, *Acheson*, 138.

78. Carl Kaysen oral history interview, July 11, 1966, p. 85, John F. Kennedy Library, Boston. We are grateful to Frank Gavin for providing this reference.

79. See, for example, Brinkley, *Acheson*, 174, 202.

80. Acheson to Truman, July 10, 1965, in Dean Acheson, *Among Friends: Personal Letters of Dean Acheson*, ed. David McLellan and David Acheson (New York: Dodd, Mead, 1980), 273.

81. See Trachtenberg, *Constructed Peace*, 304–311. Acheson, however, deliberately gave the Europeans a very different impression. Note especially his discussion of the issue in an April 20, 1961, meeting with de Gaulle, and especially his reference to a system that "would permit Europe to take its own decision on the nuclear matter." *Documents diplomatiques français* 1961, 1:495.

82. White House meeting, October 20, 1961, FRUS 1961–63, 14:518–519. Emphasis in original.

83. Quoted in Frank Costigliola, "LBJ, Germany and the 'End of the Cold War,'" in *Lyndon Johnson Confronts the World: American Foreign Policy, 1963–1968*, eds. Warren Cohen and Nancy Tucker (New York: Cambridge University Press, 1994), 195. Acheson was complaining about what he viewed as Johnson's weak response to de Gaulle's decision in 1966 to take France out of the NATO military organization.

84. Brinkley, *Acheson*, 133.

85. *Notes of Council on Foreign Relations Study Group on Nuclear Weapons and U.S. Foreign Policy, November 8, 1954, meeting, p. 12, Hanson Baldwin Papers, box 125, folder 23, Yale University Library.

86. An account Acheson gave in 1952, implying that the issue emerged only in the course of the New York meeting, was particularly misleading. For the quotation and a discussion pointing out how inaccurate that account was, see McGeehan, *German Rearmament Question*, 48–49.

87. This point is suggested by the structure of the discussion of this issue in the Princeton Seminar: after establishing the basic point that the Pentagon had insisted on the package plan and was thus responsible for what happened in September (pp. 911, 915), Acheson and Nitze then felt free to ease up and talk about how the real reason why the German rearmament issue could not have been played down and "kind of weaved in gradually" did not have to do with the JCS, but rather with what McCloy was doing (p. 916). They then went on to say that McCloy, in fact, probably performed a service in forcing people to face the issue then and there (pp. 922–925).

88. John Lewis Gaddis, *We Now Know: Rethinking Cold War History* (Oxford: Clarendon, 1997), 201.

89. Gaddis, *We Now Know*, 199–203, 288–289. The idea here of internal political norms projected outward was also a theme in the "democratic peace" literature of the 1990s. See for example Bruce Russett, *Grasping the Democratic Peace: Principles for a Post-Cold War World* (Princeton: Princeton University Press, 1993), 119.

90. R. W. Seton-Watson, *Britain in Europe, 1789–1914* (Cambridge: Cambridge University Press, 1938), 547; Lady Gwendolen Cecil, *Life of Robert Marquis of Salisbury*, vol. 3 (London: Hodder and Stoughton, 1931), 136.

91. See especially Geir Lundestad, *"Empire" by Integration: The United States and European Integration, 1945–1997* (Oxford: Oxford University Press, 1998) and Pierre Mélandri, *Les Etats-Unis face à l'unification de l'Europe, 1945–1954* (Paris: A. Pedone, 1980). Note also an important series of interpretative articles on the subject by Klaus Schwabe: "Die Vereinigten Staaten und die Europäischen Integration: Alternativen der amerikanischen Außenpolitik," in *Die Europäischen Integration vom Schuman-Plan bis zu den Verträgen von Rom*, ed. Gilbert Trausch (Baden-Baden: Nomos, 1993); "The United States and European Integration," in *Western Europe and Germany: The Beginnings of European Integration, 1945–1969*, ed. Clemens Wurm (Oxford: Berg, 1995); and "Atlantic Partnership and European Integration: American-European Policies and the German Problem, 1947–1969," in *No End to Alliance: The United States and Western Europe: Past, Present, and Future*, ed. Geir Lundestad (New York: St. Martin's, 1998).

2

"A General Named Eisenhower": Atlantic Crisis and the Origins of the European Economic Community

Paul M. Pitman

In January 1957, the French government staged a parliamentary debate to build support for its conduct of the negotiations on the common market (or European Economic Community [EEC]). Referring to the Suez Crisis, which had unfolded over the previous months, one speaker who favored the common market sardonically thanked Egyptian Colonel Gamal Abdul Nasser and Soviet Marshal Nikolai Bulganin for helping the West Europeans understand the need for unity. In response, a leftist deputy shouted, "Is there not also a general named Eisenhower?"[1] This brief exchange at the Palais Bourbon epitomizes the continental reaction to the international crises that climaxed in November 1956. Indeed, by the winter of 1956, many in France felt that tensions with the country's allies had contributed more than conflicts with its enemies to the drive toward economic integration.

Already in the fall of 1956 it was clear that dissatisfaction with the United States had helped revive the European movement. In October, Janet Flanner, Paris correspondent for the *New Yorker,* had written in her diary that the Europeans appeared to be moving together not only because of the challenge from Egypt but also because of frustration with America:

> Secretary Dulles' . . . semi-idealistic press remarks that good might even come of the Suez difficulties if they stimulated European federation brought a grim smile from French politicians. It is true that lately there has been revived talk on the continent about a united Europe, but the feeling of union unfortunately seems to be founded largely on a common dislike of Mr. Dulles.[2]

Then in early November, the spectacular climax of the Suez Crisis, along with the bloody suppression of the Hungarian revolution by Soviet and Warsaw Pact forces, highlighted Europe's weakness in a world dominated by the two superpowers. Seen from Western Europe, the crisis demonstrated yet again British perfidy and American unreliability. Publicists and politicians alike argued that one of the main lessons of Suez was that the European governments should unite their forces in the EEC.

But did the Suez Crisis really tip the balance toward the formation of a six-country customs union and away from alternate designs for the European economic order? Did a fleeting geopolitical conjuncture determine the Continent's institutional path, thereby reshaping the social and economic development of the Atlantic zone? For decades, the idea that one of the results of the Suez Crisis was the establishment of the common market has often been taken for granted. First expounded in authoritative contemporary analyses, the link between the crisis and breakthrough in the negotiations on European integration has since become a standard element in general histories of postwar international relations.[3] Thus in the first archive-based account of the negotiation of the common market treaty, which primarily draws upon the papers of the German delegation to the EEC talks, Hanns Jürgen Küsters claims that the Suez Crisis prompted the French government's realization that geopolitical imperatives required that it drop its long-standing objections to the common market, thereby opening the way for the conclusion of the EEC Treaty.[4] In a more recent contribution, Küsters baldly states that "the successful outcome of the EEC negotiations was an historical accident, initiated by Nasser's Suez crisis in November 1956."[5]

In the most fruitful challenge to such views, Alan Milward, Frances Lynch, and associated scholars have argued that Suez hardly mattered for the EEC negotiations. Not that geopolitics was always irrelevant to the evolution of the European economic order: in fact, French efforts to contain West Germany's industrial potential and military revival inspired earlier integration schemes such as the European Coal and Steel Community (ECSC) and the European Defense Community (EDC).[6] But Europe's security problems had mostly been settled in October 1954, when the Paris Accords sanctioned German rearmament within an Atlantic framework. From this point on, the only remaining "security" concern relevant to European integration was how to guide West Germany's industrial exports into channels that would benefit social and economic advance throughout Western Europe. According to Milward and his associates, after the winter of 1954, it was not geopolitical factors but the political and economic imperatives of the postwar social settlements that accounted for decisions to pursue economic integration. They have traced the process by which the customs union treaty emerged logically (but not inevitably) from debates on the future of the European economic order that began in the early postwar years and came to focus on a customs union in the early 1950s. Throughout, decisions about economic integration did not result from mere historical accidents. Rather, national negotiating positions reflected long-term economic policies hammered out by top elected

officials and high-level bureaucrats, who sought export-led growth, technical modernization, full employment, and social welfare through controlled
trade liberalization. More fundamentally, across Western Europe foreign economic policy-making reflected the new postwar determination to pursue
economic and social goals that would strengthen political coalitions that included the organized working class, farmers, and the lower middle class.[7]

As for the supposed influence of the Suez Crisis on French policy, Frances
Lynch's trenchant account shows that Paris's crucial decision to endorse the
common market came in early September 1956—at a time when the French,
apparently in the expectation that the United States would tacitly support (or
at least acquiesce in) an invasion of Egypt, were still formulating the plan to
seize the Suez Canal with their British and Israeli partners, two months before the humiliations that supposedly swung France's governing class behind the European cause. Instead of Suez, Lynch points to the proposal for
a Free Trade Area that would include all members of the Organisation for European Economic Cooperation (OEEC), put forward by the British in July
1956, which strengthened the view in France that the country could not depend on existing arrangements to protect French interests.[8] Recent work in
political science has likewise tended to de-emphasize geopolitics. Andrew
Moravcsik, for example, argues that commercial interest, as articulated by
major producer groups, was the main factor that drove the integration
process in the 1950s; in his analysis, "geopolitical ideology" and "security ex-
ternalities" were only influential at the margin.[9]

The establishment of the common market is one of the most highly cele-
brated and best documented episodes in postwar Europe's history. Our interpretation of this event has significant implications, not only for our understanding of the origins of the European communities, but also for our views of
the intrinsic character of European integration and its meaning for global politics. This chapter examines the long-term policy developments that shaped
the French and German decisions to construct a new economic and political
order on the Continent. Instead of arguing that either economic goals or strategic ambitions were the primary drivers of foreign economic policy in the mid-
1950s, it attempts to show that the two sets of concerns *acted together* to shape
decisions in both France and Germany. The first section sets the stage: it ana-
lyzes the politics of European trading and monetary arrangements, surveying
the forces behind alternative regional designs. The main point here is that as
late as the summer of 1956, the future of the common market plan, and more
generally the form that European integration was likely to take, remained anything but certain. The second section considers the role of geopolitical considerations in driving the integration process well before Suez. The focus in
that section is on continental responses to Atlantic strategic developments in
the mid-1950s, especially on the implications of the nuclearization of NATO
war plans. The basic point here is that the security issue had by no means been

resolved when the Paris Accords were signed in October 1954; on the contrary, at about that time policy-makers in France and Germany began to explore the possibility of a European nuclear force independent of the United States. The third section retraces the French and German decisions to establish the common market in the fall and winter of 1956. It argues that the Suez Crisis, which both symbolized and deepened tensions between the continental powers and the "Anglo-Saxons," triggered the establishment of the Common Market, but that the key decisions were not taken in a vacuum: long-term policy goals determined what happened during this crucial phase of the European integration process.

THE POLITICS OF EUROPEAN TRADE

Until January 1959, when the common market first came into effect, Europe's trade was regulated through intergovernmental cooperative arrangements, the most important of which were sponsored by the OEEC. The OEEC trading system rested on two main pillars, gradual trade "liberalization," that is, the removal of quantitative restrictions (but not tariffs) on imports from other OEEC countries, and the more significant European Payments Union (EPU), which arranged multilateral settlement of bilateral payments imbalances between the same countries. By making trade with the rest of the world, especially the United States, less attractive, the OEEC countries had constructed a discriminatory trading system that embraced more than half of the free world's trade, including that of the West European countries, the members of the Sterling Area, and the various elements of the Franc Zone. This framework had nurtured Western Europe's postwar economic miracle, the trade-driven growth that had lowered unemployment while accommodating increases in both wages and workplace democracy. The solidarities and disputes that emerged in this structure would shape the debate over Europe's economic future.[10]

Starting in the early 1950s, as the European economy emerged from the rearmament boom sparked by the Korean War, discontent with the perceived shortcomings of the OEEC system stimulated discussions of the future of the region's economic order. While existing structures continued to provide indispensable props for the European political economy, many on both sides of the Atlantic saw them as temporary expedients whose continued functioning threatened the realization of their long-term goals. On the Continent, the Dutch government put forward plans for a customs union that would give the smaller countries access to the markets in France, Germany, and the United Kingdom, which were still shielded by high tariffs. At the same time, the British government began to campaign vigorously for the restoration of currency convertibility as a way not only to revive Sterling's prewar role as a reserve currency, in particular for the Commonwealth countries, but also to block the emergence of a customs union on the Continent. In contrast, the French cabinets of this period opposed both regional tariff reductions and convertibility, favoring instead a customs union with the Franc zone buttressed by bilateral commercial agreements with France's major trading partners, especially West Germany.[11]

The West European governments faced choices between three contending visions of the future of the region's economic order: the further consolidation of the European market centered on the ECSC countries, known as the "Six,"* a liberalized free-world market in which currencies would be freely convertible, and a revival of the French and British colonial economic blocs. As a result of the teleological bias in both the popular and academic literatures, accounts of these debates have focused almost exclusively on the emergence of the common market and virtually ignored support for Atlantic or imperial schemes. Although there have been attempts to argue that the British proposal for an OEEC-wide Free Trade Area stood some chance of adoption, no study has attempted to weigh the political support across Europe for the three serious contenders. For the purposes of this chapter, it suffices to note that all three alternatives were taken seriously enough to frame debates on foreign economic policy in both France and Germany.

In the 1950s European policy-makers still paid special attention to signals from Washington. Like its Democratic predecessor, the Eisenhower administration, which took office in January 1953, stoutly backed the formation of a West European political and economic bloc capable of anchoring Germany to the West and countering Soviet influence on the Continent.[12] But the new administration sought to cut military spending and foreign aid in order to protect America's long-term economic health and civic vitality, which it identified with decentralized government and a competitive market order. The administration also sought to shift U.S. aid from Europe to the Third World, where Soviet economic initiatives increasingly appeared to threaten Western influence. These considerations, which inspired the famous "New Look" in military strategy, also drove efforts to rethink foreign economic relations.[13] Nonetheless, just as the Eisenhower administration would end up maintaining its ground forces in Europe, it would also continue to give European economic unification priority over a worldwide liberal market order. But the mixed messages that emerged from the Washington policy process cast serious doubt on America's willingness to tolerate continued European discrimination against imports from the dollar zone. In Europe the impact of rumors about political battles in the administration and Congress may well have been more significant than the United States government's steadfast policies.

In the summer of 1953 Eisenhower sponsored the first serious review of foreign economic policy since the debate on the Marshall Plan. Published in

---

*That is, Belgium, France, Germany, Italy, Luxembourg, and the Netherlands.

early 1954, the report of the bipartisan Commission on Foreign Economic Policy (CFEP) declared that it was time to end the Marshall Plan settlement—which had always been seen as a temporary expedient—under which the Europeans had come to trade more intensively with each other but systematically discriminated against imports from the United States, despite receiving substantial economic aid. The CFEP called for a return to something like the Bretton Woods program of multilateral trade and currency convertibility. Logically enough, the commission also argued that in order to overcome the worldwide dollar shortage, which blocked progress toward liberalizing international trade and payments, the American market should be opened to imports from the rest of the free world economies. Likewise, the government should encourage increased private direct investment instead of continuing to provide foreign aid.[14]

The Eisenhower administration endorsed the CFEP's call for "Trade, not Aid." But the American government failed to follow through either at home or abroad. The president made considerable efforts to convince Congress to reduce quota and tariff barriers that excluded European products from the American market, but the victorious commander on the European Front in World War II was no match for homegrown protectionism. And despite public endorsements of convertibility, Washington repeatedly put off the magic day when currencies would be exchanged freely.[15] Likewise, although much aid was redirected toward developing countries, the Eisenhower administration continued to provide massive amounts of military and economic assistance to the Europeans because it seemed necessary, *inter alia*, to push the Germans to rearm quickly and to encourage the French to meet their NATO obligations despite the drain imposed by the war in Algeria.

Although its policy came under fire from the Treasury, Congress, and the public, the Eisenhower administration was clearly willing to live with European trade preferences in the interest of achieving the greater strategic goal of building a second great power mass within the West capable of resisting the Soviet threat. In 1955 and 1956 American diplomacy focused on supporting the proposal for a six-power European Atomic Energy Community (EURATOM), which appeared to offer a way to channel continental nuclear ambitions into a supranational framework. It paid relatively little attention to the common market negotiations, presumably because most observers expected protectionist forces in France to block economic integration. Still, Washington backed the formation of a six-member customs union, hoping it would adopt a liberal external policy. American analysts did note the danger that the common market might form a protectionist trade bloc, especially if French preferences determined its external stance, but many hoped that increased intra-European trade would allow the weaker economies to modernize and eventually drop their opposition to freer trade with North America.[16] Certainly the common market offered a better way to tie German industry to the West than an OEEC-wide Free Trade Area such as that proposed by the British. The British scheme would have led to even greater losses for American exporters without deepening Europe's political integration.

Thus, although American leaders often declared their interest in a more liberal world economic system, this had no tangible effect on Washington's actual policy toward further economic integration on the Continent. It was thus ironic that America's continued diplomatic support for European unification did not carry as much weight on the Continent as the mixed signals that emerged from Washington policy debates. There is room here for just one example, drawn from the realm of monetary politics. The Americans repeatedly declined to pony up the cash needed to back British plans to make the pound convertible. Such an action would have set off a chain reaction leading to the dissolution of the EPU and thus a cut in credits to France that would force the Fourth Republic to choose between improvements in social welfare, investments in industry, and paying for the war in Algeria.[17] Although French policy-makers were no doubt relieved each time a convertibility plan was vetoed, they continued to hear dark rumors of secret negotiations between British and American Treasury officials.[18] Given that the Americans had frozen aid payments to the French as a punishment for the rejection of the European Defense Community, who could say what they might do in some later fight?[19]

The Eisenhower administration's grand strategy called for the establishment of a six-power common market, which would provide the economic underpinnings for a "united Europe as a third great force in the world."[20] In contrast, successive British governments stubbornly opposed the consolidation of "Little Europe," because it would threaten the United Kingdom's economic and political standing in the world by undermining the City of London's role as a financial center, weakening the Commonwealth's already attenuated trading ties with the British Isles, and increasing the danger that France and Germany would become America's primary political partners, thereby reducing the chances that Washington would continue to aid Britain's "independent" atomic forces.[21] However, as events would show, neither the British nor their allies and clients on the Continent were in a position to stop integration projects backed by Paris and Bonn. And American support and British weakness meant that the only real question was whether the sharp differences between the French and German visions of the New Europe could be overcome.

The French government's policy on economic integration reflected the requirements of its modernization plans, its commitment to the welfare state, and its ambitions for the reconstitution of the empire. Thus the proposal for the ECSC was designed to guarantee the success of the Monnet Plan; the EDC met the needs of the French aircraft and electronics industries; and the

Green Pool grew out of the decision to aim for permanent agricultural surpluses. More broadly, the policy-making community in Paris rejected the classical liberal view that trade should lead to further specialization in those products in which each country enjoyed a comparative advantage. Instead, the French sought to negotiate political agreements to fix a favorable structure for key industries before trade controls were lifted. Given that France's advanced social legislation put the country at a disadvantage in export markets, French leaders also made the harmonization of regulations on collective bargaining, paid vacations, women's wages, and social welfare a condition for their acceptance of a new trading system. Moreover, to compensate for the loss of direct political control over its empire, the French sought to reformulate the trade and monetary links between the members of the Union française, which would then join the European community as a unit. This arrangement promised to increase France's weight in Europe and, so the argument went, Europe's role in world politics.[22]

West German attitudes toward the European economic order were pulled between liberal ideological preferences and the practical need to guarantee economic ties with Germany's main trading partners, France and the Benelux countries. Earlier accounts of the Federal Republic's policy on the Common Market emphasized that the country's trading interests extended well beyond the Six, and that industry, represented by Professor Ludwig Erhard, the Minister of Economics, supported an OEEC-wide Free Trade Area as a step toward the restoration of currency convertibility. However, more recent research has shown that many business leaders remained skeptical about the wisdom of depending on the world market, preferring the security of established trade ties with Germany's closest neighbors.[23] A striking example of this attitude emerges in the Foreign Ministry's refutation of an attack on the common market issued by the Economics Ministry:

> The Foreign Ministry does not completely share the Economics Ministry's plan for economic conquest of the world, because such a rash . . . thrust into empty space must eventually reach its limits, whether in an economic downturn or another type of shock. At that point, the only thing that will be left will be whatever has been politically organized, namely the community of the Six (or Seven if Great Britain joins); otherwise Germany's economic expansion will fall in on itself.[24]

In line with such thinking, the competent German authorities, including the central bank, vigorously protected the trading arrangements that had grown up since 1949, and in particular the special economic relationship with France, Germany's top economic partner.[25] Of course, both industry representatives and government officials agreed on opposing the French proposals to harmonize wages and benefits, which would eliminate what many saw as key sources of Germany's export competitiveness. Even while supporting the common market scheme, Bonn's negotiators fought Paris's specific demands regarding social policy, agricultural imports, atomic energy, and subsidies to France's imperial dependencies. At the same time, the divisions within the German policy-making community meant that, when it came time to decide whether to go ahead with the common market, Chancellor Konrad Adenauer would be able to impose his own preferences, which by all accounts were shaped more by geopolitical thinking than by economic arguments.[26]

The first year and a half of the common market negotiations demonstrated the conflict between French and German visions for Europe's economic future. In the fall and winter of 1954, the Dutch had renewed the push for a customs union, in part out of fear of the consequences of the secret Franco-German trade and investment deals that accompanied the Paris Accords.[27] In May 1955, once the Federal Republic had formally joined NATO, the Dutch common market proposal, combined with a French proposal for an atomic energy pool, kicked off a new set of negotiations on six-power integration, the so-called *relance européenne*. But over the summer, the common market initiative got off to such a rocky start that the Dutch submitted further trade liberalization proposals to both the OEEC and the General Agreement on Tariffs and Trade.[28] The main sticking point in the common market talks was German opposition to French demands. The French delegation focused almost exclusively on EURATOM—it did not even receive instructions regarding the customs union until early October, shortly before the negotiations had to be suspended because the Edgar Faure government decided to call new elections.[29]

The Mollet government, which took power following parliamentary elections in January 1956, supported European integration much more strongly than any cabinet since early 1952 (when the first "Europeanist coalition" in the National Assembly had collapsed). Its leading members had impeccable Europeanist credentials, and many scholars have accepted their later claims to have secretly planned to push through the common market treaty from the moment they entered office.[30] But in the spring of 1956, Socialist influence in interministerial debates resulted in a negotiating position that threatened to block the common market negotiations once and for all. France's new position did not just strengthen earlier calls for the harmonization of labor regulations and social policy, which was only to be expected given the Mollet government's center-left orientation. The French also pushed for common macroeconomic policies and long-term industrial plans. In effect, the French now sought to use the common market to lock in expansionist Keynesian policies and sectoral planning throughout continental Europe.[31] For the government in Bonn, Paris's new position, which directly challenged the principles of Germany's *soziale Marktwirtschaft*, was simply unacceptable. As soon as the French delegation presented its new position in

Brussels, the common market negotiations came to a standstill. The Mollet government's new dirigist design made it less likely than ever that a customs union would come into being.

What would have happened if the conflict between the French and German plans for the European economy had not been overcome? It is hard to imagine that the British government would have pursued its Free Trade Area proposal seriously, because London's main goal was to avoid being shut out from European markets.[32] Instead, the West European economy probably would have continued to develop within existing frameworks. Trade certainly could have expanded significantly under the OEEC's "liberalization" program, with whatever neoimperial extensions the French and the British were able to cultivate. There probably would have been further progress toward convertibility through gradual "hardening" of settlement terms in the EPU. And it seems likely that the German authorities would have backed emergency credits to France whenever a real pinch came, both to safeguard its main trading interests and for more general political reasons.[33] But without new political understandings between the French and German governments, it was unlikely that "Little Europe" would have emerged as a defined economic bloc.

THE DEBATE OVER EUROPEAN DEFENSE

As noted above, recent historical accounts of the origins of the Common Market start with the proposition that the key security issues that had divided the Western nations during the first postwar decade were settled when West Germany joined NATO. In fact, intra-alliance arguments remained as lively as ever after May 1955. The Western powers were still divided over defense for one simple reason with many complicated consequences: the nuclearization of NATO strategy. The other problems that had troubled Atlantic relations since the late 1940s, such as burden-sharing, controls over armament levels, or competition over the production of technologically advanced armaments, never simply went away. They persisted, but the practical implications of the various solutions proposed for them changed, often dramatically, as a result of nuclearization. And all of these problems came to a head simultaneously in the summer and fall of 1956, primarily because of a sharp controversy sparked by Anglo-American plans to substitute atomic weapons for troops stationed in Germany.

Disputes over European defense have often been seen as a long struggle to reach a compromise around sensible Atlanticist policies that effectively meshed NATO's conventional "shield" and its atomic "sword." But in the mid-1950s, Western capitals had just begun to struggle with the basic political choices imposed by the spread of atomic weapons, and the conclusions to these debates were anything but foregone.[34] On the Continent, it seemed that three distinct strategic options were still open. The first option, known as "forward defense," called for stopping any Soviet attack as far east as possible, preferably along the West German border. While forward defense remained official NATO doctrine, skeptical Europeans perceived signs that the United States and the United Kingdom wished to revert to a second option, the "peripheral strategy," according to which the Western powers would allow Soviet forces to overrun most of the Continent before trying to reconquer whatever was left after a month of armored operations accompanied by nuclear strikes.[35] The European allies tended to feel that economic concerns (for the British, the defense of Sterling and Commonwealth economic ties; for the Americans, the need to roll back the garrison state) drove the efforts at strategic revision and conventional retrenchment. In response to the threat that the "maritime powers" would withdraw their ground forces or decouple their deterrent forces from the Central Front, some continental strategists favored a third option: the establishment of a "Eurafrican" bloc, armed with an autonomous nuclear deterrent and able to draw on the depth offered by France's African territories.[36] The important point to note here is that the broad directions European strategy could pursue in the mid-1950s—forward defense, peripheral strategy, or Eurafrican coalition—roughly corresponded to the three alternate schemes for the region's trade and monetary relations that were under consideration in policy circles at the same time.

Washington's commitment to "forward defense" was far from certain in the mid-1950s. As part of its grand strategy, the Eisenhower administration tried to foster the consolidation of a European power base that would allow a reduction in America's efforts to defend the Old World. But the main policy pursued by the Americans, the deployment of large numbers of tactical nuclear weapons in Western Europe along with schemes for "sharing" control of these weapons, ironically made it even more difficult to withdraw U.S. troops.[37] In the end, despite the attractiveness of British strategic proposals and the pull of isolationism, the Eisenhower administration did maintain established force levels in Europe. At the same time, as in economic affairs, it may have been not so much official American policy as continental fears based on unsubstantiated but plausible rumors about Pentagon priorities that gave the biggest push to Franco-German understanding.

The French response to the nuclearization of Atlantic strategy was straightforward. To defend the metropole, to maintain influence in the empire, to have a say in Western strategy, France needed to field an independent nuclear force. But to build a deterrent force, the French needed technical, industrial and financial assistance. Given that the British and the Americans refused to help, the French turned to West Germany. Thus the nuclearization of NATO strategy led the French to spearhead efforts to build a European bomb.[38]

Although France's strategists had been grappling with the implications of nuclear weapons for over a decade, it was in August and September 1954—just before and after the French parliament's vote to reject the European Defense Community—that the country's military authorities and political leaders first drew conclusions about the need for continental nuclear cooperation. The basic strategic views that emerged in these months are worth reviewing in some detail because they provided much of the hidden impetus behind Paris's European policies down to the end of the Fourth Republic, if not beyond. The development of France's policy toward cooperation in atomic energy shows that, rather than opposing European integration, military leaders often pointed the way.

The debate opened in response to a draft entitled the "Possibilities Plan," put forward by General Alfred Gruenther, NATO's Supreme Allied Commander, Europe (SACEUR). The Possibilities Plan provided the basis for the alliance's new strategic doctrine, which the NATO Council would formally adopt as MC-48 in December 1954.[39] In a hard-hitting response to Gruenther's plan, France's representative in NATO's Standing Group, General Jean Valluy, offered ideas that appear to have oriented the country's political response to the nuclearization of NATO strategy.[40] Valluy first pointed out that SACEUR assumed that any war fought in Europe would be decided quickly by a brief but intense atomic exchange. If the Central Front could be held during the crucial early days of a conflict, the West's overall superiority in strategic weapons would prevail. Thus NATO's chances for victory depended as never before on blocking Soviet efforts to launch rapid air strikes against tactical nuclear forces in Western Europe. To meet this challenge, Gruenther's new strategy called for "unconditional and instantaneous" atomic strikes that would destroy Soviet nuclear weapons on the ground. Provided they could be shielded from air strikes, NATO's "covering forces" deployed on the Central Front, which included units armed with tactical atomic weapons, stood a good chance of repelling a Soviet ground assault.

According to Valluy, the new NATO strategy would cause a major transformation in France's strategic situation. Forward defense of Western Europe, previously "affirmed somewhat academically," had not only become a technical necessity, it would soon be a practical possibility. But as a key staging ground for NATO's atomic attacks, Western Europe would also become a primary target for Soviet nuclear strikes. France's ground forces would have to prepare for operations in an atomic environment, while France's future nuclear forces would need to coordinate operations with the United States Strategic Air Command.

Whatever the military and budgetary implications, the new strategy's key difficulty was political. In order to preempt Soviet atomic strikes, it would be necessary to authorize NATO to launch attacks at the earliest possible moment. But the predelegation of authority to initiate atomic strikes, presumably to SACEUR, threatened to leave Europe's defense in the hands of an American general. For Valluy, the consequences were clear:

> The defense of the West, now concentrated around atomic weapons, will depend entirely on America's will. The only corrective for this subordination would be the constitution by the European nations of an atomic arsenal that would allow them to intervene with their own forces in such a new war and consequently resume a key role in the leadership of the coalition.[41]

NATO's adoption of a nuclear strategy did not simply mean that France had to adapt its conventional forces and acquire atomic weapons. It also meant that France, in association with its continental allies, needed to build and deploy a European deterrent force.

During the fall of 1954, the French high command amplified Valluy's message. An example is the response to a Foreign Ministry proposal for an armaments pool to replace the industrial side of the EDC prepared by General Jacques Faure, the top military aide to Defense Minister Emmanuel Temple (and one of the leaders of the coterie of military officers who had openly campaigned against the European Army plan). Faure argued that imposing restrictions on the German arms industry would only benefit British and American producers. Instead, within an Atlantic framework and preferably with British participation, France should produce atomic weapons with Germany in "secure" zones such as French North Africa.[42]

What did France's military leaders actually have in mind? The political implications of their proposals are clear: a European deterrent force, developed under French control on the basis of German industrial potential, could at once improve Europe's standing within the Atlantic Alliance and anchor the American nuclear guarantee. But despite their generous Europeanist rhetoric, it is unclear how far the French intended to go in sharing control of the force with the Germans. One wonders if French leaders had reached firm conclusions in this fundamental area.

During the fall and winter of 1954, the French government began to move forward, albeit tentatively and cautiously, with the proposals for a European deterrent put forward by the military. In September, the *Comité de défense nationale*, France's highest authority in military matters, debated the expense of a national deterrent force and the possibility that six-power atomic cooperation might help France pay for atomic weapons.[43] In the spring of 1955, the government sought German assistance in constructing an isotopic separation plant to produce the enriched uranium needed for the French bomb program. But the Germans, still waiting to join NATO, chose not to respond to French overtures at this time. In the coming months, the French would continue to reach out to their neighbors; for example, in July 1955 a representative of the Atomic Energy Commission met with Italian military offices to propose a joint research and development program.[44] The French government's main efforts on behalf of a "European deterrent" took place within the framework of the EURATOM negotiations, the real focus of which was, and would remain, an isotopic separation plant.[45]

Once again, Paris's main problem was to overcome opposition within the Bonn government. Although the German Foreign Ministry stood behind the EURATOM initiative, the minister responsible for atomic energy, Franz Josef Strauß, did not. Backed by industrial interests, Strauß strongly opposed key elements of the plan such as supranational controls and monopoly ownership of fissile materials, favoring instead direct ties with British and American industry.[46] In July 1956 the EURATOM talks became even more difficult as a result of the debates in the French Parliament. Facing heavy opposition to EURATOM, the Mollet government had to promise that the plan would not interfere with France's still officially unacknowledged efforts to produce atomic weapons. In Bonn, this raised once again the fear that Paris's European policy sought to limit Germany's strategic options.

Although the Germans had worried about the nuclearization of NATO strategy for some time, the Bonn government did not directly address its political consequences until the summer and fall of 1956.[47] In June 1956, German worries were stimulated when the British, determined to reduce the largest drain on the balance of payments by withdrawing troops from Germany, proposed that NATO develop a new Political Directive to endorse even greater reliance on nuclear weapons than that authorized under MC-48.[48] Then in July the *New York Times* reported plans supposedly under consideration by Admiral Arthur W. Radford, chairman of the Joint Chiefs of Staff, to reduce conventional forces and withdraw troops from Germany.[49] News of the "Radford Plan" had tremendous repercussions in Bonn. Leading German politicians, not least Chancellor Adenauer, expressed fears that the maritime powers might abandon their allies on the continent. The controversy came at a particularly awkward time, just days after the government had defended the need for eighteen months' compulsory military service before a skeptical Bundestag. The Anglo-American strategic initiatives threatened to turn Germany's twelve new divisions—for years the cause of fights over the future military balance within Western Europe—into mere "atomic cannon fodder."

The so-called Radford Crisis generated huge tensions in the relations between Bonn and Washington. It also provided a political excuse for a thoroughgoing reconsideration of the Federal Republic's rearmament plans. West Germany's political leaders acted as if they had suddenly grasped the practical implications of the strategic situation they had accepted by joining NATO. In the cabinet discussion on 20 July 1956 ministers agreed that the Federal Republic should seek to increase its influence in NATO in order to pressure its allies to maintain conventional force levels. Chancellor Adenauer stated that if Western strategy continued to switch over to nuclear weapons, the Federal Republic would have to reconsider its 1954 renunciation of the production of atomic, bacterial, and chemical weapons. And Strauß told the cabinet, "Today a nation that does not produce atomic weapons itself is déclassé."[50] Of course, the West German government has never openly admitted the extent of its interest in atomic weapons. But the nuclearization of NATO strategy explains the form taken by German rearmament. During the fall and winter of 1956, the dynamic Strauß, who took over the post of defense minister, would oversee a fundamental shift from large conscript forces toward a smaller, more professional military capable of deploying tactical nuclear weapons.[51]

The tensions between Washington and Bonn provided an opening for those within the French government who sought backing for a "European" deterrent. The French arranged for a high-ranking German representative, General Adolf Heusinger, to present his government's criticisms of the Radford Plan at a special meeting of NATO's Standing Group. During the meeting, Heusinger first noted that press coverage of the Radford Plan had weakened public support for NATO and threatened his government's efforts to raise troops. He then discussed the importance of strong "shield" forces, stressing the danger that NATO might lose a "small" conventional war if the British and Americans withdrew significant ground forces from Germany. Supporting the French war effort in Algeria, Heusinger also referred to the importance of holding North Africa as NATO's southern flank. The French member of the Standing Group, General Jean Valluy, strongly backed Heusinger's criticisms of Anglo-American proposals to depend on atomic forces to defend Europe. He also attacked the United States' policy of withholding nuclear technology from its continental Allies.[52]

In a subsequent private talk between Valluy and Heusinger, at which a number of other French and German officers were present, the fundamental compatibility between French and German strategic perspectives came out. Valluy stressed that the West European continental powers should unite their forces in order to escape complete dependence on the Anglo-Saxons. In particular, as the two strongest European powers, France and Germany needed to cooperate to break the Anglo-American nuclear monopoly. Valluy also emphasized the significance of North Africa for Europe's defense—a point that Heusinger had underlined in his presentation to the Standing Group. In the course of their conversation, the two generals also discovered that they shared similar views on a wide range of operational and command problems in NATO.[53]

France's support for Germany in NATO debates, along with Valluy's approach regarding atomic cooperation, apparently encouraged policy-makers in Bonn to reconsider the Mollet government's repeated efforts to revive bilateral armaments cooperation.[54] Thus, in the summer of 1956—just at the time when the common market talks had reached an impasse over German opposition to French proposals regarding industrial planning, welfare policy, and labor relations—French and German strategists were discovering that they shared not only reasonable fears regarding Anglo-American tendencies to revert to a peripheral strategy, but also an interest in establishing a Eurafrican defense bloc with atomic capabilities. During the following months, during one of the postwar era's most serious crises in Atlantic relations, these contradictory trends found resolution in an economic and strategic settlement that would shape the European order for decades to come.

ATLANTIC CRISIS AND EUROPEAN MARKET

The Suez Crisis intensified tensions between the United States and its main European allies. Recent historical studies have provided a detailed picture of the crisis itself, which began in July 1956 when the Egyptian government nationalized the Suez Canal and ended the following November when an Anglo-French attempt failed to retake the canal by force. But its broader consequences for international and transnational relations remain to be explored.[55] For the purposes of this chapter, it suffices to note that it was not Moscow's threats of atomic reprisals but Washington's moves against Sterling that convinced the British government to abandon its French (and Israeli) partners in the middle of an otherwise brilliantly successful military operation. French and German leaders reacted to Soviet threats, American sabotage, and British withdrawal with bitter anger at Great Britain's fecklessness and dark speculations regarding the possibility that the two superpowers might find condominium mutually beneficial.[56] As Chancellor Adenauer reportedly said during his visit to French Premier Guy Mollet at the turning point in the crisis on 6 November, the only way the European powers could play a decisive role in world affairs would be to build Europe. No doubt seeking to play on French resentment toward the English and the Americans, the chancellor added, "Europe will be your revenge."[57]

The German statesman's remarks apparently hit the mark. But what did his geopolitical posturing have to do with mundane negotiations on European trade? Conclusive documentary evidence shows that the French and German governments had already taken the basic decisions on the common market and EURATOM in September and early October 1956, well before the high point of the Suez Crisis in November. One could argue, along with scholars such as Milward, that geopolitical factors in general, and Suez in particular, did not count for much in these decisions, which were really driven by the requirements of national economic and social programs.[58] I submit that a review of French and German foreign policy-making shows that the overlapping disputes with the Americans over both economic and security issues, which came to a head just as Paris and Bonn reformulated their European strategies, provide a fuller explanation for the new diplomatic alignment that resulted in the common market treaty.

Thus Suez triggered sharp political reactions, but these reactions were not the fundamental cause of the political shift in Europe that occurred in the fall of 1956. Policy-makers in Paris and Bonn interpreted the disloyal behavior of the maritime powers in light of years of bruising fights over international economic relations, Atlantic strategy, and policy toward the Third World. American actions during the crisis certainly did not reverse European attitudes toward Atlantic ties. Instead, by dramatizing long-standing concerns, Suez underscored the need to lessen Europe's strategic and economic dependence on the United States, a goal that many continental leaders had already come to see as essential. The recurring rumors about convertibility, the possibility of American support for the Free Trade Area, the controversy over the nuclearization of NATO strategy, and the repercussions of the war in Algeria clearly weighed more heavily than the Suez Crisis in France's acceptance of a liberal customs union and Germany's support for the "European" bomb program.[59] This chapter is too short for a full account of the domestic and international bargains that resulted in the formation of the European Communities. But even a brief overview of the shifts in French and German policy toward Europe in the late summer and early fall of 1956 can illustrate how the crisis in Atlantic relations facilitated the consolidation of Little Europe.

The Mollet Government was run by "good Europeans," but they failed to pursue their designs for the regional economic order until early September 1956, when top ministers accepted the principle of integration through trade liberalization and dropped their springtime proposals for pan-European industrial planning and demand management. In subsequent interministerial negotiations, the principal players on the French side, including representatives of producer interests, elaborated further demands regarding subsidies for imperial development, agriculture, and safeguard clauses designed to make the treaty acceptable to Parliament.[60] France's negotiating partners sometimes interpreted these new demands as fresh evidence that the Fourth Republic might never be ready to accept the common market. But in Paris, a page had been turned.

What accounts for the decision by the French government to change course on Europe at this particular time? Although many factors may be adduced, the decisive cause was the realignment in domestic politics that resulted from the developments in Algeria.[61] The Socialist-led government's vigorous prosecution of the war destroyed the center-left alignment that had emerged from the January 1956 elections and led to the gradual reconstitution of a new "Europeanist coalition" in Parliament, which included the main center and right parties.[62] One consequence, which further weakened support on the left, was a scaling back of the government's ambitious social and economic programs and the imposition of measures associated with a war economy. France's intransigent stand in Algeria also sharpened ongoing conflicts in NATO over policy toward the Third World and brought new tensions with Washington.[63] Ironically, what critics bitterly termed "National-molletisme"—the Socialist government's play for nationalist support—opened the way for economic liberals such as Foreign Minister Christian Pineau and his advisor, economist Robert Marjolin, acting in accord with organized business and the farming lobby, to seize the initiative on the common market. The decision by Mollet and his close advisors to put the empire and Europe ahead of socialism coincided with a renewed push for military cooperation with West Germany, which won additional support from conservative political forces, including Gaullists such as Defense Minister Maurice Bourgès-Maunoury who had earlier sponsored the EURATOM proposal.[64]

As always, for the Europeanist government in Paris the key question was how to line up support in Bonn. After putting forward his government's new line in Brussels, European Affairs Minister Maurice Faure traveled to Berlin and Bonn to present his case to German leaders. In talks with German Foreign Minister Heinrich von Brentano, Faure linked progress in European integration to Franco-German armaments collaboration. He apparently surprised von Brentano by suggesting that EURATOM might also be extended to military uses of atomic energy. Faure also noted that the French would not oppose German acquisition of tactical nuclear weapons.[65] Like General Valluy, Faure suggested that cooperation with France would help, rather than hinder, German efforts to acquire atomic weapons.

In the meantime, Mollet attempted to reinforce ties with London before settling on partnership with Bonn. During a meeting with British Prime Minister Anthony Eden in early September, the French Premier proposed reviving Jean Monnet's June 1940 proposal to merge the British Commonwealth and the French Union. In the run-up to the Suez operation, Mollet remained attentive to the sensibilities of his British partners.[66] But during a visit to Bonn at the end of the month, he agreed with Adenauer that the danger that the Anglo-Saxons would return to the "peripheral strategy" meant it was necessary to build "Little Europe." Mollet argued that Franco-German cooperation was needed both to complete the negotiations on the EEC and EURATOM, the success of which would encourage British participation in European affairs, and to revive continental armaments cooperation. In response, Adenauer stated that his government would weigh France's proposals regarding military cooperation when setting its positions on EURATOM and the common market.[67] The Mollet government, long aware of Britain's lack of support for French policies in Europe, and no doubt especially frustrated by London's dithering preparations for the Suez invasion, had apparently decided to bet on the Franco-German axis. And the Federal Republic's leaders clearly welcomed France's choices.

Paris's campaign for German support soon paid off. Chancellor Adenauer dominated the formulation of the Bonn government's position on the EEC and EURATOM, strongly favoring entente with France against the Atlanticists in his government, such as Economics Minister Ludwig Erhard, who argued that Germany should pursue a new economic *Weltpolitik*.[68] In public, the chancellor continued to stress the need for full British participation in European affairs,[69] but in government deliberations he staunchly supported "Little Europe." Even scholars who argue that the common market was established primarily as an extension of domestic economic policy or in the pursuit of commercial advantage acknowledge that the Federal Republic's stance on Europe was decided by Chancellor Adenauer, and that Adenauer's policy was driven above all by geopolitical considerations.[70] But they have not noted that the German government's discussions of the EEC and EURATOM really turned on two specific issues: Europe's place in the Atlantic Alliance and questions of nuclear strategy. First, the Europeans needed to unite in order to maintain support from the Americans. Thus Adenauer argued in early October that if the Europeans did not conclude the EEC and EURATOM treaties quickly, American isolationism might gain the upper hand. When an economic downturn came, Washington might decide it could no longer bear the burden of keeping its markets open, let alone the cost of leading Europe's defense.[71] Second, Europe, rather than NATO, might be the best way for Germany to regain the right to produce atomic weapons. As the chancellor put it during a cabinet meeting on 19 December 1956: "Europe will have a longer life than NATO. It is now necessary to push ahead with the unification of Europe and to produce atomic weapons in the Federal Republic."[72] The basic message was clear: the unreliability of transatlantic ties required tighter European economic and military cooperation. The strategic issues and the economic issues were thus very tightly bound up with each other.

The showdown over Bonn's European policy came on 5 October 1956, several weeks before the launch of the Suez operation. Adenauer imposed acceptance of a negotiating position that took account of the main French demands, overriding opposition from Economics Minister Erhard and Atomic Energy Minister Strauß. In one of his many efforts to block the common market, Erhard suggested that the six-power talks should be postponed pending further consultations with the British regarding the Free Trade Area. The Chancellor, seconded by the representative of the Foreign Ministry, opposed any delay on the grounds that the British were only pursuing the Free Trade Area because of the danger that Britain would be excluded from the common market. Led by the chancellor, the cabinet rejected Erhard's objections one after the other. When the discussion turned to EURATOM, Strauß argued that the atomic energy community would represent more of a sacrifice than an advantage for the Germans. Adenauer's response, as recorded in the official cabinet minutes, was unequivocal: "[The Chancellor] wanted to use EURATOM as the quickest way to gain the option to produce nuclear weapons." This was just what the French had been hinting at since the summer. Adenauer further argued that EURATOM would be worthwhile even though Germany would not be able to catch up with France's lead in research for some time.[73]

Despite decisions by the French and Germans to favor six-power integration, the negotiations on the EEC and EURATOM continued to face major obstacles. Indeed, the October Foreign Ministers conference reached an impasse because the French and German representatives were unable to reach a workable compromise on two crucial problems: harmonization of social policies and ownership of fissile materials. Mollet and Adenauer overcame this deadlock during a meeting held in Paris on 6 November, at the high point of the Suez Crisis. The French dropped their demand that regulations on overtime pay be harmonized, in exchange for the right to invoke safeguard clauses on behalf of industries harmed by competition from countries with longer work weeks. And the Germans finally accepted the idea that EURATOM would enjoy a monopoly over fissile materials unless the community was unable to provide sufficient supplies, in which case member states would be authorized to make purchases from third parties.[74] At the same time, the Germans also agreed to French proposals regarding closer cooperation in weapons development, under WEU auspices if possible, or on a bilateral basis if necessary.[75] Negotiating over the heads of their European partners, the two governments had formulated a compromise settlement of the main outstanding issues, a settlement that would find its way almost unchanged into the EEC and EURATOM treaties.

CONCLUSION

French and German dissatisfaction with the Atlantic system drove the political decisions that led to the establishment of the European Communities. The Suez Crisis mattered, but only as a trigger, not as a fundamental cause. The special circumstances of the Suez Crisis spurred the decision by the leaders of France and Germany to cooperate in establishing European structures that would form an autonomous zone of economic policy and strengthen the Continent's influence in NATO. Suez also pushed public and parliamentary opinion in both Paris and Bonn toward European integration as an alternative to Atlantic cooperation, making it possible to strike a deal with little worry about the domestic repudiation that had killed the EDC. But the package deal agreed on by the French and Germans in November 1956—a liberal customs union flanked by sectoral agreements for agriculture, imperial development and, last but not least, strategic industries—represented a practical compromise between the key policy requirements of long-standing French and German economic and strategic programs. The reorganization of the European economic order was thus the result, not of any single incident, however dramatic, but of persistent tensions within the Atlantic system acting upon domestic economic policy processes.

Continental perspectives on European integration reflected the experience of years of disputes with the "Anglo-Saxon" powers. Fundamental questions regarding the durability of Atlantic economic ties and the reliability of extended deterrence pushed the French and German governments toward a new strategic and economic partnership years before Colonel Nasser nationalized the Suez Canal. As part of its grand strategy, the United States consistently supported European unity, but in practice its support seemed to do little to bring the Europeans together. Rather, the United States played a crucial role in the integration process by making attempts—often unsuccessful—to limit its European engagements in order to protect America's domestic economic health and social vitality. As much as any specific policy pursued by the United States, it was these attempts to lighten its Atlantic burdens that generated the feeling that, as Chancellor Adenauer put it in November 1956, Europe needed to "unite against America."[76]

NOTES

This essay began as a paper presented at the June 1996 meeting of the Society for Historians of American Foreign Relations in Boulder, Colorado. I thank Monika Dickhaus, James Ellison, Douglas Forsyth, Wolfram Kaiser, Lawrence Kaplan, Vojtech Mastny, Timothy Naftali, Leopoldo Nuti, Lorenza Sebesta, Mark Sheetz, Hubert Zimmermann, and two anonymous reviewers for the *Journal of European Integration History* for helpful suggestions and advice. I remain responsible for all remaining errors of fact or interpretation.

1. *Journal officiel de la République française, Assemblée nationale, Débats,* 17 January 1957, p. 107.

2. Janet Flanner, *Paris Journal, 1944–1965* (New York: Atheneum, 1965), 324.

3. See for example Alfred Grosser, "Suez, Hungary, and European Integration," *International Organization* 11 (1957): 470–480; David Reynolds, *One World Divisible: A Global History Since 1945* (New York: Norton, 2000), 128–129.

4. See Hanns Jürgen Küsters, *Fondements de la communauté économique européenne* (Brussels: Office des publications officielles des Communautés européennes and Éditions Labor, 1990), esp. 211–216, 356; this is an updated edition of Küsters' original study, *Die Gründung der Europäischen Wirtschaftsgemeinschaft* (Baden-Baden: Nomos, 1982). In a parallel study on EURATOM, Peter Weilemann also underlined the importance of the Suez Crisis for French policy. See Peter Weilemann, *Die Anfänge der Europäischen Atomgemeinschaft: Zur Gründungsgeschichte von EURATOM, 1955–57* (Baden-Baden: Nomos, 1983), 131.

5. Hanns Jürgen Küsters, "West Germany's Foreign Policy in Western Europe, 1949–1957: The Art of the Possible," in *Western Europe and Germany: The Beginnings of European Integration*, ed. Clemens Wurm (Providence: Berg, 1995), 69.

6. Alan S. Milward, *The Reconstruction of Western Europe, 1945–51* (Berkeley and Los Angeles: University of California Press, 1984), ch. 12; Frances Lynch, "Resolving the Paradox of the Monnet Plan: National and International Planning in French Reconstruction," *Economic History Review*, 2nd ser., 37, no. 2 (May 1984): 229–243.

7. Alan S. Milward, "Entscheidungsphasen der Westintegration," in *Westdeutschland, 1945–1955: Unterwerfung, Kontrolle, Integration*, ed. Ludolf Herbst (Munich: Oldenbourg, 1986), 231–245; idem, *The European Rescue of the Nation-State*, 2d. ed. (London and New York: Routledge, 2000); esp. ch. 4; idem, "The Springs of Integration," and "The Social Bases of Monetary Union?" in *The Question of Europe*, eds. Peter Gowan and Perry Anderson (London and New York: Verso, 1997), 5–20, 149–161; Alan S. Milward, et al., *The Frontier of National Sovereignty: History and Theory, 1945–1992* (London and New York: Routledge, 1993).

8. Frances Lynch, "Restoring France: The Road to Integration," in Milward, et al., *The Frontier of National Sovereignty*, esp. 59–60, 86–87; cf. Milward, *European Rescue of the Nation-State*, 214–215. For another argument that Suez had little effect on the negotiation of the Rome Treaties, see Wilfried Loth, "Vertragsverhandlungen bei abklingender Europabegeisterung: eine zeitgeschichtliche Einordnung," *Integration* 3 (1987), esp. 110–111, 113.

9. Andrew Moravcsik, *The Choice for Europe: Social Purpose and State Power from Messina to Maastricht* (Ithaca: Cornell University Press, 1998), ch. 2; cf. Hubert Zimmermann's review of *The Choice for Europe* in the *Journal of European Integration History* 5, no. 2 (1999): 142–145.

10. For the OEEC background to the process of European integration, see Richard T. Griffiths, "The European Integration Experience, 1945–58," in Keith Middlemas, et al., *Orchestrating Europe: The Informal Politics of European Union, 1973–95* (London: Fontana, 1995), ch. 1; idem, ed., *Explorations in OEEC History* (Paris: Organisation for Economic Cooperation and Development, 1997).

11. Paul Marsh Pitman III, "France's European Choices: The Political Economy of European Integration in the 1950s," Ph.D. diss. (New York: Columbia University, 1997), ch. 1; Wendy Asbeek Brusse, *Tariffs, Trade, and European Integration, 1947–1957: From Study Group to Common Market* (New York: St. Martin's Press, 1997).

12. Geir Lundestad, *"Empire" by Integration: The United States and European Integration, 1945–1997* (Oxford: Oxford University Press, 1998), ch. 4–5.

13. On the Eisenhower administration's grand strategy and its domestic rationales, see Marc Trachtenberg, *A Constructed Peace: The Making of the European Settlement, 1945–1963* (Princeton: Princeton University Press, 1999), 147–156; John Lewis Gaddis, *Strategies of Containment: A Critical Appraisal of Postwar American National Security Policy* (Oxford: Oxford University Press, 1982), ch. 5; Robert Griffith, "Dwight D. Eisenhower and the Corporate Commonwealth," *American Historical Review* 87 (1982): 87–122; Aaron L. Friedberg, *In the Shadow of the Garrison State: America's Anti-Statism and Its Cold War Strategy* (Princeton: Princeton University Press, 2000), ch. 2–3.

14. Federico Romero, "Interdependence and Integration in American Eyes: From the Marshall Plan to Currency Convertibility," in Milward, et al., *The Frontier of National Sovereignty*, 155–181; Council on Foreign Economic Policy, *Report to the President and Congress* (Washington: United States Government Printing Office, 1954), esp. 1–10, 14–15, 43–52, 72–75.

15. Burton I. Kaufman, *Trade and Aid: Eisenhower's Foreign Economic Policy, 1953–1961* (Baltimore: Johns Hopkins University Press, 1982), ch. 2–3; Romero, "Interdependence and Integration in American Eyes," 160–165.

16. See, for example, Memorandum of Conversation, Couillard with State Department Officials, 21 December 1955, *Foreign Relations of the United States, 1955–57* (FRUS, 1955–57) (Washington, D.C.: United States Government Printing Office, 1986), 4: 374–76; Record of Dulles-Strauß Talks, 14 May 1956, ibid., 4: 438–441; Report of the Subcommittee on Regional Economic Integration to the Council on Foreign Economic Policy, 15 November 1956, ibid., 482–86.

17. Milward, *European Rescue of the Nation-State*, 383–420; Paul M. Pitman, "The French Crisis and the Dissolution of the European Payments Union, 1956–58," in *Explorations in OEEC History*, ed. Griffiths, 219–227.

18. See for example O[livier] W[ormser], "Note a.s. convertibilité de la livre," 19 January 1953, Ministère des affaires étrangères (MAE), Paris, Direction économique, Service de coopération économique (DECE) 197; idem, "Note pour l'Ambassadeur, Secrétaire général, a.s. nouvelles perspectives dans le domaine de la coopération économique et financière internationale," 4 May 1954, DECE 197.

19. On American financial pressure in September and October 1954, see Irwin M. Wall, *The United States and the Making of Postwar France, 1945–1954* (Cambridge: Cambridge University Press, 1991), 286–295.

20. Eisenhower quoted in Trachtenberg, *A Constructed Peace*, 150.

21. For the best account of what motivated British policy, see James R. V. Ellison, *Threatening Europe: Britain and the Creation of the European Community* (London and New York: Macmillan and St. Martin's Press, 2000).

22. This account of French policy follows Frances Lynch's pathbreaking analysis of the Fourth Republic's foreign economic policy, as well as the results of my own research on military-industrial and imperial projects. See Frances Lynch, *France and the International Economy: From Vichy to the Treaty of Rome* (London and New York: Routledge, 1997) and Pitman, "France's European Choices." See also Gérard Bossuat's detailed account, *L'Europe des français, 1943–1959: La IVe République aux sources de l'Europe communautaire* (Paris: Publications de la Sorbonne, 1996).

23. Thomas Rhenisch, *Europäische Integration und industrielles Interesse: Die deutsche Industrie und die Gründung der Europäischen Wirtschaftsgemeinschaft*, Beihefte der Vierteljahrschrift für Sozial- und Wirtschaftsgeschichte, no. 152 (Stuttgart: Franz Steiner Verlag, 1999).

24. "Gemeinsamer Markt," 4 October 1956, 210-225-30-01/1208/56, Politisches Archiv des Auswärtigen Amts (PAAA), Berlin, Büro Staatssekretär 155, vol. 2. For further explication of this document, see Werner Abelshauser, "'Intégration à la carte': The Primacy of Politics and the Economic Integration of Western Europe in the 1950s," in *The Construction of Europe: Essays in Honour of Emile Noël*, ed. Stephen Martin (Dordrecht: Kluwer Academic Publications, 1994), 17–18.

25. See the superb study by Monika Dickhaus, *Die Bundesbank im westeuropäischen Wiederaufbau: Die internationale Währungspolitik der Bundesrepublik Deutschland, 1948 bis 1958*, Schriftenreihe der Vierteljahreshefte für Zeitgeschichte, vol. 72 (Munich: Oldenbourg, 1996).

26. On Bonn's European policy, see Hanns Jürgen Küsters, "Der Streit um Kompetenzen und Konzeptionen deutscher Europapolitik, 1949–1958," in *Vom Marshallplan zur EWG: Die Eingliederung der Bundesrepublik Deutschland in die westliche Welt*, ed. Werner Bührer, Ludolf Herbst, and Hanno Sowade (Munich: Oldenbourg, 1990), 335–370; for Adenauer's dominant role in West German foreign policy, see Gottfried Niedhart, "Außenpolitik in der Ära Adenauer," in *Modernisierung im Wiederaufbau*, ed. Axel Schildt and Arnold Sywottek (Bonn: Dietz, 1993), 805–818.

27. Andreas Wilkens, "Das Programm von La Celle-St. Cloud: Der Aufbau der deutsch-französischen Wirtschaftsbeziehungen, 1954–57," *Revue d'Allemagne* 25 (1993): 565–580.

28. On Dutch policy see Richard T. Griffiths, "The Beyen Plan," and "The Common Market," in *The Netherlands and the Integration of Europe, 1945–1957*, ed. Richard T. Griffiths (Amsterdam: NEHA, 1990), 165–182 and 183–208.

29. See Pinay to Félix Gaillard, chief of the French Delegation to the Intergovernmental Committee, 12 July 1955, enclosing "Instructions pour la Délégation," Archives nationales (AN), Paris: Secrétariat général du comité interministériel pour les questions de coopération économique européenne (SGCI), 121.9; O[livier] W[ormser], "Note pour le Président [Pinay]," 10 October 1955, MAE: Office Files of Olivier Wormser, Directeur des affaires économiques et financières (DE) 11; "L'Instauration d'un marché commun en Europe," *Le Monde*, 13 October 1955.

30. For example, see Moravcsik's accounts of the Mollet government's European policy, which depend almost exclusively on evidence from memoirs and oral history interviews that were prepared decades later: Andrew Moravcsik, "Why the European Community Strengthens the State: Domestic Politics and International Cooperation," Harvard University Center for European Studies Working Paper, no. 52 (Cambridge: CES, ca. 1994), 30–36, and the more cautious version in idem, *The Choice for Europe*, 103–122, 137–50.

31. Although the thrust of the Mollet government's internal debates on European policy appeared in the press, previous historical accounts have missed the significance of the resulting negotiating position. Key archival sources, which have apparently been overlooked or neglected by other scholars, include: "Projet de mémorandum du gouvernement français sur l'établissement d'un marché commun (deuxième rédaction)," 22 May 1956, Alain Savary Papers, Fondation nationale des sciences politiques, Paris, SV 19; Présidence du Conseil, "Résumé des décisions du comité interministériel du lundi, 28 mai 1956," 28 May 1956, SGCI 121.9.

32. See Ellison, *Threatening Europe*, ch. 3.

33. See Pitman, "The French Crisis and the Dissolution of the European Payments Union, 1956–58."

34. The best account of Atlantic strategic affairs in the 1950s is Trachtenberg, *A Constructed Peace*, ch. 4–6. National perspectives appear in Jan Melissen, *The Struggle for Nuclear Partnership: Britain, the United States, and the Making of an Ambiguous Alliance, 1952–1959* (Groningen: Styx Publications, 1993); Ian Clark, *Nu-*

clear Diplomacy and the Special Relationship (Oxford: Clarendon, 1994); Georges Soutou, *L'Alliance incertaine: les rapports politico-stratégiques franco-allemands, 1954–1996* (Paris: Fayard, 1996), ch. 2–3; Bruno Thoß, "Der Beitritt der Bundesrepublik Deutschland zur WEU und NATO im Spannungsfeld von Blockbildung und Entspannung (1954–1956), in *Die NATO-Option*, vol. 3 of *Anfänge westdeutscher Sicherheitspolitik, 1945–1956*, ed. Militärgeschlichthiches Forschungsamt (Munich: Oldenbourg, 1993), 1–234.

35. For the terms "forward defense" and "peripheral strategy," see Marc Trachtenberg, *History and Strategy* (Princeton: Princeton University Press, 1991), 153–160.

36. On the development of the Eurafrican idea in postwar strategic thought, see Claude d'Abzac-Epezy and Philippe Vial, "In Search of a European Consciousness: French Military Elites and the Idea of Europe, 1947–54," in *Building Postwar Europe: National Decision-Makers and European Institutions, 1948–63*, ed. Anne Deighton (London: St. Martin's Press for St. Antony's College, 1995), 1–19.

37. See Trachtenberg, *History and Strategy*, 160–168.

38. On the Fourth Republic's atomic policy, see Maurice Vaïsse, "Le Choix atomique de la France (1945–1958)," *Vingtième Siècle*, no. 36 (December 1992), 21–30 and Dominique Mongin, *La Bombe atomique française, 1945–1958* (Brussels and Paris: Bruylant and Librarie générale de droit et de jurisprudence, 1997), esp. pt. 4. An account of Paris's quest for aid appears in Pitman, "France's European Choices," ch. 6.

39. On MC-48 see Marc Trachtenberg, "La Formation du système de défense occidentale: Les Etats-Unis, la France, et MC-48," in *La France et l'OTAN*, ed. Maurice Vaïsse, Pierre Mélandri, and Frédéric Bozo (Brussels: Editions complexe, 1996), 115–127.

40. Valluy to Guillaume, No. 542/DFGP/TS, "Plan de possibilités," 13 August 1954, Papers of Pierre Mendès France, Institut Pierre Mendès France, Box CED 2. For further material on the French response to the nuclearization of NATO war plans, see other documents in the same box, including H[ervé] A[lphand], "Note pour le Président [Mendès]," 14 August 1954.

41. This quotation appears on pp. 5–6 in Valluy's letter, cited above.

42. [General Jacques Faure], Cabinet du ministre, Ministère de la Défense nationale, "Fiche," ca. 12 September 1954, DE 10.

43. This account follows the version of the minutes published by Roger Wybot, one of the principals in the "affaire des fuites," a scandal sparked by press reports of leaks from the Comité de défense nationale. Facsimile of "Procès-verbal du Comité de défense nationale," 10 September 1954, in Philippe Bernert, *Roger Wybot et la bataille pour la DST* (Paris: Presses de la Cité, 1975), annex.

44. See Leopoldo Nuti, "Le Rôle de l'Italie dans les négociations trilatérales," *Revue d'histoire diplomatique* 104 (1991), 142.

45. Pierre Guillen, "La France et la négociation du traité d'EURATOM," *Relations internationales*, no. 44 (Winter 1985): 391–412.

46. Peter Fischer, *Atomenergie und staatliches Interesse: die Anfänge der Atompolitik in der Bundesrepublik Deutschland, 1949–1955*, Internationale Politik und Sicherheit, Bd. 30, Nuclear History Program, no. 3 (Baden-Baden: Nomos, 1994), 201–223, 274–282.

47. For the development of West German policy on atomic energy and nuclear weapons see Peter Fischer, "Die Reaktion der Bundesregierung auf die Nuklearisierung

der westlichen Verteidigung (1952–1958)," *Militärgeschichtliche Mitteilungen* 52 (1993): 105–132; idem., *Atomenergie und staatliches Interesse*; Hans-Peter Schwarz, *Der Staatsmann*, vol. 2 of *Adenauer* (Stuttgart: Deutsche Verlags-Anstalt, 1991; reprint, Munich: Deutsche Taschenbuch Verlag, 1994); and Axel F. Gablink, *Strategische Planungen in der Bundesrepublik Deutschland, 1955–1967: Politische Kontrolle oder militärische Notwendigkeit?* Internationale Politik und Sicherheit, Bd. 30, Nuclear History Program, no. 5 (Baden-Baden: Nomos, 1996).

48. See Dulles-Makins meetings, 29 June and 13 July 1956, and Eden to Eisenhower, 18 July 1956, FRUS, 1955–57, 4: 84–92.

49. "Radford Terms New Arms Vital to Service Cuts," *New York Times*, 14 July 1956.

50. See "Gespräche über Rüstungsbeschränkungen in den USA und England," 20 July 1956, in *Die Kabinettsprotokolle der Bundesregierung*, vol. 9, 1956 (Kabinettsprotokole 1956), comp. Ursula Hüllbüsch, ed. Friedrich P. Kahlenberg (Munich: Oldenbourg, 1998), pp. 484–489. The passage cited from Adenauer appears on p. 486, that from Strauß on p. 487. Compare the further discussion of the same themes, "Radford-Plan," 26 July 1956, *Kabinettsprotokolle 1956*, 501–502.

51. Strauß was named defense minister on 16 October 1956. A fine survey of the Umrüstung crisis appears in Christian Greiner, "Die Militärische Eingliederung der Bundesrepublik Deutschland in die WEU und die NATO 1954 bis 1957," in *Die NATO-Option*, vol. 3 of *Anfänge westdeutscher Sicherheitspolitik, 1945–1956*, ed. Militärgeschichtliches Forschungsamt (Munich: Oldenbourg, 1993), 707–786. Compare Strauß's account in Franz Josef Strauß, *Die Erinnerungen* (Berlin: Siedler, 1989), 268–334

52. "Aufzeichnung über die Sitzung der Standing Group am Freitag, den 27.7.56, 10.30 Uhr," Bundesarchiv Militärarchiv (BAMA), Freiburg im Breisgau, BW 17/37, ff. 84–87.

53. Heusinger, "Aufzeichnung über ein Gespräch mit General Valluy von der Standing Group und Mr. Allan Dulles vom CIA," BAMA: BW 17/37, ff. 93–96. (Note that Heusinger met Valluy and Dulles separately.) For an account of this exchange that draws on additional, still classified German sources, see Gero von Gersdorff, "Westeuropäische Verteidigungskooperation und atlantische Bündnispräferenz: Wege westdeutscher Zielsetzungen, 1949–1958," in *Aus der Ohnmacht zur Bündnismacht: Das Machtproblem in der Bundesrepublik Deutschland, 1945–1960*, ed. Franz Knipping and Klaus-Jürgen Müller (Paderborn, Munich, Vienna, and Zurich: Ferdinand Schöningh, 1995), 227.

54. In April and September the Mollet government put forward memoranda calling for intensive Franco-German collaboration in the armaments sector. See *Documents diplomatiques français* (DDF) 1956, 2: 394, n. 2; "Mémorandum," 25 September 1956, DDF 1956, 3: 201–202.

55. Unfortunately, most recent studies concentrate almost exclusively on Anglo-American relations. While these are relatively easy to research, they are not the only significant aspects of the affair. Representative works include Keith Kyle, *Suez* (London: Weidenfeld and Nicholson, 1992); Diane Kunz, *The Economic Diplomacy of the Suez Crisis* (Chapel Hill: University of North Carolina Press, 1991); and Thomas Risse-Kappen, *Cooperation Among Democracies: The European Influence on U.S. Foreign Policy* (Princeton: Princeton University Press, 1995), ch. 4. Broader approaches appear in Brian McCauley, "Hungary and Suez, 1956: The Limits of Soviet and American

Power," *Journal of Contemporary History* 16 (1981): 777–800; Winfried Heinemann and Norbert Wiggershaus, eds., *Das internationale Krisenjahr, 1956: Polen, Ungarn, Suez,* Beiträge zur Militärgeschichte, 48 (Munich: Oldenbourg, 1999); and Irwin M. Wall, *France, the United States, and the Algerian War* (Berkeley, Los Angeles, and London: University of California Press, 2001), ch. 2.

56. See "Procès-verbal des entretiens franco-allemands [6 November 1956]," DDF 1956, 3: 234–237.

57. Christian Pineau, *1956, Suez* (Paris: Robert Laffont, 1976), 191. Compare the account of this meeting in Wilhelm G. Grewe, *Rückblenden, 1976–1951* (Frankfurt am Main, Berlin, and Vienna: Propyläen, 1979), 283–290.

58. See Milward's works cited in note 8 above.

59. See Winfried Heinemann, "1956 als das Krisenjahr der NATO," in *Das internationale Krisenjahr 1956,* ed. Heinemann and Wiggershaus, 615–637.

60. This process is well-documented in SGCI 122.21.

61. For more supporting evidence, see Pitman, "France's European Choices," 304–320; compare the late René Girault's penetrating analysis, "La France entre l'Europe et l'Afrique," in *Il Rilancio dell'Europa e i trattati di Roma,* ed. Enrico Serra (Baden-Baden: Nomos, 1989), 351–378.

62. For these political developments, see Jacques Chapsal, *La Vie politique en France de 1940 à 1958,* 2d ed. (Paris: Presses universitaires de France, 1990), ch. 15; Jean-Pierre Rioux, *L'Expansion et l'impuissance, 1952–58,* vol. 2 of *La France de la Quatrième République,* rev. ed. (Paris: Éditions du Seuil, 1983), 117–127; Georgette Elgey, *La République des tourmentes, 1954–1959,* pt. 3 of *Histoire de la IVe République* (Paris: Fayard, 1992), 1: 407–456.

63. See Heinemann, "1956 als Krisenjahr der NATO," 616 and, more generally, Matthew Connelly, "Taking Off the Cold War Lens: Visions of North-South Conflict during the Algerian War for Independence," *American Historical Review* 105 (2000): 739–769.

64. Although Bourgès pursued a career as a Radical party politician, he maintained close ties with the Gaullists. See Paul Marcus, *Maurice Bourgès-Maunoury: un républicain indivisible* (Biarritz: Atlantica, 1997); *Année politique, 1956* (Paris: Presses universitaires de France, 1957), 69, 71.

65. Earlier accounts of these talks have followed the published French records, which omit all reference to Faure's crucial comments on atomic weapons. See "Conversation entre M. Maurice Faure et M. Erhard à Berlin, le 16 septembre 1956," DDF 1956, 2: 384–387; Bonn to Paris, 17 September 1956, DDF 1956, 2: 387–388; "Conversation entre MM. Maurice Faure, von Brentano et Hallstein, lundi 17 septembre, à 16 heures," DDF 1956, 2: 392–394; "Conversation entre MM. Faure, le chancelier Adenauer et Hallstein, lundi 17 septembre, à 17 h. 15," DDF 1956, 2: 395–396; Bouverat, "Aufzeichnung [on Faure-von Brentano-Hallstein talks, 17 September 1956]," 19 September 1956, PAAA: Abt. 2, bd. 922.

66. As yet, French archives have divulged little related to this initiative, which may have simply been a tactical maneuver designed to keep the British on board at a delicate moment. The best source remains the extensive documentation in Public Record Office, Kew: PREM 11/1352.

67. Paris to Représentants diplomatiques de la France à l'étranger, 2 October 1956, DDF 1956, 2: 493–496; [Karl] Carstens, "Kurzprotokoll über die Besprechungen

zwischen dem Herrn Bundeskanzler, dem Herrn Bundesminister des Auswärtigen und dem Herrn Staatssekretär des Auswärtigen Amtes und dem Herrn französischen Aussenminister und Staatssekretär Faure am 29. September 1956," 1 October 1956, PAAA: Abt. 2, bd. VS-3666. I wish to take this occasion to thank the archivists who helped process my request to declassify this document.

68. In addition to Daniel Koerfer's classic account of the Adenauer-Erhard feud, *Kampf ums Kanzleramt: Erhard und Adenauer* (Stuttgart: Deutsche Verlags-Anstalt, 1988), see Hanns Jürgen Küsters, "Adenauers Europapolitik im Gründungsphase der europäischen Wirtschaftsgemeinschaft," *Vierteljahresbefte für Zeitgeschichte* 42 (1994): 646–673 and Ulrich Enders, "Integration oder Kooperation? Ludwig Erhard und Frantz Etzel im Streit über die Politik der europäischen Zusammenarbeit, 1954–1956," *Vierteljahresbefte für Zeitgeschichte* 45 (1997): 143–171; Bruno Thoß, "Die Doppelkrise von Suez und Budapest in ihren Auswirkungen auf Adenauers Sicherheits- und Europapolitik 1956/57," in *Das internationale Krisenjahr, 1956*, ed. Heinemann and Wiggershaus, 573–588.

69. Cf. Adenauer's 25 September 1956 speech to the Grandes conférences catholiques in Brussels in Konrad Adenauer, *Reden, 1917–1967: Eine Auswahl*, ed. Hans-Peter Schwarz (Stuttgart: Deutsche Verlags-Anstalt, 1975), 327–332.

70. See, e.g., Milward, *European Rescue of the Nation-State*, 197–198, 329–331; Moravcsik, *Choice for Europe*, 90–95, 136–137.

71. "Weiterentwicklung Europas," 3 October 1956, *Kabinettsprotokolle 1956*, 610. Adenauer's argument responded to the same press conference that Janet Flanner had commented on in her diary (see note 3 above). See also Adenauer's 19 December 1956 comments on British and American disengagement from NATO, "Tagung des Atlantikrates in Paris," 19 December 1956, *Kabinettesprotokolle 1956*, 776.

72. Adenauer's argument prefigured current European views on Atlantic ties, as shown by recent comments made by a German official: "While we believe that NATO will remain important to Germany in the next five to ten years, the future of our foreign and defense policy lies with the European Union, not NATO." Adenauer cited in Christian Greiner, "Die Bundesrepublik Deutschland als 'Machtfaktor' in der NATO, 1954–57," in *Aus der Ohnmacht zur Bündnismacht*, eds. Knipping and Müller, 210 (note that a more recently published version of the 19 December 1956 cabinet minutes replaces the reference to producing atomic weapons with a euphemism; see "Tagung des Atlantikrates in Paris," 19 December 1956, *Kabinettsprotokolle 1956*, 775); unidentified German official cited in Seth G. Jones, "Letter to the Editor," *Foreign Affairs* 80, no. 5 (September–October 2001), 180.

73. "Gemeinsamer Markt und EURATOM," 5 October 1956, *Kabinettsprotokolle 1956*, 620–629. The quote from Adenauer appears on page 626. Further details on the cabinet debate appear in "Ergebnisprotokoll über die Ressortsbesprechung im Auswärtigen Amt am 6. Oktober über die Probleme des Gemeinsamen Marktes und EURATOM," Bundesarchiv (BA), Koblenz: B 138/722.

74. Adenauer and Mollet approved a package deal on the EEC and EURATOM that had been hammered out by Robert Marjolin and Karl Carstens. The secondary literature contains several different versions of what the deal supposedly included; for the actual text of the agreement, see Enclosure to Letter, Adenauer to Balke, 7 November 1956, BA: B 138/723.

75. Ariane Illig, "Aufzeichnung," 9 November 1956, PAAA: Büro Staatssekretär, Bd. 278; [Jean François-Poncet], "Note à l'attention de M. Jurgensen," 20 November 1956, MAE: Europe, Généralités, 1945–60, 185.

76. See "Procès-verbal des entretiens franco-allemands [6 November 1956]," DDF 1956, 3: 235.

3

Trigger-happy Protestant Materialists? The European Christian Democrats and the United States

Wolfram Kaiser

The study of international relations, in the United States especially, is dominated by two basic theoretical approaches: realism and liberalism. Realists focus on policy-making at the state level; policy is analyzed in terms of power and geopolitical interest and domestic political forces are not seen as playing a major role in the making of foreign policy. Liberals, on the other hand, emphasize the role of interest groups in foreign policy-making in pluralist democracies: policy makers tend, in their view, to respond to pressure from well-organized groups, especially from groups that are important in electoral terms. Socioeconomic and commercial interest is generally seen—as, for example, in the liberal intergovernmentalist analysis of postwar European integration—as the principal source of such pressure.[1] The realist and liberal approaches differ in many ways, but both proceed from the assumption that political leaders make rational choices—choices based on recognizable interests.

Most contemporary historical studies of the Cold War and of U.S.–European relations are based, if only implicitly, on that same sort of assumption—even when those studies are not directly informed by either sort of theory. Those works generally treat foreign policy as the outcome of rational, interest-based choices by elites, and tend to ignore the wider cultural context in which decision-making takes place. Historians, moreover, tend as a rule to focus on intergovernmental relations; nongovernmental transnational communities, on the other hand, do not receive much attention. In today's world, a world characterized by rapid globalisation and growing interdependence, the role of transnational actors—nongovernmental organisations, for example—clearly cannot be ignored. But even in the early postwar period, transnational groups were already playing a major role in the Atlantic world.

It is important to deal with these issues in a way that takes such realities into account. Such an approach is in fact available: international politics can be approached from what has come to be called a "constructivist" point of view. Constructivists do not view power and influence in essential materialist terms. They emphasize the importance of such factors as identity, ideology, and historical consciousness; they study their impact on interest formation and preferences; they seek to show how foreign policy-making processes are culturally embedded, how policy choices are path-dependent, and how international conflict can result from clashes of culture and not just interests.[2]

This chapter will deal in that spirit with the West European Christian Democrats and with their attitudes toward the United States during the early Cold War period.[3] This sort of approach is particularly appropriate in this case. In the West European parliamentary democracies with their strong party traditions, political parties were bound to play an important role in foreign policy-making. Ideas and attitudes developed in a party context—a context shaped by history, religion, ideology, and culture in general. Focusing on political parties can thus help bring out the role that culture played in shaping perceptions, and sometimes in shaping policy. And focusing on political parties not just in a national, but rather in a transnational context, can bring out some important aspects of what was going on in relations between the United States and Europe as a whole.

The Christian Democrats formed an important and quite cohesive transnational community in postwar continental Western Europe. They were initially the largest party in every state in the European Coal and Steel Community (ECSC), founded in 1951–1952, and the European Economic Community (EEC), founded in 1957–1958—in some cases, they were the dominant party—and had a decisive influence on national foreign policies and on the development of European institutions. Those national parties were linked to each other in various ways. On the formal level, they cooperated, from 1947 on, within the framework of the Nouvelles Equipes Internationales (NEI)—an organization that developed eventually into the European People's Party (EPP), now the largest faction in the European Parliament. And leading Christian Democratic politicians also met informally (and secretly) in Geneva between 1947 and 1955 to discuss, above all, questions relating to European integration and to East-West relations. They also got together in the Assembly of the Council of Europe (from 1949 on) and in the parliaments of the ECSC and the EEC, and of course there were frequent meetings at the governmental level.[4] In these meetings, basic political, social, and economic issues were regularly discussed; the Christian Democratic leaders were especially interested in the question of Western Europe's future role in the world and thus in the question of Europe's relationship with the United States.

At first glance, the Christian Democrats' relationship with the United States in the postwar period might appear very harmonious. After all, the Christian Democrats opted, in principle, for a market rather than a centrally planned economy. They were very anti-Communist. They championed the idea of European integration with at least some supranational elements; the U.S. government, which sought to strengthen Western Europe against the Soviet Union in the Cold War, supported the same general policy. The Christian Democratic parties also strongly supported NATO. A clear majority rejected the Gaullist alternative of a Western Europe under French leadership; that majority rejected the Gaullist idea that the possibility of serious transatlantic friction could be accepted. As a result, U.S. administrations assisted a number of key Christian Democrat-led governments: financially and logistically in the early postwar period, as in the case of Italy at the time of the 1948 elections,[5] and with favourable publicity, as in the case of the Federal Republic of Germany, when Konrad Adenauer visited the United States in April 1953 in order to bolster his party's chances in the Bundestag elections of September of that year.[6]

But a closer examination reveals a pronounced ambivalence on the part of the European Christian Democrats toward the United States. In no way did support for European integration imply to them that Europe was to be unified according to the U.S. model. For the Christian Democrats, the integration process not only derived from European traditions, collective experiences, and values; many Christian Democratic leaders were frankly hostile to what they regarded as the liberal, competition-driven American system, a system in their view marked by excessive Protestant individualism and materialism. The Christian Democrats were equally ambivalent about U.S. political leadership in NATO and in international politics in general. The Europeans needed American military protection, but they also had distinctive views on international issues, especially on detente and on Third World development, when this increasingly became a battlefield of the Cold War. Due to the very tight constraints imposed by the Cold War and the West European need for security, the underlying cultural differences did not always spill over into open policy conflict. But the Cold War is now over, and these differences may in the future come to have a greater impact on relations between America and Europe.

DEFENSE OF A EUROPEAN MODEL

U.S. policy toward Western Europe after 1945 was rooted in a strong belief that it was America's mission to bring peace and democracy to a declining continent that had completely torn itself apart in two civil wars—a continent that had lost all sense of direction and that no longer had a legitimate claim to a world role.[7] In contrast to Europe, the United States was a shining example of freedom and liberty enshrined in its federal constitution, and of a dynamic society that facilitated technological innovation and economic progress, bringing wealth for all. This model seemed so obviously attractive that the U.S. government initially expected after the end of the Second World War that it would easily get transferred through imitation. It was only after 1949 that the Americans intensified their propaganda efforts in Western Europe. The Truman administration firmly believed that Western Europe should opt for a federal system similar to the U.S. model and with a common market in order to overcome the European tradition of national conflict. Indeed, it attempted to induce such a solution with its demand for a coordinated European reconstruction plan as a precondition for Marshall Plan aid, but failed and ended up with the entirely intergovernmental Organisation for European Economic Cooperation (OEEC) created in 1948.[8]

In their own collective memory and political propaganda (about Konrad Adenauer, Robert Schuman and Alcide De Gasperi being the "founding fathers" of the "core Europe" organisations ECSC and EEC), the West European Christian Democrats cultivated the idea of themselves as the avant-garde of a more integrated, supranational Europe. Of all the main political groups in Europe, they were most predisposed toward some form of supranationalism, and they also had a certain interest as a party—and indeed as a transnational group of parties—in championing such a constitutional solution for Western Europe. Yet given their historical and ideological predispositions and their distinct party interests, they were by no means inclined to forge a unified Europe on the American model—a model the Christian Democrats did not understand well and never discussed as a possible reference point for Europe. In fact, their whole approach to European unification—an approach rooted in historical memory and long historical experience—had little in common with the American myth about how their own unified nation had been established. The Americans thought of the establishment of their own nation as marking a sharp break with the past. But the European goal was to build on the past—to build on the traditions and values that had defined Western Europe as a distinct and self-conscious culture.

What were those traditions, and why in particular were the Christian Democrats interested in building a Europe with at least some federal or supranational elements? The Christian Democrats never differentiated dogmatically between federalist and intergovernmental forms of organising the new Europe after 1945. In a September 1948 resolution, for example, the NEI spoke of an "economic and political union of the free Europe," with an organisation that could be "federal or confederal and which will result in unity while maintaining diversity."[9] But the Christian Democrats were willing in principle to consider arrangements that had at least some supranational components, and their readiness to do so was mainly due to three factors: the everyday experience of the mainly Catholic Christian Democrats with the "supranational" religious authority of the Pope and the Catholic hierarchy; the idea of a Christian Abendland, or occidental European cultural space, and the intellectual and rhetorical evocation of the "supranational" worldly order of the Carolingian Empire in the Middle Ages; and, finally, the principle of subsidiarity in the Christian Democrats' economic and social programme—that is, the notion of multi-level governance as the ideal form of social organisation within the nation-state.

Compared to the interwar Catholic parties, most Christian Democratic parties after 1945 aimed at an interconfessional or nonconfessional structure.[10] Yet even the French *Mouvement Républicain Populaire* (MRP), which publicly distanced itself from the Catholic Church to achieve its full integration into the Republican consensus and to broaden its electoral appeal, received most of its votes from practicing Catholics. Some 75 percent of them voted for the MRP in the elections of 1945 and 1946.[11] In the biconfessional Netherlands, 80 to 90 percent of Catholics voted for the Catholic People's Party.[12] The German Christian Democratic Union and Bavarian Christian Social Union (CDU/CSU) were formally interconfessional, but most of its leaders, members, and voters were still Catholics.[13] And supranational European state structures were fully compatible with Catholic religious "supranationalism," which was regarded as natural and legitimate.

More importantly, while experience of the two world wars with totalitarian dictatorships led the Christian Democrats to fully embrace democratic ideas, those experiences also led them to look back toward the universalism of the religiously unified Europe of the Middle Ages. For them, the "supranational" Carolingian Empire had major symbolic importance. French intellectuals and politicians, including Napoleon, tried to appropriate this Empire for the national heritage and memory of France, and German nationalists and later the National Socialists had opposed it with their own Germanic Saxon myth. After the war, however, the Christian Democrats Europeanized the Carolingian Empire, which was largely coterminous with the small "core Europe" of the ECSC and the EEC. In their transnational meetings, they regularly evoked the idea of a Christian Europe united against external threats, from Charlemagne to the defeat of the Ottomans in the battle of Kahlenberg near Vienna in 1683, as Heinrich von Brentano, the CDU/CSU faction leader in the Bundestag, did in a speech at the NEI congress in Bad Ems in 1951.[14]

Christian Democrat-inspired political rituals, such as the Aachen Karls Prize established in 1950 to honour public figures for their contribution to European integration, were designed to support the related Abendland idea.[15] The Abendland theme was rooted in the European Catholic discourse of the interwar period, and it of course had a strongly anti-Communist coloration.[16] At Bad Ems, West German chancellor Konrad Adenauer spoke of the "great dangers which are threatening Christianity, Christian culture and all of Western Europe"; the integration of that "core Europe" was essential if "the Christian Abendland" was to have any hope of surviving the Communist Soviet threat.[17] Three years earlier, Georges Bidault, the French Prime Minister, had characterised Soviet Communism in one of the Geneva meetings in a (distorted) analogy with the Middle Ages as "a new Islam which will not retreat one inch, but from which we have everything to expect and to fear."[18]

In their anti-Communism, the Christian Democrats could relate to American Protestants like John Foster Dulles.[19] Their shared anti-Communism meant that European Christian Democratic parties had little trouble adopting the American "free world" idea and sometimes used the terms "European Abendland," "civilisation," and "Christian West" interchangeably. But the Abendland myth had specifically continental European anti-Protestant connotations—connotations that reflected a deep cultural divide *within* the "free world." In their discourse on the roots of totalitarianism and the world wars, the Christian Democrats insisted that Protestantism promoted rapid industrialisation, with all of its adverse social consequences, and led to excessive individualism and materialism. This helped to destroy the old moral order and left the interwar democracies helpless in the face of the totalitarian challenge. As P. J. S. Serrarens, the Dutch leader of the European Christian trade union movement, pointed out at the NEI congress in Luxembourg in 1948, the Reformation had been responsible for "destroying European unity" and for the rise of nationalist conflicts.[20] Lutheran Prussia was singled out for criticism in Christian Democratic circles for its supposedly catastrophic influence on the course of German history.[21] More generally, the Christian Democrats tended to take a negative view of predominantly non-Catholic countries like Britain and America. Certain Catholic politicians who had taken refuge in those countries during the Second World War had come back with a more positive view of Anglo-Saxon Protestantism and the political traditions with which it was associated, but they had only a marginal influence on Christian Democratic politics after 1945.[22]

The third reason for the predisposition of European Christian Democratic parties toward supranational solutions had to do with the importance of the principle of subsidiarity in their economic and social doctrine. As the former MRP parliamentarian Henri Teitgen insisted at the NEI congress in Tours in 1953, the organisation of the new Europe should reflect the principles of Catholic social thought as it was laid down in the Papal Encyclical Quadragesimo Anno of 1931.[23] Teitgen suggested abandoning the dogmatic debate about whether Europe should be organized on an intergovernmental or on a federal basis; he wanted a mixed constitutional structure in which decision-making would take place either by consensus or by majority vote—that is, in whatever way was most appropriate in the circumstances. His preference—and this was in accordance with Catholic social thought—was for decision-making to take place as a rule at the lowest possible level. The basic organizing principle for society was that decision-making would not be concentrated on just one level, but that instead governance would take place on a number of levels, from the family on up to the state—and this indeed is what the whole concept of "subsidiarity" meant. As a result, it was much easier for the Christian Democrats than for the Socialists to adopt the idea of shared sovereignty exercised at different levels (including the supranational level) in Western Europe; the Socialists were for the most part still preoccupied with the idea of centralised economic policy-making at the national level.

In addition, certain more mundane party interests were also involved. The Christian Democrats believed that before the war, the idealism of the young had drawn them to totalitarian ideologies; young Europeans therefore now needed a "safe" ideal to believe in. "Europe" would be that ideal, and if the Christian Democrats could establish themselves as the "European" parties, they would profit electorally. Supranational structures also resulted in the self-exclusion of Britain (without a Christian Democratic party tradition) from the new organisations, as the story of the Schuman Plan of 1950 shows; this increased the degree to which the sort of Europe that was being constructed would have a distinct Christian Democratic flavor. From that point on, the French and German Christian Democrats in particular strongly supported the idea of a more integrated "core Europe" and continued to do so even after they began to advocate the enlargement of the EEC in 1963.[24] This was a Europe that they dominated politically until well into the 1960s; their ability to determine the sort of Europe that would take shape would have been diluted if the British and Scandinavian Socialists had been involved. A broadening of Europe would have led also to increased U.S. influence, especially through Britain. The Franco-German rapprochement went so far in this context that French representatives in the NEI and the Geneva Circle resurrected the idea of an eternal rivalry between France and Britain. Of all of the MRP politicians, it was Pierre-Henri Teitgen—a hero of the French resistance who had been captured by the Germans and had escaped from the train taking him to a concentration camp—who said to his German counterparts at a meeting in January 1955 to discuss the future of Western Europe after the failure of the European Defense Community: "The English are our eternal enemy."[25]

After 1945 the Christian Democrats were thus not simply interested in building a "United States of Europe" on the American model. Instead, their policies were solidly based on European traditions; they were rooted in their own political ideology and in their own understanding of history. Such policies turned out more or less by accident to be compatible with the American preference for a supranational Western Europe in the early Cold War. But the fact that the small "core Europe" was built on traditions and ideas that were largely alien to the U.S. experience (where the dominant political culture was strongly influenced by Anglo-Saxon Protestantism) meant that there was always a certain potential for transatlantic conflict. This is especially true, since the European Christian Democrats not only rejected the Soviet idea of a centrally planned economy, but also rejected what they saw as the American laissez-faire philosophy. While the Cold War and the need for security forced the Christian Democratic parties to become more "pro-American" in foreign policy than they would otherwise have been, they were keen to develop a domestic European "third way."[26]

Although the Catholic Christian Democrats were fully converted to democratic, multiparty government after 1945, they remained quite hostile to European liberalism, just as the Pope and the Catholic Church had opposed liberalism during the European culture wars of the nineteenth century.[27] As they saw it, liberalism had not only facilitated the rise of totalitarian ideologies by undermining traditional value systems, but the overly rapid industrialization that liberalism had made possible led to social and economic instability—to mass unemployment and to extremes of wealth and poverty—and thus paved the way for the totalitarian movements of the twentieth century. And the country that, in the eyes of the European Christian Democrats, represented these liberal traditions in the most extreme form was no longer Britain; by 1945 at the latest, it had become the United States. The Christian Democrats rejected what they saw as America's prevailing ideology—its extreme individualism and materialism.

The search for a "third way" between liberalism on the one hand and Socialism and Communism on the other is reflected in all the Christian Democratic party programmes after 1945. The MRP, while relatively liberal on economic matters (at least by French standards), tended to take a more dirigiste approach in the area of social policy.[28] The "Christmas programme" of the Belgian *Parti Social Chrétien* (PSC/CVP) was influenced by the Christian Workers' Movement and called for reorganizing the state along neo-corporatist lines as a way of dealing with the problems of an excessively polarized society.[29] The Dutch *Katholieke Volkspartij* (KVP) entirely shared these neocorporatist ideas. Until 1958, that party was part of a governing coalition with the Social Democrats; together with their partners, they built a welfare state second only to Sweden's. The *Sociaal-Economische Raad* (Social-economic Council) played a crucial role in the trilateral coordination of government policy between government, trade unions, and employers.[30] In Italy, the left-Catholic *corrente* (wing) of the Christian Democratic party gained more and more influence throughout the 1950s, with Amintore Fanfani and Aldo Moro responsible for more interventionist economic policies, including the nationalisation of the energy industry.[31] Even in the Federal Republic, where Economics Minister Ludwig Erhard took a neoliberal approach—that is, where policy was based on the concept of a "social market economy"—the left-Catholic wing insisted on a rapid extension of the welfare state as the *Wirtschaftswunder* (economic miracle) ran its course in the 1950s and 1960s.[32]

But the key point to note here is that Christian Democratic "third way" ideas and policies were not framed in purely national terms: the "third way" concept developed also in a transnational context. At the very first multilateral meeting of Christian Democratic party representatives at Luzerne in 1947, which resulted in the formation of the NEI, the national secretary of the Belgian PSC, Désiré Lamalle, emphasized that European Christian Democrats had to devise a "third way" between capitalism and statism, "that is, to find the means to harmonize the necessities of individual development with the interests of all," and that, he thought, would require some degree of economic planning.[33] In their political message for 1949, the NEI emphasized that it was essential in the context of the Marshall Plan to give "all workers their social security through a statute which will guarantee that everyone, wherever they are, will profit equally from the results of the European and international division of labour."[34] In their economic resolution at the NEI congress in Sorrento in April 1950 they spoke of a "right to work" and demanded that the fight against unemployment be one of the "essential objectives" of European cooperation.[35] The political rhetoric of social solidarity and security and the actual welfare state measures that were adopted can certainly be understood as a response to what the Communists and Socialists were promising, but they also formed part of the Christian Democratic belief system.

At the European level as well, "third way" thinking was not simply a matter of rhetoric. On the contrary, the "core Europe" organisations implemented policies based on these ideas thanks largely to the influence of the Christian Democrats. Those policies (in the ECSC) were designed in particular to benefit the declining coal and steel industry and (in the EEC from the 1960s on) to assist the agricultural sector.[36] European policies for these sectors aimed at a managed transformation; a reduction in the workforce and improvements in productivity were to be achieved in consultation with trade unions and employers' organisations. The guiding principle in the EEC beginning in the mid-1950s was to avoid even temporary unemployment and socially disruptive, rapid urbanization in order to protect local communities and guarantee social cohesion. These goals required highly protectionist policies; this sort of thinking was one of the main factors shaping the EEC's Common Agricultural Policy (CAP) in the 1960s. To some extent, the CAP reflected the Christian Democratic parties' fears of losing rural votes. Yet it was also in line with their ideological preference for small-scale farming and medium-sized companies as important cornerstones of a less individualistic, less materialistic culture than that of the United States.

The Christian Democrats, the dominant political force in continental Western Europe after 1945, played a key role in designing the "core Europe" organisations that came into being in that period. But in taking the lead in this area, those parties did not draw on the U.S. model. If anything, the Christian Democrats designed the new Europe in such a way as to avoid what they saw as the social excesses of American capitalism. "Free world" rhetoric was rooted in a sense of external threat. It was the Soviet menace that pulled Europe and America together: the effect was to de-emphasize the cultural divide that separated the United States from a Christian Democratic Western Europe. It is thus not surprising that Christian Democratic "third way" policies could lead to transatlantic policy clashes when common core security interests were not involved—especially in trade, where the first "chicken wars" were fought between the EEC and the United States in the 1960s.

EUROPEAN AUTONOMY AND GLOBAL INFLUENCE

Christian Democratic ambivalence toward the United States was not, however, limited to domestic political issues. It also extended to the U.S. leadership role in the Atlantic Alliance and to American foreign policy more generally. Within the security constraints imposed by the Cold War, the Christian Democratic parties were keen to retain the greatest possible independence and influence for their "core Europe." Despite the totalitarian experience and the two world wars, they regarded such influence as historically and culturally justified and also essential in view of their critical appraisal of U.S. leadership qualities and of the danger, as they saw it, of renewed American isolationism. Their claim to a stronger European role within the "free West" is reflected, for example, in their policy on the European Defense Community (EDC), on the issue of détente in the mid-1950s, and on the question of policy toward the Third World.

Even Adenauer, who very early on opted for a policy of alignment with the West and rejected the idea of a European "third force" equally distant from both superpowers, saw integration as a means of establishing Europe as an influential "third power in the world."[37] Henri Teitgen insisted in his speech at the NEI congress in Bad Ems that Western Europe had to unite in order to achieve a substantial degree of autonomy within the Atlantic Alliance. Christian Democrats had to protect Europe from degenerating into a mere "vassal state" of the United States.[38] At the NEI congress in Salzburg in September 1955 the Dutch Economics Minister Jelle Zijlstra argued that if further economic integration, which was then being discussed in the Spaak Committee in Brussels, were to fail, Europe would lose all influence on world affairs. "The old Europe," he said, "will be nothing but a small border region between the world powers; moreover, it will be a 'contested territory' which will run the danger of becoming the battleground of another 'Korea conflict'."[39] Thus, the emerging "core Europe" had to become integrated in order to retain its cultural individuality, protect its socioeconomic system from external pressures, and continue to exercise some influence in the world—

goals that implied that Europe and America, while both part of the "free world," were to a certain extent in competition with each other.[40]

The Christian Democrats wondered whether the United States was qualified to lead the Western world; they wondered about how committed the Americans were to the defense of Western Europe. It was clear to them, therefore, that Europe needed as much autonomy as possible. The Catholic Christian Democrats, moreover, were often appalled by the moralistic evangelical anti-Communism, embedded in a predominantly Protestant political culture, of many U.S. politicians, who tended to frame the conflict between democracy and Communism in black and white terms—who tended to see the conflict as a fight of good against evil. Christian Democratic party activists were used to the greyer tones of European politics: collaborating with the Communists in the resistance to the German occupation; dealing with severe social problems by adopting highly interventionist policies; and even at times cooperating with the Communists at the local level, as in the Tuscany of *Don Camillo e Peppone,* where the Catholic priest and the Communist mayor practice the new policy of peaceful coexistence.[41] The persecution of hapless intellectuals and artists with Communist leanings such as in the McCarthy era was unlikely to win many Communists over to the cause of parliamentary democracy in much of Western Europe. Worse, the Americans' missionary zeal, Christian Democrats feared, could lead to a crusade against the USSR: the Americans had had a finger on the trigger ever since their arrival on the new continent; they might launch a preventive war against Russia and be too quick to use nuclear weapons; the result might well be the destruction of Europe. Yet, as the Dutch KVP politician Emmanuel Sassen put it in the Geneva Circle in December 1950, "one cannot maintain peace by making war."[42]

At the same time, however, the Christian Democrats were well aware that Western Europe depended on U.S. military protection, and always worried that America might return to isolation, thereby possibly withdrawing that protection. As Adenauer put it in the Geneva Circle in June 1949, "America does not understand Europe." Public opinion in the United States, he argued, was very unstable. The Americans might some day agree to "an entente with the Soviet Union at the expense of Europe."[43] When U.S.–Soviet relations did improve during the 1953–1956 period, the Christian Democratic parties feared a much-reduced American interest in Western Europe. Herbert Blankenhorn, Adenauer's advisor in the chancellory, warned in the Geneva Circle in June 1953 after Winston Churchill's summit proposal that the isolationists around Senator Robert Taft were gaining in influence and that their ideas had already, to a certain extent, penetrated the U.S. administration.[44] Otto Lenz, a CDU member of the Bundestag and another advisor to Adenauer, argued at the NEI congress in Salzburg in September 1955 that the Americans could not be relied upon forever, especially in times of peaceful coexistence, to retain the same interest in Western Europe, and that it could by no means be taken for granted that they would be prepared to intervene "if and when things flare up again in Europe."[45] These fears of American isolationism later became a recurring theme in Christian Democratic discourse in the context of the never-ending debate on burden sharing in NATO.[46]

The desire for relative autonomy and the fear of U.S. isolationism were two of the main driving forces behind the Christian Democrat support for the EDC from 1950 on.[47] In the final negative vote in the French *Assemblée Nationale* in August 1954, the MRP was the only parliamentary faction that voted almost unanimously in favour of the treaty.[48] As the former French MRP foreign minister Robert Schuman put it at a rally of the West German *Europa-Union*, to be content with the British alternative solution of the intergovernmental Western European Union combined with West Germany's accession to NATO would amount to "the definite abandonment of a *European* solution to which we [Christian Democrats] remain attached over and above all other preoccupations."[49] Only an institutionalised "core Europe" defense organisation linked to the Atlantic Alliance would give Europe a distinctive voice vis-à-vis the U.S. and provide a stable, independent structure in the case of serious friction within NATO or of U.S. withdrawal from Europe.

The same rationale explains the general Christian Democrat interest in détente between the blocs. The NEI set up a special committee in 1956, headed by the former Belgian foreign minister Paul Van Zeeland, to discuss and coordinate Christian Democrat policy on détente issues.[50] The party representatives, it soon became clear, could not agree on Van Zeeland's more farreaching proposals for a demilitarized Central Europe. The Germans and Dutch in particular were concerned that the withdrawal of NATO troops from West Germany would reduce NATO's forward defense capabilities in the event of war; they also thought that there was a real risk that in the medium-term some sort of disengagement arrangement might even lead to U.S. troop withdrawals from Western Europe. On the other hand, it was clear that the Soviet bloc was internally unstable, as the unrest in Poland and the Hungarian Revolution in 1956 demonstrated; but with the Soviet leadership prepared to use military force to keep the Warsaw Pact together, it seemed necessary to search for alternative ways to induce some degree of liberalisation in Eastern Europe. For the Christian Democrats, the ultimate goal throughout the Cold War remained to overcome not so much the division of Germany, which was in some ways convenient as it reduced the potential economic strength and political influence of the Federal Republic, but of Europe as a whole. Christian Democrat détente initiatives were not only designed to enhance security and to weaken Soviet control over Eastern Europe, but ultimately, as Van Zeeland put it, to allow "the reconstitution of the traditional Europe," including East-Central Europe, so that it could again exercise much greater influence on world affairs.[51]

The Christian Democrats' search for autonomy from the United States was also reflected in their collective attitudes toward decolonisation and in their views on Third World issues more generally; they were particularly interested in working with the Christian Democratic parties in Latin America. Catholic parties had not been the main political force behind European colonial expansion in the nineteenth century, but now, after the Second World War, they refused to support what they saw as rushed decolonisation. They regarded American anti-colonialist rhetoric with deep suspicion; the U.S. aim, they thought, was to expand America's global influence at Europe's expense.[52] The Christian Democrats insisted from the start that the so-called overseas territories ought to become linked to an economically integrated "core Europe." In one of its first resolutions, the NEI emphasized that organic ties between Western Europe and its colonies (which, it recognized, might in the future become independent states) were crucial and ought to be maintained.[53] The idea of "Euroafrica"—that is, of institutionalised economic and political bonds between Western Europe and Africa, which at that time was seen as a continent with great potential—was not just a French preoccupation.[54] Josef Müller, the Bavarian CSU leader, suggested, for example, in March 1949 that only a Western Europe with strong links with its colonies— colonies that were important sources of raw materials and that provided growing markets for European finished products—would be strong enough and independent enough to prevent "a clash of the blocs."[55]

Indeed, a number of initiatives that were undertaken—the establishment of an EEC investment fund for overseas territories and then, after decolonisation, the policies that culminated in the Yaoundé and Lomé conventions on trade and aid between the European Union and the former European colonies—were ultimately rooted in this sort of thinking. And Third World issues were often a source of friction in transatlantic relations during the Cold War and beyond; the Americans, for example, recently complained about the European Union's banana regime, which disadvantaged some Central American countries and the large U.S. fruit companies that controlled their banana production.[56] But the Christian Democrats have always tended to look at such problems in a very different way. The real issue for them has to do with their former colonies' socioeconomic development. During the 1950s and 1960s, they resisted the Americans' tendency to view Third World issues in confrontational Cold War terms. At the NEI congress in Paris in September 1960, Roger Reynaud, a French MRP member of the ECSC High Authority, insisted that Europe should concentrate on fighting poverty and underdevelopment in the Third World, and not on opposing the Soviet Union there.[57] Albert Coppé, the Belgian PSC/CVP Vice-President of the High Authority, added that the Christian Democratic parties should not allow themselves to be identified with economic liberalism in the Third World. The "core Europe" would have to play a crucial role there because Russian and U.S. policies were "equally deplorable." The United States had nothing to offer but freer trade through the General Agreement on Tariffs and Trade (GATT), when the main economic problem of these countries had to do with the extreme fluctuations in the price of raw materials. The United States, moreover, appeared to support any regime as long as it was anti-Communist.[58] Coppé was especially critical of the recent U.S. threats against Cuba and military intervention in Nicaragua and other Central American countries. One year earlier, at the NEI congress in Freiburg in Germany, the Belgian NEI president August de Schryver had already warned that Third World countries should be allowed to develop their own forms of governance, but that Western Europe and the United States should under no circumstances support military dictatorships.[59]

The Christian Democratic parties were especially critical of U.S. policy in Latin America, where they had close links with the emerging Christian Democratic movement. They organized a first intercontinental congress of Christian Democratic parties in Paris in November 1956.[60] Four years later, in the autumn of 1960, the NEI founded an intercontinental study center in Rome with the Bohemian-born Dutch KVP politician Karl Josef Hahn as its first director; the aim was to reach out to Christian Democratic movements outside of Europe. The Christian Democratic parties in Latin America were far to the left in terms of their socioeconomic programme; they supported far-reaching land reform, nationalisation, and redistributive measures. They had close links with the Catholic movement from below, a movement led by local priests who regarded social action as important as religious service.[61] Their far-left Catholic programme was regarded by European Christian Democratic parties as legitimate in view of the extreme inequalities of wealth in Latin America. The European Christian Democrats held America responsible to a considerable extent for conditions there: the Americans supported socially conservative and often corrupt regimes, and even supported military dictatorships as long as those regimes served the interests of the large landowners and major U.S. companies.[62] With Africa it had been different: the European Christian Democratic parties wanted to cultivate strong ties with that continent, even though they had no significant party contacts there. But in the Latin American case, a centerpiece of their policy was support for the Christian Democratic movement there, and they were very critical of U.S. policy in this region throughout the Cold War period.

CONCLUSION

Samuel Huntington has argued that the end of the Cold War marked the beginning of a new era of conflict. He sees a "clash of civilizations"—a clash, above all, between the Christian-inspired and democratic "West" and other cultural spaces, especially Islam.[63] That view appeared to be confirmed by the terrorist attacks of 11 September 2001—which, thanks to the media, was experienced as a global event by people around the world. But the Huntington view is highly simplistic: it overemphasizes cultural differences (and thus the potential for conflict) *between* larger "civilizations," and plays down the importance of cultural differences *within* cultural spaces, and especially within the "West" itself. During the Cold War period, countries within the Atlantic world did share some basic values, such as a belief in human rights and in democracy, and they continue to do so. But as the case of Christian Democratic attitudes toward the United States demonstrates, below the surface of "free world" rhetoric the differences were substantial. Christian Democracy had indigenous continental European roots that had little in common with the U.S. model. Christian Democrats viewed that model very critically and wanted to preserve a European socioeconomic "third way." They knew Europe was dependent on U.S. military protection, but still they wanted to retain as much autonomy as possible in the foreign policy area: their goal was to chart a course in world affairs in line with their own belief system—with their own historical experiences as they understood them. They wanted to pursue their own policy toward the Third World in general, and toward Latin America in particular. But the Christian Democrats worked closely with the United States throughout the Cold War period. If even they felt such ambivalence toward America, it is only to be expected that the Social Democrats, currently the second largest political group in the European Parliament, would feel even greater ambivalence, albeit for different reasons.

Cultural differences within the Atlantic world are unlikely to disappear as a result of globalisation. Despite the unifying forces of global competition and international stock markets and mergers and acquisitions, the European Union and most of its member states have responded to these pressures by adjusting their established patterns of informally cooperative or institutionalized, corporative decision-making, not through the wholesale adoption of the U.S. model. How to devise a new "third way" for the twenty-first century is of course a contested issue in European politics. But what is not contested is whether Europe needs to make its own choices—choices rooted in its own values, its own culture, its own history. A distinct culture means a distinct policy: it is not surprising therefore that Europe and America clash head-on on many global issues—over the Kyoto protocol on climate change, for example, and on issues related to the International Court of Justice. Those differences have little to do with geopolitics, and are not to be explained solely in terms of varying economic interests; in such cases, culture is the fundamental variable. And what that means is that in the future as in the past, a certain degree of tension is inevitable in U.S.–European relations. That relationship was never a marriage of love; it was rooted in necessity and its terms had to be continually renegotiated. And if that was so in the past, when the Cold War brought the two sides together, it is likely to remain so in the future.

NOTES

1. Andrew Moravcsik, *The Choice for Europe: Social Purpose and State Power from Messina to Maastricht* (Cornell: Cornell University Press, 1998).

2. For a brief theoretical and bibliographical introduction to constructivism as applied to the integration process, see Ben Rosamund, *Theories of European Integration* (Basingstoke: Macmillan, 2000), 171–174.

3. For introductions to European Christian Democracy after 1945, see Michael Gehler, Wolfram Kaiser, and Helmut Wohnout, eds., *Christian Democracy in 20th Century Europe* (Vienna: Böhlau, 2001), Emiel Lamberts, ed., *Christian Democracy in the European Union (1945/1995)* (Leuven: Leuven University Press, 1997); Tom Buchanan and Martin Conway, eds., *Political Catholicism in Europe 1918–1965* (Oxford: Clarendon Press, 1996).

4. On the organisational structures and content of the transnational contacts of European CD parties after 1945, see Michael Gehler and Wolfram Kaiser, *Europäische Christdemokraten: Transnationale Parteienkooperation in NEI und Genfer Kreis 1947–1965. Darstellung und Dokumente* (forthcoming).

5. On U.S. policy toward Italy after the war, see the articles in the special issue 4, no. 3 (2002) of the *Journal of Cold War Studies*. See also Leopoldo Nuti, "The United States and Italy at the End of the Second World War," *Annales du Monde Anglophone* (forthcoming); James E. Miller, *The United States and Italy, 1940–1950: The Politics and Diplomacy of Stabilization* (Chapel Hill: North Carolina University Press, 1984); and John L. Harper, *L'America e la ricostruzione dell'Italia, 1945–1948* (Bologna: Il Mulino, 1987).

6. Frank Schumacher, *Kalter Krieg und Propaganda: Die USA, der Kampf um die Weltmeinung und die ideelle Westbindung der Bundesrepublik Deutschland, 1945–1955* (Trier: WVT, 2000), 252–254. On U.S. policy toward Germany after the war, see also Hermann-Josef Rupieper, *Der besetzte Verbündete. Die amerikanische Deutschlandpolitik 1949–1955* (Opladen: Westdeutscher Verlag, 1991) and Thomas Alan Schwartz, *America's Germany: John J. McCloy and the Federal Republic of Germany* (Cambridge, Mass.: Harvard University Press, 1991).

7. On the American "mission" ideology, see also H. W. Brands, *What America Owes the World: The Struggle for the Soul of Foreign Policy* (Cambridge: Cambridge University Press, 1998).

8. The "Europeanisation" of the Marshall Plan is strongly emphasized in Alan S. Milward, *The Reconstruction of Western Europe 1945–51* (London: Methuen & Co., 1984). For a U.S. perspective, see Michael J. Hogan, *The Marshall Plan: America, Britain, and the Reconstruction of Western Europe, 1947–1952* (Cambridge: Cambridge University Press, 1987).

9. NEI, Résolutions du Congrès de la Haye sur l'organisation de l'Europe, 17–19 septembre 1948, Katholieke Documentatie- en Oderzoekcentrum Leuven (KADOC), Archief de Schryver, 7.2.4.3.

10. On the confessional and social basis of European CD parties after 1945, see also the chapters in part II of Lamberts, *Christian Democracy*, and the chapters on the postwar period in Gehler et al., *Christian Democracy*.

11. Pierre Letamendia, *Le Mouvement Républicain Populaire: Histoire d'un grand parti français* (Paris: Beauchesne, 1995), 281.

12. Jac Bosmans, "Das Primat der Innenpolitik. Die niederländische Christdemokratie in der ersten Nachkriegszeit," in *Christian Democracy*, eds. Gehler et al., 370–384, 377.

13. Cf. Frank Bösch, *Die Adenauer-CDU. Gründung, Aufstieg und Krise einer Erfolgspartei 1945–1970* (Stuttgart: DVA, 2001).

14. Entwurf von Hassel für einen Vortrag für MdB von Brentano bei der NEI-Tagung in Bad Ems, September 1951, Bundesarchiv Koblenz (BA) N 1351 (Blankenhorn)/8a. Brentano did give the speech in accordance with this draft.

15. Cf. Sabine Schulz, *Der Aachener Karlspreis* (Aachen: Meyer & Meyer, 1988); Helmut Reuther, ed., *Der internationale Karlspreis zu Aachen. Zeugnis europäischer Geschichte, Symbol europäischer Einigung: eine Dokumentation 1950–1993* (Aachen: Transcontact-Verlagsgesellschaft, 1993).

16. The Abendland myth already played an important role in Catholic-inspired attempts at Franco-German reconciliation in the interwar period. See Guido Müller and Vanessa Plichta, "Zwischen Rhein und Donau. Abendländisches Denken zwischen deutsch-französischen Verständigungsinitiativen und konservativ-katholischen Integrationsmodellen (1923–1957)," *Journal of European Integration History* 5, no. 2 (1999), 17–47. For the postwar period see also, albeit only in the German context, Axel Schildt, *Zwischen Abendland und Amerika: Studien zur westdeutschen Ideenlandschaft der 50er Jahre* (Munich: Oldenbourg, 1999).

17. Stenogramm der Rede des Herrn Bundeskanzlers anlässlich der NEI-Tagung in Bad Ems am 14. September 1951, 15.30 Uhr, Kursaal, Bad Ems, BA N 1351 (Blankenhorn)/8a.

18. Geneva Circle, 21 October 1948, Protocol by Felix Hurdes, Institut für Zeitgeschichte Innsbruck, Karl Gruber-Archiv (KGA), Karton 4.

19. On Dulles, generally, Ronald W. Pruessen, *John Foster Dulles: The Road to Power* (New York: Free Press, 1982), Richard H. Immerman, ed., *John Foster Dulles and the Diplomacy of the Cold War* (Princeton, N.J.: Princeton University Press, 1990). On Dulles and Europe see also Manfred Görtemaker, "John Foster Dulles und die Einigung Westeuropas," *Die Christen und die Entstehung der Europäischen Gemeinschaft*, eds. Martin Greschat and Wilfried Loth (Stuttgart: Kohlhammer, 1994), 159–187.

20. P. J. S. Serrarens, Le problème allemand, son aspect politique, NEI, Session de Luxembourg, 30–31 Janvier et 1er Fevrier 1948, Bundesarchiv Bern (BAR), JII.181 1987/52.

21. On the Christian Democrats and Germany after the Second World War, see in greater detail Wolfram Kaiser, "Deutschland exkulpieren und Europa aufbauen. Parteienkooperation der europäischen Christdemokraten in den Nouvelles Equipes Internationales 1947–1965," in *Christian Democracy*, eds. Gehler et al., 695–719, 710–714.

22. On Catholic politicians in exile and their changing views of Britain and the U.S., see Wolfram Kaiser, "Co-operation of European Catholic Politicians in Exile in Britain and the USA during the Second World War," *Journal of Contemporary History* 35, no. 3 (2000), 439–465.

23. Henri Teitgen, L'Autorité supranationale et la notion de souveraineté. Aspects politiques, Congrès de Tours, 1–6 septembre 1953, Bundesarchiv Bern (BAR) JII.181 1987/52, 2382.

24. Un Appel pour l'Europe. Déclaration de la Conférence des Présidents des Partis Démocrates Chrétiens de l'Europe des Six, 8 February 1963, Algemeen Rijksarchief Den Haag (ARA), Archief Dr. W.P. Berghuis, 357. The declaration in favour of enlargement in principle was not motivated by any enthusiasm for British EEC membership, but by opposition to de Gaulle's attempt, as the CD parties saw it, to undermine the supranational character of the EEC or even to replace it with entirely intergovernmental structures.

25. Geneva Circle, 31 January 1955, Protocol by Karl von Spreti, ACDP I-172-31.

26. For the importance of their "third way" for the electoral success of the CD parties in Western Europe after 1945 see also R. E. M. Irving, *The Christian Democratic Parties of Western Europe* (London: George Allen & Unwin, 1979), xix.

27. Cf. Christopher Clark, "The New Catholicism and the Culture Wars," in *Culture Wars: Secular–Catholic Conflict in Nineteenth-Century Europe*, eds. Christopher Clark and Wolfram Kaiser (Cambridge: Cambridge University Press, forthcoming 2003); John W. Boyer, "Catholics, Christians, and the Challenge of Democracy: The Heritage of the Nineteenth Century," in *Christian Democracy*, eds. Gehler et al., 23–59.

28. Bruno Béthouart, "Le Mouvement Républicain Populaire. L'entrée des catholiques dans la République française," in *Christian Democracy*, eds. Gehler et al., 313–331, 324.

29. Emiel Lamberts, "The Zenith of Christian Democracy in Belgium. The Christelijke Volkspartij/Parti Social Chrétien 1945–1968," in *Christian Democracy*, eds. Gehler et al., 332–347, 332–333. See also Jean-Louis Jadoulle, "L'évolution du programme du PSC/CVP (Noël, 1945–1968)," in *Un parti dans l'histoire (1945–1995). 50 ans d'action du Parti Social Chrétien* (Leuven: Duculot, 1996), 343–364.

30. Bosmans, "Der Primat," 377–379.

31. Cf. Carlo Masala, "Die Democrazia Cristiana 1943–1963: Zur Entwicklung des partito nazionale," in *Christian Democracy*, eds. Gehler et al., 348–369, 358.

32. Cf. Anthony J. Nicholls, *Freedom with Responsibility: The Social Market Economy in Germany, 1918–1963* (Oxford: Clarendon Press, 1994), Volker Hentschel, *Ludwig Erhard. Ein Politikerleben* (Munich: Olzog, 1996).

33. Aussprache, Convenium christlicher Politiker Europas, Luzern, 27 February to 2 March 1947, BAR JII.181 1987/52, 2372.

34. Botschaft der NEI für 1949, Östereichisches Staatsarchiv (ÖstA), Archiv der Republik (AdR), BKA/AA, II-pol, Int. 14, Zl. 80.755-pol/49.

35. Wirtschaftliche Entschließung, NEI-Kongreß, Sorrent, 12–14 April 1950, Archiv für christlich-demokratische Politik St. Augustin (ACDP) IX-002-011/4. See also Robert Houben, Der Stand der Doktrin, Bericht, NEI-Kongreß, Freiburg/CH, 12–14 September 1952, BAR JII.181 1987/52, 2356.

36. By way of introduction, see Dirk Spierenburg and Raymond Poidevin, *The History of the High Authority of the European Coal and Steel Community: Supranationality in Operation* (London: Weidenfeld and Nicolson, 1994); Gisela Hendriks, "The Creation of the Common Agricultural Policy," in *Widening, Deepening, and Acceleration: The European Economic Community 1957–1963*, eds. Anne Deighton and Alan S. Milward (Baden-Baden: Nomos, 1999), 139–150.

37. Speech by Adenauer at a meeting of the CDU in the British zone, 19 October 1948, quoted in *Konrad Adenauer und die CDU der britischen Besatzungszone*

1946–1949: Dokumente zur Gründungsgeschichte der CDU Deutschlands, ed. Konrad-Adenauer-Stiftung (Bonn: Eichholz-Verlag, 1975), 492–499, 499. See also Konrad Adenauer, *Erinnerungen 1945–1953* (Stuttgart: DVA, 1965), 211.

38. Henri Teitgen, Der politische Friede—der soziale Friede, Bericht, NEI-Kongreß, Bad Ems, 14–16 September 1951, KADOC; Archief A. E. de Schryver, 7.2.4.5.

39. Jelle Zijlstra, Die Europäische Integration, Bericht, NEI-Kongreß, Salzburg, 16–17 September 1955, BAR JII.181 1987/52, 2383.

40. Proponents of the idea of Europe as a "third force" in foreign policy who became converted to Western integration as a result of the emerging Cold War confrontation were particularly keen to retain the highest possible degree of European autonomy within the Atlantic Alliance in order to sustain a separate West European socioeconomic order. See, for example, Wilfried Loth, "German Conceptions of Europe during the Escalation of the East-West-Conflict, 1945–1949," in *Power in Europe? Great Britain, France, Italy, and Germany in a Postwar World, 1945–1950*, eds. Josef Becker and Franz Knipping (Berlin/New York: Walter de Gruyter, 1986), 517–536, 530.

41. For the gradual softening of U.S. attitudes toward the non-Communist left in Western Europe from 1956, see also (with regard to the case of the Italian PSI and the DC's cooperation with it) the chapter by Leopoldo Nuti in this book.

42. Geneva Circle, 11 December 1950, Protocol by Victor Koutzine, ACDP I-009-017.

43. Geneva Circle, 10 June 1949, Protocol by Victor Koutzine, ACDP I-009-017.

44. Geneva Circle (at Baarn, Netherlands), 29 June 1953, Protocol by Jacques Mallet, Archives Nationales Paris (AN) 457 AP 59.

45. Aussprache (contributions in German only), NEI-Kongreß, Salzburg, 16–17 September 1955, ACDP IX-002-017.

46. See in this context Hubert Zimmermann, *Money and Security: Troops, Monetary Policy, and West Germany's Relations with the United States and Britain, 1950–1971* (Cambridge: Cambridge University Press, 2001).

47. See also Michael Gehler and Wolfram Kaiser, "Transnationalism and Early European Integration: The Nouvelles Equipes Internationales and the Geneva Circle 1947–57," *The Historical Journal* 44, no. 3 (2001), 773–798.

48. For MRP and NEI policy on European integration during 1954–1956 see in greater detail Wolfram Kaiser, "Une bataille est perdue, mais la guerre reste à gagner—Das Scheitern der Europäischen Verteidigungsgemeinschaft 1954 und der Durchbruch zur horizontalen Wirtschaftsintegration," *Die Europäische Union und ihre Krisen*, ed. Romain Kirt (Baden-Baden: Nomos, 2001), 79–95, 85–93.

49. Quoted in Raymond Poidevin, *Robert Schuman, homme d'Etat 1886–1963* (Paris: Impr. Nationale, 1986), 381. Emphasis added.

50. Kommission Ad Hoc I, Paris, 11 February 1956, BAR JII.181 1987/52, 2362.

51. Ost-West-Kommission, Paris, 1 February 1957, BAR JII.181 1987/52, 2362.

52. See, for example, Geneva Circle, 13 February 1950, Protocol by Victor Koutzine, AN 457 AP 59.

53. Entschließung, Politischer Ausschuß, NEI-Kongreß, Den Haag, 17–19 September 1948, Archiv für christlich-soziale Politik Munich (ACSP), Nachlaß Josef Müller.

54. For France see, by way of introduction and in relation to the EEC treaty negotiations, René Girault, "La France entre l'Europe et l'Afrique," in *The Relaunching of*

Europe and the Treaties of Rome, ed. Enrico Serra (Brussels: Bruylant, 1989), 351–378. For the Christian Democrat position on this issue before the start of the EEC negotiations, see also the answers of the national NEI groups to question 9 in Robert Houben, Fragebogen zur Wirtschafts- und Sozialpolitik in der europäischen Integration in Vorbereitung auf den NEI-Kongreß in Brügge, 10–12 September 1954, Antworten der CDU/CSU, 8 July 1954, and of the French equipe (MRP), no date (July 1954), KADOC, Archief R. Houben, 246.2./3.

55. Josef Müller, Rede zur Gründung der NEI-Equipe des Saarlandes, Saarbrücken, 6 March 1949, ACSP, Nachlaß Josef Müller.

56. This conflict was eventually resolved in the context of the Cotonou Agreement between the EU and the ACP (African–Carribean–Pacific) countries, which made the relationship compatible with the rules of the World Trade Organization (WTO). Cf. Genevra Forwood, "The Road to Cotonou: Negotiating a Successor to Lomé," *Journal of Common Market Studies* 39, no. 3 (2001), 423–442.

57. Roger Reynaud, Bericht, NEI-Kongreß, Paris, 22–24 September 1960, ACDP IX-002-022.

58. Aussprache, NEI-Kongreß, Paris, 22–24 September 1960, ACDP IX-002-022.

59. August de Schryver, Die aktuelle politische Lage, NEI-Kongreß, Freiburg/D, 30 May 1959, ACDP IX-002-021.

60. See Roberto Papini, *The Christian Democrat International* (Lanham, Md.: Rowman & Littlefield Publishers, 1997), chapter 3, an account largely based on the author's personal experience as a collaborator of Karl Josef Hahn in the study center in Rome.

61. By way of introduction, see the chapters on Latin America in Thomas Kselman, ed., *Christian Democracy in Europe and Latin America* (South Bend, Ind.: Notre Dame University Press, forthcoming 2003).

62. See, for example, Karl Josef Hahn, "Eine Aufgabe für Europa. Die Anfänge einer christlichen Demokratie in Lateinamerika," *Rheinischer Merkur*, 9 February 1962.

63. Samuel Huntington, *The Clash of Civilizations and the Remaking of World Order* (New York: Simon & Schuster, 1996).

4

The United States and the Opening to the Left, 1953–1963

Leopoldo Nuti

The political system that took shape in the Western world after World War II was not simply a system of interstate relations. That system also had a major domestic political component. For the Europeans especially, the question of their relations with the United States was of fundamental importance during the Cold War period—and that meant in particular that it was bound to be important even in domestic political terms. As for the Americans, they were deeply interested in what was going on politically within the main European countries, and framed their policies toward them with such concerns in mind. Given the power of the United States, and the dependence of the Europeans on American power, it was natural that those policies would have a major impact on domestic political life within Europe.

The point applies to one degree or another to all of the European countries in the Western bloc—and perhaps above all to the Federal Republic of Germany, in whose domestic political affairs the Americans were very deeply involved from the outset. But West Germany, although the most important case, was also a very special case. So to understand how the international system, and in particular American policy, affected the political life of Western Europe as a whole, it makes sense for analytical purposes to focus on another major European country.

The aim here, therefore, is to examine how American policy affected political life in Italy. To make that analysis manageable, I want to focus on one specific issue: the question of an "opening to the left" in Italian politics in the period from 1953 to 1963. This was perhaps the most central issue in Italian politics in that period. In 1953 the Italian elections failed to provide the Christian Democrats with the absolute majority that their leader, Alcide De Gasperi, had sought. This partial electoral failure of the largest pro-Western

Italian party marked the end of the first phase of the country's postwar history and ushered in a period of uncertainty. For the next ten years, De Gasperi's successors strove with limited success to recapture their party's hegemonic position in the Italian political system. But the coalition governments the Christian Democrats put together generally ended up lasting no more than a year.

The key issue during that period was thus whether greater stability could be introduced into the system by broadening the base of the governing coalition by bringing in Pietro Nenni's Italian Socialist Party, the PSI. Until the mid-1950s, that party had been closely allied with the Italian Communist Party. The question, therefore, was whether a fundamental reorientation of the PSI, away from the Communists and toward the center, could be effected. In the mid-1950s, the Christian Democrats thus began to explore the possibility of some kind of "opening to the left." The PSI, for its part, was tempted to work out an arrangement of that sort: becoming one of the governing parties would clearly benefit the party and its supporters. But at the same time, the Socialists were reluctant, for both political and ideological reasons, to cut their ties so completely with their Communist former allies. So the process took a long time to run its course, and the PSI did not enter into a coalition government with the Christian Democrats until the end of 1963.

What role did the Americans play in all this, and what policy did they pursue in this area? According to most scholarly and journalistic accounts, the story can be divided into two very distinct parts. In the first period, the period of the Eisenhower administration, the Americans firmly opposed any dialogue between the Christian Democrats and the PSI because of the deep mistrust the administration as a whole—and above all, the U.S. ambassador to Italy for much of that period, Clare Booth Luce—felt toward Nenni and his party. In the second phase, it is argued, the Kennedy administration found itself divided between those who wanted to stop interfering with Italian politics and give Italy more autonomy in its domestic political choices, and those who remained deeply opposed to any opening to the left. The administration remained divided for almost the entire Kennedy period. It was only in mid-1963 that the conflict was resolved, when the American supporters of a Christian Democrat-PSI rapprochement won out. That group, composed mostly of highly ideological, liberal Kennedyites, saw in the dialogue between the Christian Democrats and the PSI a chance to shake Italian politics loose from the perilous conservative stagnation of the 1950s and encourage a reprise of dynamic reformism that Italy had experienced in the early postwar period.

This type of account is not entirely incorrect, but it is somewhat overschematized and is misleading in particular areas. Many writers, for example, spend a good deal of time talking about Ambassador Luce and her blatantly aggressive policy toward the Italian left. Mrs. Luce is mostly remembered for her brash anti-Communist stance, her often clumsy intrusions in Italian union and industrial affairs, and her alarmist declarations against the red peril. She is usually criticized for a basic incapacity to understand the subtle nuances of the Italian political system, its arcane and complex mechanisms, and the psychology and the mentality of its protagonists. In short, the most common portrait of ambassador Luce is something of a caricature, one that can be summed up in the classic image of the bull in a China shop.[1] But whatever her flaws, her importance should not be overstated. She did not, in fact, play a very important role in the story. Real policy, in this as in practically every other area, was actually made in Washington.

The U.S. government as a whole, during the early Eisenhower period, did take a hard line on matters relating to the Italian left. Indeed, the Americans took a hard line on many such issues throughout the world at that time. The most important document laying out U.S. policy toward Italy in the 1950s was NSC 5411/2 of April 13, 1954, and some extracts from that basic policy document are worth quoting at length. According to that document, the U.S. government was to try, using "all practicable means":

a. To reduce the strength and effectiveness of the Italian Communist party and of pro-communist groups
b. To prevent Italy from falling under the domination of the Italian Communist party or of the present Italian Socialist party.

The American government was also to:

Continue to make full use of U.S. political means and, as practicable and appropriate, economic and military aid to:

a. induce the Italian government to adopt measures striking at the organizational basis of Communist power and undermining Communist financial and political strengths.
b. induce private Italian groups, particularly Italian employers and free labor movements, to combat Communism vigorously.

Finally, "whenever possible and advantageous," the United States was to "seek to accomplish the above by conditioning U.S. assistance on anti-Communist actions taken by the Italian government and private Italian groups."[2]

The very tough and highly interventionist policy outlined here provided the warrant for what are commonly viewed as some of Mrs. Luce's most notorious initiatives, including her threat to assign U.S. Offshore Procurements (OSP) contracts only to those factories where non-Communist trade unionists held a clear majority within the workers' assemblies. But it is quite clear that policy itself was decided on not by her, but by the political leadership in Washington.

But does it make sense to see the policy outlined in NSC 5411/2 as reflecting the deep-seated and unchanging view of the Eisenhower administration? Did that document simply formalize a policy that was implemented as soon as that administration came to power in January 1953, was maintained intact for the next eight years, and was only abandoned when a new administration took office in 1961? Well, not quite, and it is important, when interpreting American policy during the Eisenhower period, to emphasize certain elements of change within that period and also certain elements of continuity with what came before and would come later.

First of all, one should note that the policy of the early Eisenhower administration had its roots in a reappraisal of U.S.–Italian policy that had begun in the last years of the Truman presidency. Between 1951 and 1953 many officials in the Truman administration had criticized an American policy that encouraged the Italian government to fight the Italian Communists only by encouraging economic and social reforms. Those officials advocated the adoption by De Gasperi or his successors of a tougher, more aggressive line against the Italian Communists. And the plan that emerged, the notorious "Demagnetize" (later relabeled "Clydesdale") plan approved by the Psychological Strategy Board toward the end of the Truman administration, was the real source of the subsequent Eisenhower policy; the basic idea here was that the Italian government should be encouraged by Washington to pursue a political and psychological offensive against the Communists.[3]

And as for the Eisenhower period itself, policy toward the end of that period was rather different from what it had been at the beginning. On the Italian question as in so many other areas, American policy had mellowed in the course of the 1950s; by the end of that period, the early hard line had softened considerably. The general assumption that there was no basic change in Eisenhower's Italian policy during the eight years of his presidency, the common belief that until the Kennedy administration stepped in, the basis of Washington's Italian policy remained frozen in stone, is quite mistaken.

In purely formal terms, it might, however, seem that American policy had not changed. The basic U.S. policy document for Italy, NSC 5411/2, was only replaced by a new policy document, NSC 6014, in 1960, and that new policy document was not radically different from its predecessor.[4] But one should not be misled by the formal policy documents. The key point to note is that in practice, beginning in late 1956, the Eisenhower administration adopted a less aggressive policy, a policy whose profile was less clear-cut than the previous one, and less easily defined.

That new policy was rooted in the sense, as the number two man in the U.S. embassy in Rome put it in mid-1956, that the "battering ram" approach was no longer a suitable tool in the new political climate. That policy was bankrupt in any case, according to that official, for the simple reason that the governing parties in Italy had simply refused to adopt a policy of direct confrontation with the left. In such circumstances, a subtler policy, a policy that would try to exploit the weaknesses and the internal tensions of the Italian left in order to disorganize it and generate more confusion within its ranks, might well be in order.[5]

One key event marking the beginning of that shift in policy was the American trip of Amintore Fanfani, the new general secretaryof the Christian Democratic Party, in the summer of 1956. Following Fanfani's visit, the Eisenhower administration began to move away from the old hard line and toward a rather bland encouragement of a policy of moderate reformism. Fanfani, in fact, became a kind of privileged interlocutor of the U.S. government, especially after the 1958 elections and the formation of his cabinet in July of that year. He was the man, as the Americans saw it, who might be able to bring about major reforms—reforms that might reduce support for the left while at the same time generating doubts and confusion within the ranks of the PSI.

So one has the sense that policy was beginning to shift, albeit gradually and in relatively minor ways, during the late Eisenhower period. In 1958, for example, a U.S. embassy official was allowed to begin a dialogue with some members of Nenni's wing of the PSI, the so-called autonomists. Those discussions then became almost a daily feature of the embassy's routine; but until that point talks of that sort had been utterly out of the question.[6] This does not mean that the embassy had suddenly come to support the idea of an "opening to the left" and had decided to help Nenni break with the Communists and get into the government. The shift was by no means that sharp or that extreme. But in the final years of the decade, the U.S. line, as reflected in day-to-day embassy practice, had clearly softened. The Socialists were no longer beyond the pale, and the Americans were now encouraging them to take their distance from the Communists.[7]

Another point worth noting in this context has to do with the British—both the British government and the British Labour Party. The conservative government, while perhaps not openly favoring the opening to the left, sought to influence events in a more indirect way: it supported certain key public figures in Italy who *were* directly involved in promoting the dialogue between the Christian Democrats and the PSI. The British, for example—unlike the Americans at that point—favored the election of Giovanni Gronchi as president of the Italian Republic in 1955; this is important in this context because Gronchi was one of the warmest supporters of a rapprochement between the Socialists and the Christian Democrats.[8] Britain was also the first government to try to cultivate the sympathies of Enrico Mattei, head of the state-run Italian oil company ENI and an outspoken champion of the opening to the left.[9]

The British Labour Party played an even more important role. The Labour Party had broken with the PSI a few years earlier, when the Italian Socialists had allied themselves with the Communists in the 1948 elections.[10] But now, in the mid- and late 1950s, it was rebuilding its ties with the PSI, and it was using those new links to encourage Nenni to pull away from the Communists and move toward the Christian Democrats. Leading Labourites, for example, went to Italy to try to encourage Nenni to move in that direction. And the Labour Party did more than just offer advice and moral support: during the January 1959 PSI Congress in Naples, Nenni managed to score an outstanding victory against his opponents inside the party thanks in part to a substantial Labourite contribution.[11]

The Americans seemed on the surface to disapprove of these Labour Party initiatives. The U.S. embassy in Rome, for example, gave a strongly negative assessment of their possible impact on Italian politics and judged them as hasty, ill-timed and based on an imprecise evaluation of Nenni's policies.[12] The Americans, moreover, decided eventually to take some direct countermeasures. They made the British aware of their misgivings, and they covertly warned some trusted members of the Socialist International against what they saw as a premature readmission of Nenni's party into its fold; the PSI, in their view, would first have to give stronger proof of its loyalty to the West.[13]

But the American attitude on this issue is by no means clear-cut, and there may have been more to American policy than met the eye. The Labour Party activities were, in fact, in line with what one U.S. embassy official in Rome had recommended in 1956. He suggested a plan for helping the PSI in a more "social democratic" direction, a plan that in some ways seemed to foreshadow what the Labour Party later ended up doing. That official thought the U.S. government might "consider having less-than-first rank European (not Italian) Social Democrats develop informal and unpublicized but close personal relations" with leaders of the anti-Communist wing of the PSI. The goal would be "to establish a channel of communication and, if possible, gently to influence their thinking." If those "relationships developed satisfactorily," that official thought that "the possibility of some financial aid through the channel of the European party in question could be considered."[14]

Given this type of thinking, one wonders whether a kind of "good cop, bad cop" strategy had been adopted: the British, perhaps, would take care of removing the rough ideological edges from Nenni's party, helping guide it toward the goal of social democratic respectability, while the Americans would be responsible for making sure that an official certificate of good behavior was not issued prematurely.

Whatever was going on here—and not all the evidence, especially from intelligence agency sources, bearing on the issue has been released thus far—the point to bear in mind is that the process that led to the opening to the left was quite complex, even in its international dimensions. America was not the only foreign player; governments were not the only actors. And one does get the sense that this part of the story was by no means of negligible importance: in the late 1950s, the British Labour Party had a major effect on Nenni and on the policy of the PSI.

The policy of the British left was, as it turned out, quite similar to the policy that the more liberal wing of the Kennedy administration favored, beginning in 1961. There was a debate within the new administration about the policy it should pursue toward Italy. Some have argued that the debate was centered on the opportunity to "lift the American veto" to the Italian natural inclination to spontaneously pursue the opening to the left. In reality, however, the clash centered on the desirability of openly encouraging a center-left coalition and of covertly supporting Nenni in his fight inside the PSI to crush the pro-Communist factions of the party.[15] Arthur M. Schlesinger, Jr., Robert Komer, Averell Harriman, and other members of the new administration believed that without a clear-cut signal from Washington, Italian politicians would never dare to bring about an opening to the left. In their view, Nenni was engaged in a life-and-death, no-holds-barred struggle for the control of his party, a struggle whose outcome would shape the political future of Italy for many years to come. As they saw it, the United States could not just sit still and watch passively while Nenni lost a fight whose outcome could well determine the future of Italian democracy. It was thus important not only that the United States support the opening to the left, but also that the Kennedy administration study what could be done to provide the beleaguered Nenni with some material support.[16]

And this question of financial support, it should be noted, is the crucial part of the story. In most accounts it is ignored or, at best, merely hinted at, and, given the limitations on source availability, much of this story remains unclear. But in the sources that are available, there are important clues here and there: the idea of financing the PSI was raised first by Arthur Schlesinger and CIA's Dana Durand in the summer of 1961, and debated between the State Department, the CIA, the embassy, and the White House throughout the following months.[17] Some liberal American trade union leaders, such as Walter and Victor Reuther of the United Automobile Workers (UAW) and Gus Bellanca of the Amalgamated Clothing Workers (ACW), then proposed to the Special Group of the NSC that they help the administration implement a major covert plan to build up a PSI-oriented, anti-Communist, trade union.[18] The available documentation shows that the project was turned down by the end of June 1962, but one should also note that by the end of 1962 the PSI began to receive a modest amount of financial support from the UAW and the ACW to build up its trade union support and free it from Communist control.[19] While there is no documentary evidence of direct approval of this initiative by the President, it is hardly conceivable that after a year and a half of heated debate the UAW and the ACW could go ahead *without* telling the administration and *without* some tacit approval of what they were doing.

So the policy that Schlesinger and his allies championed had some impact on what was actually done, but their views were not universally shared within the government. Many diplomats and government officials were in fact on the other side on this issue. They felt that someone like Nenni could not yet be trusted to become a member of a government of a member-state of NATO, and preferred therefore either to move more cautiously in the direction of a center-left coalition or even support a return to a more conservative formula. And standing above, or outside, the debate was the president himself—at least for most of his brief period in office. Kennedy, during that period, neither openly supported Schlesinger and his allies nor reined them in; in effect, he gave them ample freedom to maneuver. The result was a policy that for quite some time oscillated between the old and new approaches.

The great change came only in the summer of 1963. At that time, during his trip to Italy, Kennedy had a long conversation with Nenni during a reception in the Quirinale gardens. He thus signaled his personal support for the opening to the left. The extraordinary importance of that event was reflected in people's reactions at the time: open relief and satisfaction on Nenni's side, perplexity if not outright resentment on the side of some of the other Italian politicians who watched the scene.[20]

How is this move of Kennedy's to be understood? America's relations with Europe took a sharp turn for the worse in January 1963. The French leader, General Charles de Gaulle, was openly defiant, and Kennedy needed to rally the Europeans behind his new policy of détente with the Soviet Union. In Italy, by shifting his weight in favor of an opening to the left, the U.S. president probably hoped to kill two birds with one stone. Not only would a center-left cabinet hopefully stabilize Italian politics by bringing the Socialists into the government, but it would also have the beneficial effect of making sure that the foreign policy of the new Italian coalition would follow the U.S. approach toward détente and would not be inclined to support De Gaulle's challenge. The French general, as a matter of fact, was the veritable *bête noire* of the Italian Socialists.

So, looking at this period as a whole, what conclusions are in order? In particular, what impact did American policy have on developments within Italy? Under Eisenhower, the Americans played a fundamental role, but essentially a negative one. In the early Eisenhower period especially, the main effect of American policy was to strengthen those Italian forces opposed to a rapprochement between the Christian Democrats and the PSI. The ties between the Americans and the more conservative Italians were reinforced by various covert actions, especially in the financial area. Even as late as 1957–1958, for example, U.S. food aid was illegally resold by the Christian Democrats, who then used the proceeds for electoral purposes.[21]

But even during that period, there were limits to what the Americans could do. The United States might be able, in effect, to block an opening to the left, but it could not get the Italian government to pursue a really tough anti-Communist policy. De Gasperi's heirs—Pella, Scelba, and Segni—all shied away from the idea of a full-scale attack on the Italian Communist Party, the largest such party in Western Europe. After a puzzling encounter with the director general of the Italian Ministry of Foreign Affairs, Massimo Magistrati, Mrs. Luce herself remarked that the much-vaunted offensive against the Communists would be enacted at the speed of "cold molasses."[22]

The United States, moreover, was unable to reduce the influence of the Communists to the point where they became an entirely marginal actor in Italian politics. The central goal of weakening the Italian Communist Party, in fact, proved quite elusive. The results achieved, whether through encouraging bold reformist efforts or through pressing the Italian governments to adopt a harshly repressive policy, always fell very short of the mark. And that strategic failure was accompanied by a number of smaller tactical ones, which clearly show the limits of the American influence: the failure to prevent the election of Giovanni Gronchi as president of the Republic, for example, or the failed attempt to launch Fanfani as the new, dynamic reformist leader of the Christian Democratic Party in 1957–1958.[23]

As for the Kennedy period, again American policy played a key role. Limited though American support for the PSI was, the new U.S. attitude symbolized by Kennedy's meeting with Nenni in 1963 was regarded as a truly momentous shift in Italian political circles, and helped pave the way for the eventual admission of the Socialists into the government. By granting the PSI a full aura of respectability, and by letting the Reuther brothers and the ACW grant some limited covert assistance as well, the Kennedy administration undermined the position of those groups within Italy who counted on Washington to prevent—or, at least, to not facilitate—the opening to the left.

But is this how the question of American influence is to be conceptualized? Does it make sense to break the story down into two sharply defined phases? Perhaps it would make more sense to see a more complex process at work, a process unfolding over time, a process in which American and Italian attitudes interacted with each other. The Americans may have blocked an opening to the left in the 1950s; but the key point to note here is that that attitude also helped bring about a major shift in the character of the PSI. Nenni's policies changed dramatically in the 1953–1963 period; and indeed the moderate left in the Western world as a whole, as Donald Sassoon has shown, was transformed during that period. That transformation was characterized by the marginalization of the neutralist and philo-Soviet elements within the West European Socialist parties, and, on domestic issues, by a move toward a reformist, social democratic philosophy, especially in the German Social Democratic Party and in the British Labour Party, but also, to a certain extent, in the Italian PSI.[24]

These fundamental changes are of course not to be understood in purely geopolitical terms. It is important, however, to realize that the international environment played an important role in bringing them about. The Socialist parties needed to shed their neutralist, anti-NATO trappings if the United States was not going to throw its very considerable weight into the political scales within their own countries, and effectively keep them from ever becoming true governing parties. On the other hand, if they did evolve in a pro-NATO direction, the Americans would have an interest in bringing them in—that is, in broadening the base of the pro-NATO coalition. The effect was to help pull the Socialists to a more moderate position on foreign and defense policy issues; and when that happened, the Americans—and the European conservatives as well—found it much easier to take an accommodating position on the question of political participation at home.

One should note, moreover, that one of the things that made it relatively easy for this process to run its course was that American objections to the idea of bringing the Socialists into the government, in Italy as elsewhere in Western Europe in the 1950s, primarily had to do with the foreign, and not the domestic, policies those leftist parties called for. In the Italian case, the Americans feared that bringing the PSI into the government would help push Italian policy toward neutralism. Italy under the Christian Democrats pursued a strong, pro-Western policy; the Americans' main concern was that an opening to the left might well change all that. The focus, in other words, was overwhelmingly on foreign and military policy: the U.S. government did not really object to the idea of bringing the Socialists into the government because it was afraid of the sort of domestic policy a coalition that included the PSI would pursue. Indeed, the Americans generally believed that far-reaching political and social reforms were of vital importance—if only to weaken the grip of Communist propaganda on the poorest sections of the population. To be sure, U.S. pressure on Italy to pursue a reformist policy was halting and far from constant. It sharply decreased in the early Eisenhower years and became strong again only during the Kennedy period. But the Americans were never opposed to reform as a matter of principle, and the effect of this emphasis on the foreign policy side of the question was to lower the bar—to limit the sort of objections the Americans might have had to the inclusion of the Socialists in the government—and thus make it easier for the PSI to both change its policy and join a coalition that had America's blessing, and for the United States to support a development of that sort.

One can thus see the basic structure of the process that was at work. And the point needs to be stressed that the fundamental political changes that took place within Italy in this period are to be understood in *process* terms. To the quite considerable extent that they had an international taproot, those changes are not to be understood as the product of one-time shifts resulting from the changes of administration in Washington. The opening to the left took place at a particular point in time—after the PSI moderated its position, and after the American attitude softened. But these things did not happen overnight. There was a process at work, a process that took many years to run its course. The fact that it took so long meant that the PSI had the time to adjust to new realities and move toward a foreign policy position that would not jeopardize Italy's international position. And that, in turn, meant that the rapprochement between the Socialists and the Christian Democrats, when it was finally worked out, took place on less slippery and less dangerous ground than it would have if the "opening" had taken place in the early 1950s.

Throughout the whole period of the opening to the left there was thus a very close connection between the evolution of the international system and the evolution of the domestic Italian one—between the gradual beginning of détente on the international level and the first steps of the dialogue between the Christian Democrats and the PSI. Many commentators, especially in Italy, have claimed that the opening to the left is to be understood in purely domestic political terms. Even Nenni himself argued along these lines.[25] But it is quite clear that the international environment, and external pressures, played a fundamental role both in the *timing* of these developments and in the *way* they were implemented. The Americans in particular played a crucial role in defining the environment in which Italian politicians lived and acted. If one wants to understand even the internal history of Italy in that period, one must never lose sight of that fact.

This is not to say, of course, that this was all there was to the story—that every single turn or move inside the Italian political system can be explained by referring to a deus ex machina, which from the outside was pulling the strings and cunningly manipulating its pawns on the Italian chessboard. The Italians, obviously, were by no means simply passive objects of American pressure who played no real role of their own. The channels of influence ran both ways, and Italian politicians, both conservatives and moderates, made use of the international situation for their own political purposes. Many conservatives were afraid of the possible domestic repercussions of détente and warned the Americans about the effect it would have on the political situation within Italy—that is, they warned the Americans that a rush toward détente might have very serious repercussions in terms of Italian politics, and indeed might undermine the political position of America's best friends in Italy.[26] They cultivated their relationship with the United States, and especially, when they could, with the American president, in large part for domestic political reasons. They often used foreign policy arguments instrumentally: those arguments were useful tactically in political maneuvering at home. Perhaps the most striking example of this was the attempt of some conservative Italian politicians in late 1963 to disrupt the negotiations that led to the first government based on an alliance between the Christian Democrats and the PSI by citing (non-existent) American pressure on Italy to join a U.S.-sponsored Multilateral Force.[27]

On the other hand, those who favored the opening to the left—Gronchi, Mattei, Nenni, and so on—threw their weight into the scales on the pro-détente side, again, in large part, for domestic political reasons. They understood that a more relaxed international climate would legitimize their own policies and make it easier for them to accomplish their goals at home.

What emerges, then, from a study of this question is a strong sense of the interconnectedness of these various elements of both domestic and international political life. One has the sense of one overarching system coming into being, one with both internal and transnational aspects. The Cold War political system deeply influenced political life within every major Western country. But the extraordinary political changes that took place within those countries had far-reaching effects that went well beyond state borders.

The rallying of the moderate left to the NATO system was, in particular, a development of great *international* importance. It meant that the defense of Europe could now rest on a more solid domestic political base. It meant that the Americans could disengage from too great an involvement in internal European political affairs. It also meant that a certain element of rigidity was being removed from European political life, and that an element of brittleness was being removed from the NATO system itself. That system would no longer depend for its viability, in domestic political terms, on the support of conservative and centrist elements alone. And all of this ultimately made for a more stable political order in Europe, both internationally and domestically. But one can see why that sort of system came into being only by looking closely at how this process ran its course within individual Western countries. This is why a study of the opening to the left within Italy, a case that shows that process at work in an exceptionally clear way, is of fundamental historical interest.

NOTES

1. A striking example is Giangiacomo Migone, "Stati Uniti, FIAT e repressione antioperaia negli anni cinquanta," *Rivista di storia contemporanea*, no. 2 (1974). Some of the memoirs of Italian politicians also take this general view. See, for example, Giulio Andreotti, *Gli USA visti di vicino* (Milano: Mondadori, 1989). Note also James E. Miller, "Roughhouse Diplomacy: The U.S. Confronts Italian Communism," *Storia delle Relazioni Internazionali* 5, no. 2 (1989), 306. Alessandro Brogi, *L'Italia e l'egemonia americana* (Firenze: Nuova Italia, 1996) correctly relates Mrs. Luce's behavior with the strategic choices of Eisenhower's administration.

2. NSC 5411/2, U.S. policy toward Italy, April 13, 1954, in U.S. National Archives (NA), Record Group (RG) 59, Records Relating to State Department Participation in

the Operations Coordinating Board and the NSC: Lot File 62 D 430, box 79, folder "5411 memoranda."

3. Psychological Operations Plan for the Reduction of Communist Power in Italy (code name "Clydesdale"), February 15, 1952, in Harry S. Truman Presidential Library (HSTPL), papers of Harry S. Truman, records of the Psychological Strategy Board, folder "091-Italy." For an analysis of the "Demagnetize" plan, see Maria Eleonora Guasconi, *L'altra faccia della medaglia: Diplomazia psicologica e sindacale nelle relazioni Italia-Stati uniti durante la prima fase della guerra fredda (1947–1955)* (Messina: Rubbettino, 1998); Mario Del Pero, *L'alleato scomodo: Gli USA e la DC negli anni del centrismo (1948–1955)* (Roma: Carocci, 2001): 149–156.

4. NSC 6014, Draft Statement of U.S. Policy Toward Italy, August 16, 1964, in U.S. Department of State, *Foreign Relations of the United States* (FRUS), 1958–1960, vol. 7, part 2, p. 600. Henceforth, references to this source will be cited in the following form: FRUS 1958–60, 7(2): 600. After some slight changes, this document was approved as an official statement of policy and was issued as NSC 6014/1 on December 20, 1960.

5. Jernegan to Jones, 26 June 1956, in NA, RG 59, Central Decimal Files (CDF) for 1955–1959, box 3605, 765.00/6-2756 (document released through the F.O.I.A.).

6. Author's interview with George Lister, Washington, June 1991. Lister had his first meeting with a member of the PSI when he saw Riccardo Lombardi. "Memorandum of Conversation with PSI Leader Riccardo Lombardi," February 3, 1958, in NA, RG 59, CDF 1955–1959, box 3608, 765.00/2-358.

7. Report by the Operations Coordinating Board: Operations Plan for Italy, July 8, 1959, in FRUS 1958–60, 7(2): 529.

8. Ilaria Favretto, "La nascita del centro-sinistra e la Gran Bretagna: Partito socialista, laburisti, Foreign Office," *Italia Contemporanea*, no. 202 (March 1996), 5–43, note 36.

9. The first step was the purchase by ENI (*Ente Nazionale Idrocarburi*) of a British nuclear reactor for its power plant in Latina, the first nuclear reactor to be sold to Italy. The British embassy in Rome, in particular, dedicated much attention to building up its relationship with Mattei (to the point where one of Mattei's opponents, Giuseppe Saragat, called him a "British agent"). In 1960, the UK ambassador was the first to suggest to the foreign office that it was necessary to try to mediate the delicate controversies between Mattei and the British oil companies: Sir Ashley Clarke to Sir Paul Gore-Booth, August 11, 1960, in British Public Record Office (PRO), FO 371/153362, RT 1532/10.

10. On this episode see A. Varsori, "Il Labour Party e la crisi del socialismo italiano (1947–1948)," in *I socialisti e l'Europa,* ed. Fondazione Brodolini (Milano: Angeli, 1989), 159–210.

11. See Palewski to Mollet, October 23, 1958, in Office Universitaire de Recherche Socialiste (OURS), Archives Guy Mollet, "Dossier sur le PSI avant le 33ème Congrès du 16 janvier 1959"; and Barbour to Dulles, January 21, 1959, in NA, RG 59, CDF 1955–1959, box 3609, 765.00/1-2159.

12. Ambassador Zellerbach explicitly denied to Giuseppe Saragat that the U.S. embassy approved of the British maneuvers. Embassy Rome to the Department of State, "Conversation with On. Giuseppe Saragat and Notes on Visit of British Labour MP, Alfred Robens," in NA, RG 59, CDF 1955–1959, box 3608, 765.00/7-2458.

13. In February 1959 members of the State Department had a lively exchange of ideas on this matter with some British diplomats: Memorandum of Conversation, "Italian Political Situation—Evaluation of Nenni," February 4, 1959; and memorandum of conversation on "Italian Socialist Developments," February 6, 1959; both in NA, RG 59, CDF 1955–1959, box 3610, 765.00/2-459 and 765.00/2-659.

14. Jernegan to Jones, June 26, 1956, in NA, RG 59, CDF 1955–1959, box 3605, 765.00/6-2756 (document released through the Freedom of Information Act).

15. See the Oral History Interview with G. Frederick Reinhardt, and Schlesinger's comment on that interview, in the John F. Kennedy Presidential Library (JFKPL).

16. Memorandum for the deputy director of intelligence, "Suggested Lines for Briefing President Kennedy on Pending Visit of Premier Fanfani," June 1, 1961; Memorandum to Walt Rostow, "State Department Paper on Italy," July 6, 1961; suggested approach to "OPERATION NENNI," 9 August 1961; all in JFKPL, Arthur Schlesinger Papers, Subject File: Italy, box WH 12. On the issue of financial support for the PSI there are a few hints in Leo Wollemborg, *Stars, Stripes, and Italian Tricolor: The United States and Italy, 1946–1989* (New York: Praeger, 1990), and Spencer Di Scala, *From Nenni to Craxi: Renewing Italian Socialism* (New York/Oxford: Oxford University Press, 1998).

17. Leopoldo Nuti, *Gli Stati Uniti e l'apertura a sinistra. Importanza e limiti della presenza americana in Italia* (Roma: Laterza, 1999), 369–374. For the Special Group meeting, see "Meeting between Walter P. Reuther and Bob Kennedy at Gen. Maxwell Taylor's office," June 21, 1962, Walter Reuther Library, Walter Reuther Papers, Series XVIII, Appointments and Invitations, box 602, and "Minutes of Meeting of Special Group (CI)," June 21, 1962, in JFKPL, Papers of President Kennedy, National Security Files, box 319. See also Arthur M. Schlesinger journal entry for June 25, 1962 (p. 720). I am grateful to Professor Schlesinger for allowing me to consult this very valuable source.

18. L. Nuti, *Gli Stati Uniti e l'apertura a sinistra,* 467–476.

19. Ibid., 639–655.

20. The best account of this episode is the one given by William Fraleigh in his oral history interview at the Kennedy Library. For Nenni's version, see P. Nenni, *Gli anni del centro-sinistra: Diari 1957–1966* (Milano: Sugarco, 1982), entry for July 1, 1963. For a more "bureaucratic" account, see FRUS 1961–63, 13: 888–889.

21. Among the personal papers of New York Senator Victor Anfuso, for instance, there is an encoded exchange of letters between Anfuso and one of Fanfani's closest collaborators, Raimondo Manzini, which sheds some light on the true nature of the management and distribution of the relief aid provided by the United States during the period from 1957 to 1958 in accordance with U.S. Public Law 480. With Anfuso's, and possibly Eisenhower's, full approval, the food provided according to that law was illegally resold by the Christian Democrats, with the earnings used to support the electoral campaigns of different factions within the Christian Democratic Party. See Center for Migration Studies, Victor Anfuso papers, Subgroup II, Papers Pertaining to Anfuso's Activities as a U.S. Congressman, Series 31—ITALY, box 13, folder 140.

22. Luce to Dulles, April 19, 1954, FRUS 1952–54, 8: 409–414. Mrs. Luce had already expressed her doubts a few weeks before. Luce to Dulles, March 18, 1954, FRUS 1952–54, 8: 383–389.

23. In the latter case, the United States adopted the unusual and dramatic step of having the ambassador openly praise and defend Prime Minister Fanfani against his internal critics, only to see those critics triumph a few weeks later when Fanfani was forced to resign.

24. Donald Sassoon, *A Hundred Years of Socialism: The West European Left in the Twentieth Century* (London: Harper and Collins, 1997).

25. See what Nenni himself wrote about his talk with Kennedy: P. Nenni, *Gli anni del centro-sinistra, 1957–1966,* 288–289.

26. See for instance the remarks by Prime Minister Segni and Foreign Minister Pella during their 1959 visit to the United States: Memorandum of Conversation, September 30, 1959 and Memorandum of Conversation, October 2, 1959, both in FRUS, 1958–1960,7(2), docs. 242 and 256.

27. On this point see L. Nuti, "Commitment to NATO and Domestic Politics: The Italian Case and Some Comparative Remarks," *Contemporary European History* 7, no. 3 (November 1998), 361–377.

5

Hegemony or Vulnerability? Giscard, Ball, and the 1962 Gold Standstill Proposal

Francis J. Gavin and Erin Mahan

What was the character of America's international monetary relations with Europe during the early 1960s, and how were they related to the larger power political questions of the day? There is a standard interpretation of this question. During this pre-Vietnam war period, the argument runs, the United States strove to maintain hegemonic power vis-à-vis Western Europe "based on the role of the dollar in the international monetary system and on the extension of its nuclear deterrent to include its allies."[1] Since this economic dominance resulted from the structure and rules of the Bretton Woods monetary system, the Americans had no interest in reforming arrangements that were "a prerequisite for continued American global hegemony."[2] "Because it was interested in preserving the privileges it derived from the operation of the Bretton Woods regime," the United States would not "condone a structural reform" of the system that threatened "the continued preeminence of the dollar."[3] And while most of "America's allies acquiesced in a hegemonic system that accorded the United States special privileges to act abroad unilaterally to promote U.S. interests," the French did not.[4] The Fifth Republic government, led by Charles de Gaulle, deeply resented the privileges they believed the system conferred upon the American dollar and actively exploited America's balance of payments position in an attempt to force the United States to abandon the Bretton Woods system. The United States, conventional wisdom holds, was able to thwart this French effort until the American deficit ballooned in the late 1960s and early 1970s as a result of massive "guns and butter" inflation.[5]

The real story is rather different. American policy-makers had no great love for the Bretton Woods system. It was associated in their minds not with American hegemony, but with American vulnerability. The United States was running a payments deficit; the Europeans were in effect financing that deficit and were thus enabling the Americans to live beyond their means. But the Americans did not view this as a source of strength: the growing European dollar balances, which, under the rules of the system, could be cashed in for gold at any time, were a kind of sword of Damocles hanging over their heads. The U.S. government felt vulnerable and it did not like it. Kennedy feared that if the system was not reformed, the Europeans might come to the conclusion that "my God, this is the time. . . . [I]f everyone wants gold we're all going to be ruined because there is not enough gold to go around."[6]

The most surprising fact to emerge from French and American documents is that for a brief period in 1962, the French appeared willing to help the United States out of its monetary difficulties. Instead of hostility toward the dollar, Minister of Finance Valéry Giscard d'Estaing, was, for a time, cooperative. Inspired by Giscard's hints of support, Undersecretary of State George Ball and key members of the Council of Economic Advisors (CEA) crafted a monetary plan that would have essentially ended Bretton Woods while providing the Americans with time and protection to end their balance of payments deficits. The key provision of this plan was a gold standstill agreement, whereby the European surplus countries would agree to hold U.S. deficit dollars and formally limit their gold purchases from the American Treasury. In return, the United States would move aggressively to end its balance of payments deficit. At the end of the agreement (likely to be two years), a new international monetary arrangement would be negotiated with the Europeans. Surprisingly, many within the Kennedy administration were willing to sacrifice the central role of the dollar and its "seigniorage" privileges in any new system, a position that would have had much appeal for the Europeans.

While elements of the administration were enthusiastic about Giscard's hints and Ball's plan, the more financially orthodox members from the Department of Treasury and the Federal Reserve vehemently opposed the arrangement. Given the poor state of Franco-American political relations in the summer of 1962, the President was himself unsure of French motives, and in the end formal negotiations never began. Was Giscard's offer a missed opportunity? U.S. officials at the time were perplexed and scholars since then have neglected it entirely.

The analysis here is broken down into three parts. The first section provides a brief overview of the monetary problems that plagued the Kennedy administration and the efforts in 1961 and the first half of 1962 to solve them. It also explores the motivations for France's international monetary policy in the early 1960s. The second section deals with Giscard's visit to the United States in July 1962. The final section explores the furious debate within the Kennedy administration over the French finance minister's seemingly cooperative statements during his visit, and investigates why nothing came of Giscard's apparent willingness to help ease the dollar and gold outflow problem.

AMERICAN AND FRENCH MONETARY POLICY

Most historians and political scientists identify Richard Nixon as "the destroyer of Bretton Woods."[7] In reality, however, the Bretton Woods system was inherently unstable and began experiencing potentially fatal difficulties as early as the late 1950s. Economists now recognize that the system lacked an effective mechanism to adjust and settle the inevitable payments imbalances caused by shifting real currency values arising from differential national monetary policies and savings rates.[8] Postwar policy-makers eschewed the two most effective means of adjustment—"flexible" exchange rates and a pure gold standard—on principle. Mindful of the competitive devaluations during the 1930s, they believed that flexible exchange rates—where the relative value of currencies is determined by purchases and sales in an open market—were erratic, allowed destabilizing capital flows, and gave far too much control over the economy to bankers and speculators.[9] A pure gold standard, which required states with a payments deficit to transfer gold, was seen as no better. In a country that lost gold, the domestic monetary base would be decreased and aggregate domestic demand would shrink. Imports would fall, exports would rise, and the payments would balance. But the cost was deflation.[10] In an era where full employment and robust social spending were promised, it was politically inconceivable that national governments would accept a process that depressed national income and led to unemployment in order to balance international payments.[11]

At the time, however, American and European policy-makers were less concerned with the flaws of the Bretton Woods adjustment mechanism per se and instead focused on the growing outflow of dollars and gold from the United States as the biggest problem in the system. A whole series of factors—including the move to current account convertibility by the Europeans and the foreign exchange cost of America's NATO commitments—had dangerously enlarged the American balance of payments deficit in 1959 and 1960. Many observers worried that the large deficit could lead to a crisis of confidence in the dollar and spark a mass conversion into gold, rendering the dollar unusable as a reserve currency and, in the process, destroying a large portion of the world's liquidity. This problem had come to be known as the "Triffin Dilemma," after the Yale economist Robert Triffin published a book highlighting the confidence problem in his 1960 book, *Gold and the Dollar Crisis*.[12]

Fearing the potential dangers, political and economic, of a ballooning deficit and gold outflow, the new Kennedy administration pursued an aggressive strategy to correct the problem.[13] Political allies, particularly the Federal Republic of Germany, were pressured to spend surplus dollars purchasing military equipment made in the United States. Trade liberalization became a key element of the administration's foreign policy. The federal budget was scrutinized for ways to reduce U.S. government expenditures abroad. Most importantly, the undersecretary of the Treasury for International Monetary Affairs, Robert Roosa, negotiated a whole series of ad hoc arrangements to defend the dollar and limit the flow of gold from the U.S. Treasury. Currency swap and standby borrowing arrangements were implemented that allowed deficit countries to stave off attacks on their currencies.[14] The most important currency arrangement was the gold pool, a consortium of industrial nations who intervened in the London gold markets whenever the price of the dollar seemed threatened.

Roosa's efforts were quite successful in limiting the amount of gold purchased by central bankers holding U.S. dollars. But the administration's efforts to reduce the overall payments deficit were far less successful, which was a source of great frustration to President Kennedy, as this exposed the Achilles heel of America's international monetary policy. If the surplus countries of Europe—namely France and West Germany—cooperated with the United States by limiting their gold purchases, the dollar could be protected. But if this cooperation collapsed for either political or economic reasons, then the countries holding surplus dollars would have enormous leverage over the United States. "I know everyone thinks I worry about this too much," he told advisor Ted Sorensen. But the balance of payments was like "a club that de Gaulle and all the others hang over my head." In a crisis, Kennedy complained, they could cash in all their dollars, and then "where are we?"[15]

This meant that France's attitude on international monetary issues was critical. As with all questions of French policy, the first place to look was the attitude of the president, Charles de Gaulle. In the late 1950s and early 1960s, de Gaulle merely posed the overall framework for French economic policy. He realized that military power required economic strength. During this period, when the United States began experiencing balance-of-payment difficulties, France was enjoying an economic miracle of financial stability, industrial progress, and an annual growth rate of 4.5 percent. The Fourth Republic had already laid the groundwork for the upward surge in the economy when de Gaulle came to power, but prosperity had often been marred by monetary crisis.[16]

In December 1958, de Gaulle appointed a group of economic experts under Jacques Rueff, magistrate for the European Coal and Steel Community and a previous minister of finance, who drew up the plans that put the French economic house in order. The successful reforms, however, came at a political cost. Implemented by two successive finance ministers, Antoine Pinay and Wilfrid Baumgartner, the program was based on a formula of austerity and strict financial and monetary orthodoxy. Measures included higher taxes, a devaluation of the franc by 17.5 percent, strict budgetary policy, removal of the automatic tying of wages to a cost-of-living index, and reduced government subsidies. Selective liberalization of trade allowed more foreign goods into the country. The currency was replaced with a new franc worth a hundred of the old variety. And in the years that followed, the French government restricted the growth of credit in order to slow inflation. This practice of *encadrement du crédit*, however, discouraged investment because it limited industry's access to capital. The Finance Ministry also imposed a *coefficient de trésorerie* that required banks to hold 30 percent or more of their assets in treasury bonds or medium-term rediscountable credits.[17]

In the spring of 1961, Rueff began his eight-year campaign against what he saw as the subtle and insidious effects of the U.S. balance-of-payments deficit on the French economy. Rueff and many French officials, including French Prime Minister Michel Debré, believed that the United States relied on "easy money" and an expansionary monetary policy that exported inflation abroad to countries such as France. They also believed that a major consequence of the U.S. capital outflow was encouragement of American investment in the French economy.[18]

Gaullist officials held what Robert Solomon has described as a "schizophrenic view" toward multinational investment. On the one hand, French officials sought such investment because they welcomed the technological advances and influx of capital. On the other hand, they wished to see more national, and less foreign, investment in the French economy and wanted the EEC to adopt a common policy toward multinational investment. They also urged the United States to change its tax code to eliminate deferrals on taxation of overseas facilities. What the French government resented was the development of U.S. monetary seignorage that allowed the buying of European companies with dollars.[19]

Rueff had little patience for U.S. complaints about bearing the burden of Cold War security commitments. Before the Rueff plan in December 1958, many French politicians blamed the weakness of the French franc on the draining wars in Algeria and Indochina. Even though *le fardeau algérien* continued, the French franc became one of the world's strongest currencies after the Bank of France stopped increasing its domestic money supply. Rueff argued that U.S. foreign economic and military aid programs were a small proportion of GNP, hardly an intolerable burden. A practitioner of strict fiscal and monetary orthodoxy, he believed that a sharp increase in discount rate would eliminate the U.S. deficit overnight, as the French government did in 1958. The French government planned to raise its discount rate to 4 percent and the *coefficient de trésorerie* to 36 percent to combat its own inflationary cycle.[20]

In a series of lengthy letters to de Gaulle, published in *Le Monde* in early June 1961, Rueff encouraged the French president to take measures that would end the dollar's role as an international reserve currency. He implored de Gaulle to bypass Parliament and invoke the presidential emergency powers provided by the constitution of the Fifth Republic so that he could pursue policies that might force the devaluation of the dollar. Rueff considered the gold exchange standard a "prodigious collective error that allowed the United States to avoid the consequences of its economic profligacy." His views resonated with the nationalistic de Gaulle, who longed to abolish the privileges of the dollar and sterling as reserve currencies within the Bretton Woods system. Rueff also began to urge conversion of France's dollar reserves into gold as an indication of displeasure with U.S. abuses of the reserve-currency system, which accelerated French inflation.[21]

Rueff's views were shared by several high-ranking French officials close to de Gaulle. Foreign Minister Couve de Murville, an *inspecteur des finances* who had worked with Rueff at the Ministry of Finance between 1936 and 1939, echoed his polemic against the hegemony of the dollar. Étienne Burin des Roziers, who became secretary general of Élysée in the spring of 1962, was also well placed to begin shaping de Gaulle's outlook on international monetary relations.[22] Olivier Wormser, director general of economic affairs at the Ministry of Foreign Affairs, argued that Kennedy and Harold Macmillan's strong desire to stabilize the pound and the dollar was connected to Britain's bid to join the Common Market. America's international monetary policy was a convenient target for France's complaints about the relationship between Britain's application for the EEC and "Anglo-Saxon" balance-of-payments difficulties.[23]

The Ministry of Finance, however, did not share these views during the early 1960s. The Ministry was a bastion of "Atlanticism" that believed in cooperating with the United States. Wilfrid Baumgartner resisted the insistence of Rueff's coterie on ending the dollar as a reserve currency. Baumgartner had that quaint sense of gratitude toward the United States for helping France under the Marshall Plan, which was becoming increasingly out-of-fashion in Gaullist France. He also developed a close professional and personal friendship with Douglas Dillon during his ambassadorship to France under President Dwight D. Eisenhower. Baumgartner and Dillon often addressed their letters with "dear friend" as the salutation.[24]

During his tenure as finance minister, Baumgartner managed to mute Rueff's influence. Before 1962, France was one of the few European countries that *did not* convert the bulk of its dollar reserves into gold. In 1961, the United States sold no gold to France but 970 million dollars of gold to other countries.[25] And although Baumgartner refused to capitulate to the Kennedy administration's demands for expanding international liquidity, he participated in Roosa's ad hoc measures, including swap arrangements and a gold pool, which temporarily eased the recurring monetary crises.[26]

In December 1961, shortly after the creation of the gold pool, Baumgartner announced his resignation, effective the following month. Finance officials recall that even though he was not forced to retire per se, he felt too old to fight the political battles emerging within the French government over international monetary relations. To the Americans, his retirement suggested that the halcyon days of Franco-American financial cooperation might be over.[27]

U.S. FEARS AND FRENCH MOTIVES

Indeed, in May 1962, it seemed that the French might be considering a policy of putting pressure on the dollar for political reasons. Douglas Dillon told the president that a Bank of France official made a statement "which could indicate possible difficulties ahead with France. He said that it must be realized that France's dollar holdings represented a political as well as an economic problem." One of President Kennedy's great fears was that a nation or group of nations might exploit American monetary vulnerability for their own political purposes. If the French, alone or in collaboration with other surplus countries, decided to cash in all of their surplus dollars, they could run down the American gold supply. Regardless of economic motives, a French-led bloc might believe their larger political objectives were worth the cost. The United States might be forced to take politically unpopular measures in order to prevent a complete monetary meltdown, such as trade and capital controls, troop withdrawals, or an embarrassing devaluation or even a suspension of dollar-gold convertibility.[28]

A widely circulated State Department memo summarized an article that appeared in *The Statist* warning of a possible attack on the dollar by the French. President de Gaulle was "fully prepared to play [the] diplomatic trump card he holds in form of substantial French holdings of dollars." In other words, if U.S. policy toward Europe clashed with French interests, de Gaulle would pressure Kennedy by continuing to purchase gold from the United States.[29] The article went on to say that unless France were accepted as an equal power, "he would not hesitate to make himself felt by resorting to devices liable to cause grave embarrassment to the United States."[30]

What made this scenario even more alarming was the possibility that the increasingly strong Franco-German bloc was looking to weaken the U.S. grip on Western policy. It was no secret that both de Gaulle and West German Chancellor Konrad Adenauer were apprehensive about elements of the Kennedy administration's military and political policy in Europe. If both France and Germany collaborated on monetary policy, they could use their considerable supply of dollars to initiate a crippling gold crisis. Without the help of the two largest surplus countries, the U.S. might find it impossible to defend the dollar. This bloc could force the Americans to end negotiations with the Soviets over Berlin, or bring about a change in American military policy toward Europe. Maybe the French could bargain for technology to advance their nuclear ambitions. A French-led bloc could also have considerable say in designing a new international monetary mechanism in its own terms.

Were Kennedy's fears exaggerated? Franco-American relations had become so strained that the president's advisers believed the possibility of a French-inspired monetary attack could not be ruled out. In mid-May 1962, the extent of this strain, and the linkage between military and monetary policy, was revealed in a provocative discussion between President Kennedy and the French Minister of State for Cultural Affairs, André Malraux.[31] Kennedy complained that France was delaying the United Kingdom's entry into the Common Market. According to Kennedy, the U.S. supported the application despite the negative impact UK entry would have on the American payments deficit, which would serve the far more important purpose of creating a Franco-British counterweight to the Germans in the EEC. Kennedy declared that if the French preferred "a Europe without Great Britain and independent of the United States," it would create a situation in which America was bearing the enormous costs of defending Europe without any voice. If that were the case, Kennedy would bring the troops home and save $1.3 billion, an amount that "would just about meet our balance of payments deficit."[32]

When de Gaulle learned the details of Kennedy's conversations with Malraux, the French leader dismissed the possibility that the U.S. could withdraw from Europe, since America recognized that it would be lost if Western Europe were conquered.[33] De Gaulle accused the U.S. of dictating to its allies, a line of policy that was undermining its leadership. He claimed that by entering into negotiations with the Soviets over Berlin and by publicly stating that France should not have an atomic force, the administration risked a breakdown in the alliance.

Given the climate of mistrust, U.S. officials initially suspected a veiled threat when French Finance Minister Valéry Giscard d'Estaing reminded them that only cooperation "on a grand scale" could help the Americans with their dollar drain and prevent a speculative attack.[34] Giscard claimed that the United States could not handle a real run on the dollar by itself, even with the help of the IMF. Only with the collaboration of those European central banks that held large quantities of dollars could such a run be handled. What was Giscard proposing? He would not say, and the Americans did not want to appear weak by asking. Although the American deficit had decreased, gold purchases had increased, and the dollar market was weak. Giscard's hints fed into the administration's suspicions of French intentions, and combined with worsening gold outflow figures to stimulate a massive intergovernmental effort to develop plans to meet a monetary crisis.

Responding to rumors of French blackmail over the dollar, Undersecretary of State George Ball sent a memo to President Kennedy recommending that the administration take preemptive action in an upcoming meeting with Giscard. "I am seriously concerned about the tendency of our allies to view the present world financial problem as a case solely of dollar weakness rather than as a common problem for the Atlantic partnership."[35] It was time to move away from the position that the payments deficit was a narrow, technical problem to be negotiated between Treasury and European central bankers, whose views Ball described as "pre-Herbert Hoover."[36] In its efforts to move toward payments equilibrium and arrest the gold outflow, American policy was increasingly "reminiscent of Dr. Schacht"—that is, of the series of bilateral deals and clearing arrangements that the Nazi government had negotiated in the mid-1930s. Unless an explicit link was made between American military policy and the balance of payments, the U.S. would be vulnerable to "blackmail" by the Europeans. Ball believed it was time for fundamental multilateral systemic reform of the Bretton Woods edifice and not simply more ad hoc measures, even if that meant overruling the objections of the Treasury department.

Would France cooperate? Before Giscard's July 1962 visit, contact between Kennedy administration officials and the finance minister sent mixed signals. In May 1962, faced with an economic slump at home, Kennedy marveled at the performance of the French economy and considered transposing aspects of French dirigisme to the United States. The president sent Council of Economic Advisers Walter Heller and James Tobin to Paris where they met with Giscard and finance ministry officials for a study of the French economic planning process. Heller and Tobin concluded that France and other West European economies grew faster than the United States for multiple reasons. These included consistently higher levels of demand, a higher level of government investment, greater reinvestment of business earnings, a larger body of skilled labor, higher levels of capital formation, technology, productivity, and smaller defense expenditures.[37] To generate interest in economic planning within the United States, Kennedy arranged for French officials to speak to labor and business groups. The financial counselor of the French embassy, for example, gave addresses touting his country's economic plan as a successful path to increased growth.[38]

Heller and Tobin's study of French economic planning was also undertaken to convince Gaullist officials that Kennedy was serious about making the U.S. economy sound, so that they would be less worried about the devaluation of the dollar and less inclined to convert its dollar reserves into gold. Bundy told Heller before his departure for Paris that "in the current state of Franco-American relations, any friendly contact is a good thing."[39]

Although Heller and Tobin established a good rapport with Giscard during their Paris trip, the finance minister's attitude toward U.S. investment in the French economy worried Ball. On several occasions, Giscard complained that American investment in France was leading to the loss of control over key segments of the economy. Without specifying what, he implied that "measures might be taken by the French government to establish safe-guards against such a possibility."[40] The French government wanted to pressure the Kennedy administration to dissuade American companies from investing in the French economy. However, the ministry of the economy had no intention to exert that pressure by moving against the dollar.[41]

The young finance minister, who combined technocratic skill with political savvy, tried to navigate a difficult middle course between de Gaulle's increasing anti-Americanism and Atlantic monetary cooperation.[42] Like his predecessor, Giscard did not share de Gaulle's animosity toward the United States. Giscard felt that it was in France's national interest to stabilize the international monetary situation. The May stock market crash in the United States had worried the French finance minister. If the U.S. deficit persisted or worsened, the Kennedy administration might devalue the dollar, which would decrease the value of France's foreign exchange reserves and make dollar exports more competitive in Europe. According to de Lattre's memoirs, his subordinates, namely Claude Pierre-Brossolette, André de Lattre, and Pierre Esteva, practiced guerrilla tactics to combat Rueff's influence on French foreign economic policies.[43]

At the same time, however, Giscard was politically ambitious and dutiful toward de Gaulle. André de Lattre, who worked closely with him at the Ministry of Finance, recalls that "il obéissait." For Giscard, obeying meant converting dollar reserves into gold at the rate of 70 percent. In the first quarter of 1962, France converted forty-five million dollars' worth of gold, and in the second quarter, that amount increased to ninety-seven and a half million dollars. He also saw to it that France repaid its post-World War II debt of 211 million dollars.[44]

Giscard recognized that de Gaulle regarded the U.S.-dominated IMF as an "alien and objectionable organization." The French government preferred to deal with international monetary problems within the framework of the Organization of European Cooperation and Development (OECD). This preference had been evident even in 1961: the Kennedy administration got the message that the French might not be willing to cooperate on monetary stabilization "except perhaps through a restricted OECD undertaking outside of the IMF."[45]

It was not that Giscard, in adopting this approach, was trying to pursue a relatively "pro-American" policy for political reasons. He may have been willing to cooperate with the United States, but his basic idea was that "cooperation" could not be a one-way street. In exchange for French cooperation, the Americans would have to accept certain limits on their freedom of action—a kind of *"surveillance multilatérale."*[46] Among other things, Giscard calculated that using Working Group 3 within the OECD instead of the IMF would give the French government a platform to criticize an overly-expansionist U.S. domestic budget, which he identified as the primary cause of the American payments deficit.[47]

Although Giscard's visit to Washington in late July 1962 was at President Kennedy's request, the timing was propitious. De Gaulle was personally preoccupied with strategic issues and strengthening the Franco-German entente. After meeting with Adenauer in early July, de Gaulle was trying to persuade the chancellor that their two nations should develop formal lines of cooperation, a courtship that began in 1958 and would culminate in January 1963 with the signing of the Franco-German Treaty of Friendship.[48] De Gaulle and Adenauer also were preoccupied with the resignation of Supreme Allied Commander of Europe Lauris Norstad.[49]

Rueff later obtained great influence on de Gaulle's economic philosophy. But without an official capacity to implement policy and with de Gaulle immersed in defense issues, Giscard had a relatively free hand to negotiate with the United States during the summer of 1962. To the Kennedy administration's surprise, Giscard was in a cooperative mood when he visited Washington. Furthermore, he wanted any arrangements to be conducted with minimal publicity because it would strengthen his hand and not draw de Gaulle's attention.[50]

On July 20 and 21, 1962, Giscard met with Kennedy alone and later with Ball, Bundy, and Tobin. The president and these advisers conveyed their concern over the deficit and gold outflow, and their desire to "manage" these issues on the "political" level. Ball said the administration did not have any formal plan, but felt that in principle some sort of political agreement should be reached to stabilize payments among the major industrial countries. A multilateral, political solution to this issue would not only squelch calls for protectionism in the U.S., it would also demonstrate the solidarity of the Atlantic partnership. What the U.S. had in mind, Ball said, was an agreement regarding the ratio of gold to dollar holdings.[51]

The administration was surprised when the French finance minister agreed with most of what the Americans said about the problem and appeared to want little in return. Even so, Giscard tried to explain that the president should be as irked at the British, who, before 1962, converted more dollars into gold than France. As long as other European countries continued to convert their reserve dollars, France would feel compelled to follow suit. Giscard declared that the key was to avoid any unilateral action by either side. He thought that it was important for the creditor countries to establish a common payments policy while the U.S. reduced its payments deficit. Such an agreement might suspend gold takings and establish fixed reserve ratios. France was certainly willing to hold its dollars for a time, as along as others agreed as well. He thought the UK might protest, but even they might cooperate given their desire to join the Common Market.[52]

The administration was delighted that Giscard appeared to understand American difficulties. Giscard's statements alleviated the fear of a Franco-German monetary bloc. A French-led initiative to reform the payments system would save the U.S. the embarrassment of continued ad hoc measures that made the U.S. look weak. In order to be prepared for such negotiation, the administration launched an enormous effort to study and debate exactly what form an international monetary agreement should take. An interdepartmental committee on the balance of payments was created, and a "gold budget" established.[53]

Giscard was hopeful that he could convince de Gaulle to accept a gold standstill arrangement because it could potentially meet the general's long-term objective of curbing the hegemony of the dollar. The indications that he received from Ball suggested that after a two-year grace period, the G-10 nations could modify or construct a new international financial structure. Giscard did not intend to end the use of the dollar as a reserve currency, but he hoped to give the franc a place in a broadened monetary scheme that used additional currencies as reserves. He wished to establish a *unité de réserve composite* (CRU), which would be tied to gold. The creation of a CRU would address French concerns of curbing global inflation while meeting demands for expanded international liquidity.[54]

THE DEBATE OVER MONETARY REFORM
WITHIN THE KENNEDY ADMINISTRATION

From discussions with Giscard, the Kennedy administration hoped that there was now an opportunity to solve the gold outflow problem within a political, multilateral context. Giscard seemed to accept the need for a standstill agreement to give the U.S. time to bring its payments into equilibrium and begin systemic reform of the international financial system. The Treasury held over $16 billion of gold, but legally $12 billion was required to back domestic currency. There was much talk about rescinding the laws behind the domestic cover, and the Federal Reserve could take certain actions in a crisis that would release the gold without legislative action. But Congress would want a protracted debate on the issue, and that debate might upset the markets and might quite possibly set off another gold crisis.

More important than the gold cover issue was the supply of dollars held by surplus countries, both officially and in private hands. These liabilities totaled over $20 billion, which could be turned in at any time. While this was more than the gold supply backing them, it was not, by the historical standards of gold-exchange regimes, a dangerous ratio. Interest rate policy and central bank cooperation could handle any run on the dollar. But if this cooperation were not forthcoming, then the dollar liabilities were a loaded gun aimed at the American gold supply. If a Franco-German bloc formed, these overhang dollars could be used to expose American monetary weakness, and perhaps force political concessions. Therefore, it was important to take the opportunity afforded by Giscard's suggestions to create a mechanism to prevent a large American gold outflow.

Encouraged by the French finance minister's cooperative spirit, Kennedy's closest advisers began considering dramatic departures from traditional monetary policy to solve this problem. Gold guarantees, gold standstill agreements, and raising the dollar price of gold, either in concert with others or unilaterally, were all debated. The Department of State even prepared a draft memo for the president's use should he want to end the American policy of redeeming gold on demand.[55] Carl Kaysen sent Kennedy an essay by J. M. Keynes proposing an international payments system that dispensed with gold altogether. Kaysen wrote the president: "The great attention paid to gold is another myth. . . . As you said of the Alliance for Progress, those who oppose reform may get revolution."[56]

Perhaps the most discussed proposal was from George Ball. In his memo to the president, "A Fresh Approach to the Gold Problem," Ball maintained that the problem was at heart about politics, not economics.[57] Unfortunately, claimed Ball, few people in Europe, Wall Street, or even the U.S. Treasury Department understood this. For them, the gold outflow and payments deficit were signs of American profligacy, correctable through deflationary policies at home and massive cuts in military aid expenditures abroad. By pursuing Roosa's policy of "improvised expedients" and taking the posture of suppliants seeking credits, offsets, and debt pre-payments, the administration created a picture of weakness that eroded America's authority and bargaining power with the Europeans. Ball warned "this is no way to run the government of any nation—much less to exercise the leadership of the Free World."[58]

Ball argued that the answer to this problem was simple. The strength of the dollar should not be dependent on the "daily whims of private and official 'confidence' but to a structure of long-run reciprocal assurances by governments." The Europeans must be made to understand that such an agreement was in their best interest as well as ours. The Europeans, Ball claimed, would be just as hurt by a dollar crisis as the U.S. More importantly, they must recognize that the continued American defense of Europe is dependent upon safeguarding the dollar.[59] Without such reforms, President Kennedy would be forced to take aggressive, unilateral action to improve the balance of payments, such as withdrawing American troops from Europe or imposing controls on capital and restrictions on tourism. Ball argued that such policies would not be in America's interest.

Instead, Ball advocated a multilateral agreement at the *political* level, which would "insulate ourselves from the danger of excessive gold losses while we are working, by less costly measures that will, over a reasonable period of time restore equilibrium." If the latter policy was not pursued, the U.S. would continue to be vulnerable to the "confidence" game. More importantly, as long as the current rules were maintained, the U.S. would remain "subject to the blackmail of any government that wants to employ its dollar reserves as political weapons against us."[60] Ball told the president that if the United States were to "become more heavily involved in Southeast Asia" the "West Coast of South America" or the "Congo," the Europeans might be tempted to "exploit our own problems, NATO's difficulties, and our own problem with the gold flight for political purposes."[61] A multilateral gold standstill arrangement would limit America's vulnerability to this kind of pressure. Why would the Europeans agree to such a plan? Ball hinted that the United States could exploit its own political leverage. "Central bankers may regard our expenditures to defend the Free World as a form of sin," he argued, "but the political leaders of our Western allies do not."[62]

Ball provided a general outline of a temporary arrangement to stop the gold outflow. Its provisions included a massive increase in Treasury swaps with foreign central banks, a long-term loan with a consortium of European allies, large withdrawals from the IMF, and fixed gold ratios for central bank portfolios. The U.S. would have to redistribute some of its gold and perhaps guarantee dollar holdings in gold. Ultimately, Ball believed the U.S. should seek a "thorough-going" revision of the Bretton Woods system, "multilateralizing" responsibility for the creation of liquidity as Giscard indicated during his visit. The undersecretary of state was fully prepared to sacrifice the "hegemonic" role of the dollar if a new system reduced America's vulnerability.

The key to any plan was getting the Europeans to maintain the same or a smaller proportion of their reserves in gold. James Tobin of the Council of Economic Advisers (CEA) produced a plan to accomplish this.[63] To meet Giscard's demand for similar conversion policies among the European nations, Tobin suggested that the leading industrial countries determine a uniform ratio of gold to foreign exchange to which all countries would have to adhere. This would require countries with gold in excess of this ratio to sell a part of their gold for foreign exchange. Instead of only using the dollar and sterling as the reserve currency, the currencies of all participating countries (assumed to be the Paris Club) would be equally acceptable. That provision would satisfy French demands that the franc be treated as a reserve currency on par with the dollar. Each country would provide a gold guarantee for their currency against devaluation. Tobin laid out several different ways this could be done, but they would all involve the U.S. selling gold for foreign exchange and retiring dollar liabilities. Some European countries would also have to sell or buy gold. Over time, the non-gold component of reserves would decrease, and the currencies of the participating countries would increasingly share the burden borne solely by the dollar. Removing the wide variations in gold ratios would make the international monetary mechanism more predictable and manageable.

The president was keenly interested in these plans, and commissioned a small, interdepartmental group from the State Department, the CEA, and Treasury to come up with an outline of an interim international monetary agreement based on Ball's and Tobin's ideas. The group produced a plan that focused on protecting the American gold supply and strengthening the dollar. The report claimed that cyclical forces would combine with measures already taken to bring America's balance of payments into equilibrium within a few years. The heart of the plan was a proposed standstill agreement between the ten members of the Paris Club and Switzerland whereby the participants would agree to not convert the official dollar balances they held at the start of the agreement into gold. In order to accommodate increases in the dollar balances of the participants over the two years of the plan, $10 billion would be mobilized from a variety of financial sources. This would include $1 billion of American gold sales, a massive $5 billion drawing on the IMF, $2.5 billion in swaps and direct borrowings from Europe, and up to $1.5 billion in forward exchange operations taken by the Treasury Department.[64]

The purpose of this agreement was two-fold: to get the countries of Western Europe to "extend more credit to the U.S. than they might voluntarily," and to dampen speculative attacks on the dollar. Even with the plan in place, there were all sorts of potential difficulties. The two years had to be used to eliminate the "basic" deficit, and there would certainly be large-scale reshuffling and uncertainty when the arrangement ended. To make the plan work, it had to be acceptable to the Europeans, and in fact, had to be initiated by the Europeans, so that it did not look like an act of American weakness. The report did not suggest how the Europeans could be brought to accept let alone propose such a plan.

Walter Heller, the CEA chair, was extremely enthusiastic about the interdepartmental plan. It would "eliminate the whims and prejudices of currency speculators and bankers from the making of U.S. policy."[65] The administration could end the basic deficit in an orderly way, without deflation or drastic cuts in programs crucial to American foreign policy. An international, interim agreement would give the U.S. far more protection than the techniques used by the Treasury department, which were employed on a "secret, day-to-day, piecemeal, ad-hoc basis."[66] An interim agreement would also give world leaders time to scrap the Bretton Woods regime and come up with a world payments system that defended all currencies against speculative attack, internationalized the burdens of providing international money, and provided for an orderly increase in liquidity. Carl Kaysen, the National Security Council officer responsible for international monetary affairs, and Kermit Gordon, a member of the Council of Economic Advisers, went so far as to argue that devaluation could remain a potentially profitable action for the United States, even after the guarantee was paid off.[67]

Douglas Dillon was infuriated by these analyses. In a cover memo to a report written by Henry Fowler, Dillon claimed that Ball's interim reserve scheme was simply a reflection of the State Department's "reluctance to squarely tackle the more difficult but fundamentally necessary job of obtaining a more adequate sharing of the burden by our European friends."[68] The Treasury Department argued that Ball was treating the symptom, the gold outflow, and not the disease, the continuing balance of payments deficit. The interim reserve scheme would give a green light to "loosen up" on all the disciplines that the administration had established to cure the payments imbalance. Fowler agreed that international balance of payments discussions should be raised to the highest political level, but the focus should be on increased burden sharing within NATO, not reserve composition. The U.S. balance of payments would never move to equilibrium until the Europeans started paying a greater share of NATO's military costs.[69]

Dillon was even more caustic in his attack on the interim agreement, despite the fact that a Treasury representative, John Leddy, had helped write the report. In essence, the actions proposed would close the gold window for $7.9 billion of official dollar balances, an abandonment of traditional gold policy similar in scope to the U.S. devaluation of 1933.[70] The Kennedy administration would be reneging on its promise not to change its gold policy, which would shake private financial markets and scare those countries not participating in the agreement. Dillon believed that using the word "standstill" would evoke memories of the German standstill agreement of 1931, an event associated with the world economic collapse. A formal gold standstill arrangement would mean that "it would no longer be sensible" to "expect foreign monetary authorities to continue to hold dollars as an international reserve currency," thereby eliminating the "important substantive advantages" the United States enjoyed under the Bretton Woods system.[71] The plan assumed that the Europeans would agree to such a scheme, an idea Dillon found preposterous despite Giscard's cooperation. The Secretary of the Treasury found an ally in Federal Reserve Board Chairman William Martin, who said the plan for a standstill monetary agreement would "hit world financial markets as a declaration of U.S. insolvency and a submission to receivers to salvage."[72]

Dillon also forwarded a report by his undersecretary, Robert Roosa, to rebut the charge that the Treasury's actions had been "ad hoc." Roosa argued that the agreements that had been reached in the past two years between the U.S. and its allies had been very successful. It had not been a policy of ad hoc expedients, as many had claimed, but a well thought out and innovative plan to strengthen the Bretton Woods system. It only appeared ad hoc because many of the discussions held between financial officials were secretive. But the global payments system was much better prepared to absorb the shocks of any future financial disturbance. The gold pool, swap agreements, forward exchange operations, and increased IMF borrowing privileges prepared the U.S. to meet any attack on the dollar. According to Roosa, some of the ideas being discussed, both inside and outside the administration, were foolish. Devaluation, gold guarantees, or a gold standstill would damage or destroy a world payments system that had greatly benefited the U.S. and its allies.[73] Dillon believed these policies were more appropriate for the currency of a third-world country, not the U.S., and publicly tried to sabotage the idea. Kaysen was infuriated when Dillon testified before the Joint Economic Committee on August 17 and called gold guarantees a "dangerous experiment." The Secretary of the Treasury called them "a poor idea and not to be seriously considered." Dillon also ruled out changing the value of the dollar. McGeorge Bundy was worried that Dillon's public statements would preclude the changes in international monetary policy that they were considering.[74]

Surprisingly, the reformers were unconcerned with Dillon's contention that the United States might lose the benefits of "seigniorage" in a new international monetary system. During a meeting on August 20, 1962, Ball told the President that "we're not persuaded that it is at all vital to the United States that we do return to a situation in which the dollar would be the principal reserve currency. . . . [W]e can see many disadvantages as well as advantages." Kennedy appeared to agree with Ball's analysis. "I see the advantages to the Western world to have a reserve currency, and therefore it's an advantage to us as part of the Western world, but what is the national, narrow advantage?" When Dillon tried to spell out these benefits, Kaysen pointedly asked, "you wouldn't describe this as an advantage right now, would you Doug?"[75]

The president seemed to side with the reformers against Dillon. Kennedy argued that now was the time to negotiate a monetary agreement with the Europeans because "we have much more political strength with them now then we'll probably have two years from now." The Europeans "are much more dependant upon us militarily than they might be" before they "get together" to organize their own defense.[76] The administration had to get the Europeans to agree that for "a two year period that they're not going to ask" for gold while "our balance of payments situation improves and while we work on other arrangements."[77] The president concluded that the administration should "pursue" the gold standstill arrangement, "because I think this is really the area where we may be able to make some progress." Kennedy wanted the Europeans to agree that "they are all going to go easy on the taking of gold."[78]

Kennedy dispatched Assistant Secretary of State C. Griffith Johnson and Assistant Secretary of the Treasury John Leddy to sound out the possibilities of a European initiative to limit foreign purchases of U.S. gold and strengthen the international monetary system. Kennedy suggested that an acceptable arrangement would be for the Common Market countries and the UK to each set an absolute target for gold holdings, as opposed to a ratio, which could be controversial and might involve *increasing* the amount of gold held by certain countries. Another solution would be to limit the amount of gold taken from the U.S. to a small percentage, perhaps 30 percent, of the overall payments deficit. But regardless of the plan, Kennedy insisted that that should look like a voluntary European initiative. Any evidence of U.S. pressure could shake the confidence of financial markets and lead to a run on American gold.[79]

Giscard appeared ready to negotiate. While always wary of the British and any "deals" between *les Anglo-Saxons* that excluded France, he did invite the G-10 finance ministers to participate in discussions at the upcoming IMF/World Bank meeting. Anxious to maneuver without arousing de Gaulle's intervention, he asked the G-10 ministers to limit accompanying officials to two persons and to conduct their meetings without publicity.[80] But even with these precautions, Giscard and the Americans found it hard to engage in serious negotiations. For example, when Leddy and Johnson asked Giscard what British Chancellor of Exchequer Maudling's thoughts were on the subject, Giscard replied, "the two were in agreement that there should be high level secret discussions of the subject."[81] Giscard did not tell Johnson and Leddy what the "subject" actually was. Was it the hoped-for initiative to limit gold takings? Giscard would not say, and the American representatives thought it imprudent to ask. Later, British representatives asked the Americans what Giscard had said, and, after being told, observed that "the whole affair was mysterious." The next day, *French officials* said the same thing!

President Kennedy was scheduled to speak to the central bankers and finance ministers of the G-10 at the IMF/World Bank meeting. The purpose of the meeting was to tell the Europeans that the underlying cause of the American deficit was its disproportionate share of Western military and aid expenditures. This group had heard this message many times before, but the meeting would give the president the chance, as Kaysen put it, to "give them a real feeling of how central it is to your thinking. This is something that you can convey directly in a way no one else can."[82] Kaysen urged the president to tell his audience that the administration recognized the fact that "there is more than one way the system might evolve in relation to the central role of the dollar, and we do not foreclose consideration of alternative schemes of improvement for the payments system."[83] In other words, the U.S. was not wedded to the Bretton Woods system and its supposed privileges. A better system could be created that reflected the new economic strength of the Europeans. This new system would give the Europeans an "expanded role in the international monetary system."[84]

But could the administration act without the hoped-for French or European initiative suggested by Giscard? Dillon thought Kaysen's strategy was far too risky. "A statement by you that we are prepared to study new ideas and welcome new initiatives would in all probability be misinterpreted . . . as indicating a lack of confidence on your part in our ability to handle our balance of payments problem within the framework of the existing monetary system. This could have dangerous and immediate effects this fall."[85] Without a formal proposal from the French, Kennedy's speech was closer to Dillon's than Kaysen's approach, hinting that the administration was open to international monetary discussions but offering no concrete American plans. The American team adopted this position because of the fear that "open pressure on the French might lead them to think that political questions could be successfully interjected."[86]

The momentum for monetary reform subsided considerably after the IMF meeting. In the weeks ahead, the Kennedy administration's attention turned to the far more pressing matter of Soviet missiles in Cuba. By the time Kennedy returned to the dollar and gold outflow issue, America's political relations with France had deteriorated markedly.[87] It no longer seemed that monetary cooperation was in the cards. Kennedy again feared that a Franco-German political bloc would use its surplus dollars to compel changes in America's political strategies in Europe.[88]

CONCLUSION

France's international monetary policy was, at least through 1962, far more cooperative than conventional wisdom holds. But this cooperative spirit was not to last. Without assurances that other European nations would restrict "hoarding" of gold, the French government began increasing its conversion of dollars. For each of the first two quarters of 1963, the sale of U.S. gold to France was $101.1 million dollars.[89] More importantly, after 1962, Rueff and others who were against monetary cooperation with the Americans increased their influence with de Gaulle. In February 1965, de Gaulle launched his famous attack on the dollar and its privileges within the international monetary system. By January 1966, Giscard's influence had waned considerably and de Gaulle, who had come to view him as insubordinate, forced him to resign.

Ironically, during the same period official American attitudes toward American monetary reform became less timid. In 1962, the financially orthodox members of Kennedy'sadministration successfully slowed any bold American move toward international monetary reform. But by 1963 and beyond, American officials became far more interested in a whole-scale restructuring of the system. This striking shift in American foreign economic policy was made evident in a speech Lyndon B. Johnson's Secretary of the Treasury, Henry Fowler, gave before the Virginia Bar Association on July 10,

1965. "I am privileged to tell you this evening that the President has authorized me to announce that the United States now stands prepared to attend
and participate in an international monetary conference which would consider what steps we might jointly take to secure substantial improvements in
international monetary arrangements."[90] The Treasury Department, which
three years earlier had gone to great lengths to suppress any program of
monetary reform, now warmly embraced it.

But with France and the United States in vehement disagreement over
how to change the global payments system, meaningful change was elusive.
This Franco-American monetary dispute during the 1960s created a legacy of
bitterness between the two countries that lasted well beyond the collapse of
the Bretton Woods system in August 1971. It is quite possible that this enmity
might have been avoided if the Kennedy administration had embraced Giscard's cooperative suggestions during the summer of 1962, or if Giscard had
offered a less vague proposal to reform international monetary relations.

In the long run, these disagreements may not have mattered, because the
Bretton Woods system was inherently flawed and not fixable. Given the explosion of international capital flows during the 1960s, market-determined
exchange rates were probably inevitable. But it is important to note that the
Kennedy administration was not wedded to the Bretton Woods system and
felt more vulnerable than hegemonic under its rules. While they were not
sure what they wanted exactly, key officials, including President Kennedy,
were willing to contemplate fundamental changes to the system, *even* if this
meant sacrificing the dollar's central role in the global payments system.
What is perhaps even more surprising is that the French were not mono-
lithically determined to oppose the Americans in this area in the early 1960s.
Even de Gaulle was open to options that went beyond a pure gold standard,
as long as the "exorbitant privileges" of the dollar were curtailed.[91] In the
end, to characterize America and France's attitudes toward the Bretton
Woods system in terms of hegemony or empire is a vast oversimplification.
There were ambiguities and contradictions in policies on both sides of the
Atlantic, as both sides struggled to understand how to pursue their narrower
national interests without precipitating a worldwide monetary calamity. The
story behind the gold standstill forces us to reconsider not just Franco-
American relations, but also the often misunderstood relationship between
international monetary policy and transatlantic political developments during the "crucial decade" of the 1960s.

NOTES

1. Robert Gilpin, *The Political Economy of International Monetary Relations*
(Princeton: Princeton University Press, 1987), 134.

2. Diane Kunz, *Butter and Guns: America's Cold War Economic Diplomacy* (New York: The Free Press, 1997), 99. For similar interpretations, see William Borden, "Defending Hegemony: American Foreign Economic Policy," in Thomas Paterson, ed., *Kennedy's Quest for Victory: American Foreign Policy, 1961–1963* (New York: Oxford University Press, 1989), 83–85; David Calleo, *The Imperious Economy* (Cambridge: Harvard University Press, 1982), 23; David Calleo, *Beyond American Hegemony: The Future of the Western Alliance* (New York: Basic Books, 1987), 13, 44–52; Frank Costigliola, "The Pursuit of Atlantic Community: Nuclear Arms, Dollars, and Berlin," in Paterson, ed., 24–56; Paul Kennedy, *The Rise and Fall of the Great Powers: Economic Change and Military Conflict from 1500 to 2000* (New York: Random House, 1987), 434. For interpretations that see Kennedy's monetary policy as a conservative approach designed to maintain the privileged place the dollar held in the postwar "capitalist world-system," see Borden, 57–62, 84; Calleo and Benjamin M. Rowland, *America and the World Political Economy: Atlantic Dreams and National Realities* (Bloomington: Indiana University Press, 1973), 88–89; John S. Odell, *U.S. International Monetary Policy: Markets, Power, and Ideas as a Source of Change* (Princeton: Princeton University Press, 1982), 88; Susan Strange, *International Monetary Relations* (London: Oxford University Press, 1976), 82, 207.

3. Joanne Gowa, *Closing the Gold Window: Domestic Politics and the End of Bretton Woods* (Ithaca: Cornell University Press, 1983), 52.

4. Benjamin Cohen, *Organizing the World's Money: The Political Economy of Dominance and Dependence* (New York: Basic Books, 1977), 97.

5. It is quite true that by 1965, de Gaulle claimed the system allowed for "l'hégémonie américaine." See Press Conference, February 4, 1965, from Charles de Gaulle, *Discours et messages*, vol. 4, "Pour l'effort, Août 1962–Décembre 1965 (Paris: Omnibus/Plon, 1993); see also Raymond Aron, *La République impériale* (Paris: Calmann Levy, 1973); Georges Soutou, *L'alliance incertaine: Les rapports politico-stratégiques franco-allemands, 1954–1996* (Paris: Fayard, 1996), 287. But the key point that this article makes is that the views of 1965 were not the basis for French policy in 1962, which is implied in Jean Lacoutre, *De Gaulle: The Ruler, 1945–1970* (New York: W. W. Norton, 1992), 380–382. Most French scholarly interpretations about de Gaulle's criticisms against the dollar begin with the mid-1960s. For a significant but brief exception, see Henri Bourguinat, "Le général de Gaulle et la réforme du système monétaire international: la contestation manquée de l'hégémonie du dollar, " in *De Gaulle en son siècle*, vol. 3 (Paris, 1992), 110–118.

6. Discussion between President John F. Kennedy, William McChesney Martin, Chairman of the Federal Reserve, and Theodore Sorensen—August 16, 1962, 5:50–6:32 P.M., tape 13, President's Office Files (POF), John F. Kennedy Presidential Library (JFKL), Boston Mass.

7. Kunz, *Butter and Guns*, 192.

8. Excellent discussions of these questions can be found in Richard Cooper, *The International Monetary System: Essays in World Economics* (Cambridge, Mass.: The MIT Press, 1987) and Paul de Grauwe, *International Money: Post-War Trends and Theories* (Oxford: Clarendon Press, 1989).

9. Paul Volcker and Toyoo Gyohten, *Changing Fortunes: The World's Money and the Threat to American Leadership* (New York: Random House, 1992), 7–8.

10. See Barry Eichengreen, *Globalizing Capital: A History of the International Monetary System* (Princeton: Princeton University Press, 1996), 7–44. In practice, gold inflows and outflows were often "sterilized" under the gold standard, which just meant that gold was added or subtracted from the national treasuries without changing the domestic monetary base. But even with some sterilization, the gold standard was nowhere near as stable as was once thought. See Giulio Gallarotti, *The Anatomy of an International Monetary Regime* (New York: Oxford University Press, 1995). For the economic and political volatility of the "gold standard" during the late-nineteenth and early-twentieth century, and the American propensity to "sterilize" gold flows, see Milton Friedman and Alan Schwartz, *A Monetary History of the United States 1867–1960* (Princeton: Princeton University Press, 1963), 89–188; see also Milton Friedman, *Money Mischief: Episodes in Monetary History* (N.Y.: Harcourt Brace, 1994), especially the essays "The Crime of 1873" and "William Jennings Bryan and the Cyanide Process."

11. See especially Donald Edward Moggridge, *Keynes: An Economist's Biography* (London: Routledge, 1992).

12. Robert Triffin, *Gold and the Dollar Crisis: The Future of Convertibility* (New Haven: Yale University Press, 1960).

13. See Theodore Sorensen, *Kennedy* (New York: Harper and Row, 1965), 406. See also John Kenneth Galbraith's letter to the president from October 1960, in his *Letters to Kennedy* (Harvard: Harvard University Press, 1998), 29–31.

14. The swap arrangements were standby credit lines that allowed participants to draw on other participants' currencies in order to defend their own exchange rates. The increased IMF credit was arranged through a procedure called the General Arrangements to Borrow, which were negotiated at the end of 1961. While connected to the IMF, these arrangements were unique in that they gave the lending countries some discretion over the size and use of the loans. For an excellent discussion of these innovations, see Harold James, *International Monetary Cooperation since Bretton Woods* (Oxford: Oxford University Press, 1998), 159–165.

15. Richard Reeves, *President Kennedy: Profile of Power* (New York: Touchstone, 1993), 431.

16. William Hitchcock, *France Restored: Cold War Diplomacy and the Quest for Leadership in Europe, 1944–1954* (Chapel Hill: University of North Carolina Press, 1998), 12–71. See, also, Richard Kuisel, *Capitalism and the State in Modern France: Renovation and Economic Management in the Twentieth Century* (New York: Cambridge University Press, 1981).

17. Serge Berstein, *The Republic of de Gaulle, 1958–1969*, trans. Peter Morris (Cambridge, UK: Cambridge University Press, 1993), 101–124; Michael M. Loriaux, *France after Hegemony: International Change and Financial Reform*, (Ithaca, N.Y.: Cornell University Press), 168–174.

18. See, generally, Rueff, *Balance of Payments: Proposals for the Resolution of the Most Pressing World Economic Problem of Our Time*, (New York: Macmillan Co., 1967). See also François Bourricaud and Pascal Salin, *Présence de Jacques Rueff* (Paris: Plon, 1989), 243–314.

19. Robert Solomon, *The International Monetary System, 1945–1981* (New York, 1982), 54. J. Lee, "Kennedy, Johnson, and the Dilemma of Multinational Corporations: American Foreign Economic Policy in the 1960s," *Essays in Economic and Business History* 14 (1996), 322.

20. Rueff to Wilfrid Baumgartner, June 26, 1961, Wilfred Baumgartner papers, box 3BA34, folder DR 7, Fondation Nationale des Sciences Politiques (FNSP), Paris.

21. Jacques Rueff to Charles de Gaulle, May 5, 1961, Baumgartner papers, box 3BA34, folder Dr 5, FNSP. For Rueff's articles, see "Un danger pour l'occident: Le Gold-Exchanges standard," *Le Monde*, June 27, 1961; "Deux Pyramides du crédit sur le stock d'or des Etats-Unis," ibid., June 23, 1961; and "Comment sortir du système?" ibid., June 29, 1961.

22. On the French bureaucratic schism, see, Entretien biographique de Claude Pierre-Brossolette, interview 4, 32–33, Comité pour l'histoire économique et financière de la France, Ministère de l'Économie, des Finances, et d'Industrie, Paris.

23. Note, Olivier Wormser, May 30, 1961, Baumgartner papers, box 3BA48, folder Dr 2, FNSP. See also C. W. Sanders (British Board of Trade), "Points for Meeting," 26 June 1961, FO 371/158179, Public Record Office, Kew.

24. See, for example, Douglas Dillon to Baumgartner, 4 May 1961, Baumgartner papers, box 3BA48, folder Dr 1, FNSP. On Baumgartner's attitude toward cooperating with the United States, see, Entretien biographique de Claude Pierre-Brossolette, number 4, 23, Comité pour l'historie économique et financière de la France.

25. For Baumgartner's reaction to Rueff's views, see, for example, Baumgartner to Rueff, letter, June 27, 1961, Baumgartner papers, box 3BA34, folder Dr 7, FNSP. For figures on French conversion of gold, see "Tableau des transactions en or des États-Unis avec les pays étrangers," in Bourguinat, "Le général de Gaulle et la réforme du système monétaire international: la contestation manquée de l'hégémonie du dollar," in *De Gaulle en son siècle*, 125.

26. Triffin, *The World Money Maze: National Currencies in International Payments*, 249. See, also, Charles Coombs, *The Arena of International Finance* (New York: Wiley Press, 1976), 61–62.

27. Entretien biographique de Claude Pierre-Brossolette, number 4, 18–22.

28. Dillon, Memo for the President, May 25, 1962, National Security Files, Departments and Agencies: Treasury, box 289, JFKL.

29. Jones to State Department, June 13, 1962, University Publications of America (UPA), President's Office Files (POF), Treasury, 25.

30. Ibid., 1

31. Memo of Meeting between the President, Ambassador Hervé Alphand, André Malraux, and McGeorge Bundy, May 11, 1962, *Foreign Relations of the United States* (FRUS 1961–63, 13: 695–701).

32. The whole tone of this meeting calls into question the idea that Kennedy wanted to create a Pax Americana regardless of cost. "The goal of U.S. policy was to support and sustain nations which desired independence." If France wanted to lead a Europe independent *from* the United States, then Kennedy would "like nothing better than to leave Europe." Ibid., 697.

33. Gavin to the State Department, May 28, 1962, FRUS 1961–63, 13: 705–707.

34. Gavin to Rusk, July 12, 1962, UPA, National Security Files (NSF), W. Europe, France. See also Heller, Memo to the President, July 16, 1962, UPA, POF, Council of Economic Advisers, 9.

35. Ball, Memo for the President, "Visit of French Finance Minister," July 18, 1962, UPA, NSF, W. Europe, France.

36. Ibid., 2.

37. Conversation between Giscard d'Estaing and James Tobin, June 1, 1962, Heller papers, reel 24: European budget study file. For Heller's study of French economic planning, see, e.g., Heller, "Capital Budgeting Experience in Five European Countries," May 1962, Heller papers, reel 21: Budget (federal) file; and memorandum, Bundy to Heller, May 14, 1962, Heller papers., reel 24: European budget study file.

38. Remarks by René Larre (financial advisor at French embassy, Washington) at a meeting of the AFL-CIO Research Directors, Washington, D.C., May 15, 1962, Fonds trésor: Tome 15, Relations bilatérales avec les Etats-Unis, B 10917, folder: balance des paiments, Archives économiques et financières, Ministère de l'économie et des finances, Savigny-le-Temple, France. Giscard's own writings extol the benefits of economic planning. See, for example, "The Management of the Economy and Social Development" and "The New Growth" in Valéry Giscard d'Estaing, *French Democracy* (New York: Doubleday, 1977), 75–92.

39. Memorandum, Bundy to Heller, May 14, 1962, Heller papers, reel 24; file European budget study. For French perception of Kennedy's motives, see Jacques Rueff to Philip Cortney, 31 May 1962, ibid., Ribicoff file.

40. Jacques Reinstein (Minister-Counselor, U.S. embassy Paris), circular telegram, June 29, 1962, RG 84, France, box 64, folder: Investment of Capital.

41. See, for example, Larre to Giscard, "Investissements des États-Unis à l'étranger," May 18, 1962, Fonds Trésor: Vol. 15, Relations bilatérales avec les Etats-Unis B10915, folder: Politique financière, 1958–1965, Archives économiques et financières. See, generally, J. J. Servan Schreiber, *The American Challenge*, trans. Ronald Steel (New York, 1968).

42. J. R. Fears, *France in the Giscard Presidency* (London, 1981), 1–18. See, also, Entretien biographique de Claude Pierre-Brossolette, interview 5, 28.

43. For Giscard's views on the Bretton Woods system, see, for example, Giscard, Speech before the National Assembly, 17 May 1962, sur le projet de loi relatif au renforcement des ressources du FMI, Direction des Affaires économiques et financières, papiers directeurs: Olivier Wormser, vol. 63: 388–404. On French concerns about the U.S. stock market crash, see Note d'information, René Larre (Conseiller financier, embassy in Washington), June 15, 1962, Fonds Trésor: Vol. 15, Relations bilatérales avec les Etats-Unis, Côte B10915, folder: Budget, 1956–1965. On Giscard's delicate balancing act, see de Lattre, *Servir aux finances*, 150.

44. For figures on French dollar conversion, see United States Net Monetary Gold Transactions with Foreign Countries and International Institutions, 1 January 1962–30 June 1962, Fonds Trésor: Vol. 15, Relations bilatérales avec les Etats-Unis, Côte B10915, folder: Budget, 1956–1965. On debt repayment, see Note pour le ministre, July 3, 1962, Direction des Affaires économiques et financières, papiers directeurs: Olivier Wormser, vol. 119: 252.

45. Memorandum, Walter Heller to President Kennedy, May 16, 1961, Heller papers, Heller/JFK 1960–1964 series, box 5, folder: memos to JFK, 5/61, JFKL. Couve had met with Heller at the first meeting of the expanded OECD and had conveyed de Gaulle's disdain of the IMF.

46. André de Lattre, *Servir aux finances* (Paris: Comité pour l'histoire économique et financière de la France, 1999), 150.

47. Maurice Perouse (Directeur du Trésor) to Giscard d'Estaing, Compte-rendu de la 8ème réunion du Groupe de Travail No. 3 du Comité de politique économique de

l'O.C.E.D., 16–17 April at Château de la Muette, Fonds 9: Institutions Financières Internationales, côte B54754.

48. De Gaulle to Adenauer, Secrétariat général, Entretiens et messages, 1956–1966, July 15, 1962, 16: 218–219. For a concise summary of the Franco-German rapprochement, see Pierre Maillard, *De Gaulle et l'Allemagne: le rêve inachevé* (Paris: Plon, 1990), 169–202.

49. For de Gaulle's preoccupation with Norstad's resignation, see "Le général Norstad serait démissionnaire," *Le Monde*, 21 July 1962, 1. De Gaulle met with Norstad's named successor, Lyman Lemnitzer on July 23, 1962, and criticized U.S. nuclear policy within NATO. See Entretien de Gaulle-Lemnitzer, 23 July 1962, Secrétariat général, Entretiens et messages, 1956–1966, 16: 206–209, Archives of the Ministry of Foreign Affairs, Paris, France.

50. Hervé Alphand, *L'étonnement d'être: journal (1939–1973)*, 381. See, also, Entretien biographique de Alain Prate, entretien 4, Comité pour l'histoire économique et financière de la France. Rueff's other strong ally, Foreign Minister Maurice Couve de Murville, was also preoccupied with strategic issues. While Giscard was in Washington, Couve was in Geneva for talks with the Soviets on Laos and Berlin. See, Entretien Couve-Gromyko in Geneva, July 21, 1962, Secrétariat général, Entretiens et messages, 1956–1966, 16: 179–181. Dinner of the four ministers of foreign affairs in Geneva, 21 July 1962, Secrétariat général, Entretiens et messages, 1956–1966, 16: 190–195.

51. No record of Giscard's meeting with Kennedy alone has been found in either U.S. or French archives. Kennedy mentions some of the points he discussed in a later meeting with Federal Reserve Chairman William Martin. Discussion between President John F. Kennedy, William McChesney Martin, Chairman of the Federal Reserve and Theodore Sorensen—August 16, 1962, 5:50–6:32 P.M., tape 13, Presidential Recording, International Monetary Relations, Presidents Office Files, JFKL, transcribed by Francis J. Gavin. For the meeting with multiple participants, see memcon, "Payments Arrangements Among the Atlantic Community," July 20, 1962, FRUS 1961–63, 13: 733. And memcon (luncheon meeting), July 21, 1962, JFK NSF, reel 2: 154–155.

52. Ibid.

53. Memo, the President for the Secretary of the Treasury and Administrator, Aid, June 20, 1962, UPA, POF, Treasury, 25; Memo, Bundy for the President, June 22, 1962, UPA, POF, Treasury, 25; Memo, the President for the Secretary of the Treasury, June 22, 1962, UPA, POF, Treasury, 25.

54. In September 1962, Giscard began talking about a CRU, a proposal that was debated intermittently until 1965. See, for example, Loraix, *France after Hegemony*, 185–186. See, also, Samy Cohen and Marie-Claude Smoute, *La politique de Valéry Giscard d'Estaing* (Paris: Fondation Nationale des Sciences Politiques, 1985), 146–148; and Bourguinat, "Le général de Gaulle et la réforme du système monétaire international: la contestation manquée de l'hégémonie du dollar," in *De Gaulle en son siècle*, 116–117.

55. Memo, Coppock to Johnson, August 1, 1962, DDC 1993.

56. Memo, Kaysen to the President, July 6, 1962, FRUS 1961–63, 13: 138.

57. Memo, Ball to the President, "A Fresh Approach to the Gold Problem," July 24, 1962, the Papers of George W. Ball, box 15b, "Memorandum to the President on the Gold Problem," Seeley G. Mudd Manuscript Library, Princeton University.

58. Ibid., pp. 4–5.

59. Ibid., 5. Ball argued that "what we must tell our European allies is, therefore, clear enough: if we are to continue to carry our heavy share of the Free World burdens we can do so only under the conditions where our exertions in the common cause do not imperil the dollar and in fact, the whole international payments system. To create those conditions is the first and most urgent task for the Atlantic partnership."

60. Ibid., 10.

61. Presidential Recording, Tape 14, August 20, 1962: 4:00–5:30 P.M., International Monetary Relations, Presidents Office Files, JFKL, transcribed by Francis J. Gavin.

62. Ball, "A Fresh Approach to the Gold Problem," 14.

63. James Tobin, "A Gold Agreement Proposal," July 24, 1962, Acheson Papers, State Department and White Adviser, Report to the President on the Balance of Payments, 2-25-63, HSTL.

64. Memo for the president, "An Interim International Monetary Arrangement," August 9, 1962, Acheson Papers, State Department and White Adviser, Report to the President on the Balance of Payments, 2-25-63, HSTL.

65. Memo, Heller to the President, "Why we need an interim international monetary agreement," August 9, 1962, FRUS 1961–1963, 9: 139.

66. Ibid., p. 140.

67. Carl Kaysen and Kermit Gordon, Memo for the President, "Gold Guarantees," July 18, 1962, UPA, POF, Treasury, 25.

68. Dillon, Memo for the President, August 7, 1962, Acheson Papers, State Department and White Adviser, Report to the President on the Balance of Payments, February 25, 1963, Harry S. Truman Library (hereafter HSTL), Independence, Missouri.

69. Fowler, Memo for Dillon, "The Need to Couple High Level Political Negotiations for more Equitable Burden Sharing Designed to Correct the U.S. Balance of Payments with any Political Negotiations for Interim Arrangements Designed to Defend U.S. Gold Reserves," August 7, 1962, Acheson Papers, State Department and White Adviser, Report to the President on the Balance of Payments, February 25, 1963, HSTL. These memos indicated that the Treasury department had no idea how important the American troops stationed in West Germany were to the stability and security of Europe.

70. "Appraisal of Problems in the Proposal for an 'Interim Monetary Arrangement,'" August 16, 1962 (no author given but included with a cover letter to Ball from W. N. Turpin, Dillon's Special Assistant), Acheson Papers, State Department and White Adviser, Report to the President on the Balance of Payments, February 25, 1963.

71. Ibid., 4–5.

72. William McChesney Martin, Jr., Chairman of the Board of Governors, Federal Reserve System, "Commentary on 'An Interim International Monetary Arrangement' Presented by Chairman Martin," UPA, POF, Treasury, 25, 1.

73. Roosa, "The New Convertible Gold-Dollar System," and Roosa, "International Liquidity."

74. Bundy to Kaysen, August 21, 1962, NSF, Departments and Agencies, Treasury, 6/62-4/63, box 289, JFKL. Bundy asked Kaysen, "Is Doug Dillon pinning us to his position by such public statements?"

75. Presidential Recording, Tape 14, August 20, 1962: 4:00–5:30 P.M., International Monetary Relations, Presidents Office Files, JFKL, transcribed by Francis J. Gavin.

76. Presidential Recording, Tape 11, August 10, 1962: 11:20–12:30 P.M., International Monetary Relations, Presidents Office Files, JFKL, transcribed by Francis J. Gavin.

77. Tape 14, August 20, 1962.

78. Ibid.

79. Memo, President for the Secretary of the Treasury, The Undersecretary of State, and Chairman of the CEA, August 24, 1962, NSF, Department and Agencies, Treasury, 6/62-4/63/ 289, JFKL.

80. Giscard d'Estaing to the finance ministers of the Group of 10, 12 September 1962, Direction des Affaires économiques et financières, papiers directeurs: Olivier Wormser, vol.132: 347–350.

81. Memo from Dillon and Ball to the President, September 12, 1962, with attachment, Memo for Dillon and Ball from Johnson and Leddy, September 10, 1962, FRUS 1961–63, 9: 146.

82. Memo, Kaysen to the President, September 18, 1962, FRUS 1961–63, 9: 149.

83. Ibid., 149.

84. Ibid., 149.

85. Memo, Dillon to Kennedy, September 18, 1962, FRUS 1961–63, 9: 152.

86. Ibid., p. 146–147.

87. For details of the post-Nassau Franco-German revolt, see Marc Trachtenberg, *A Constructed Peace: The Making of the European Settlement, 1945–1963* (Princeton: Princeton University Press, 1999), 355–379.

88. For these fears in 1963, see Gavin, "The Gold Battles within the Cold War: American Monetary Policy and the Defense of Europe, 1960–1963," *Diplomatic History*, Winter, 2002, vol. 26, no. 1.

89. United States Net Monetary Gold Transactions with Foreign Countries and International Institutions, 1 Jan. 1963–30 June 1963, Fonds Trésor, Vol. 19, Relations monétaires—Etats-Unis, 1962–1978, Côte Z 9984, folder: Transactions d'or monétaire avec l'étranger.

90. "Remarks by the Honorable Henry H. Fowler, Secretary of the Treasury, before the Virginia State Bar Association at the Homestead, Hot Springs, Virginia, Saturday, July 10, 1965, 6:00 P.M.," Papers of Francis Bator, box 7, LBJ Library, 10.

91. See G. Grin, "L'évolution du système monétaire international dans les années 1960: Les positions des économistes Robert Triffin et Jacques Rueff," *Relations Internationales*, no. 100 (winter 1999), 389.

6

Western Europe and the American Challenge: Conflict and Cooperation in Technology and Monetary Policy, 1965–1973

Hubert Zimmermann

During his brief presidency, John F. Kennedy spent almost as much time in Western Europe as his two immediate successors combined. His tours through European capitals invariably drew cheering crowds and created a lasting image in which the American leader incorporated not only the American dream but also the inclusion of Europe in a transatlantic community that was symbolised by modernity, technological progress, and economic prosperity. Lyndon B. Johnson and Richard Nixon rarely went to Europe, and if they did, the reception was often cool. They were frequently greeted by protesters. When Kennedy affirmed in a ringing speech in Philadelphia on Independence Day 1962 that America was "prepared to discuss with a United Europe the ways and means of forming a concrete Atlantic partnership, a mutually beneficial partnership between the new union now emerging in Europe and the old American union founded here 173 years ago," politicians all over Europe (except for France) congratulated the president.[1] Henry A. Kissinger's grandiose pronouncement of a "Year of Europe" in 1973 was mostly met with disbelief and scorn.[2] Certainly, personality goes a long way in explaining such a difference; however, the contrast also denotes a dramatic change in European attitudes toward the United States. Of course, serious European-American conflicts also existed during the Kennedy administration, but they paled in comparison with the mutual disenchantment of the 1970s.

How is this shift to be explained? Many analysts assume that it was a consequence of basic structural change, that is the reemergence of a Europe that was more inclined and able to pursue its own interests, even if this resulted in a conflict with the U.S. Additionally, they point to an alleged American decline. Such an interpretation justifies Nixon and Kissinger's assertive policy toward Europe as a defensive reaction.[3] Other commentators stress the impact of more specific reasons, such as LBJ's and Nixon's mistakes in handling their allies,[4] the consequences of Vietnam, or the American neglect of Europe in favour of great power diplomacy with the Soviet Union and China.[5] Certainly, these factors were not unimportant, but such interpretations do not adequately capture the essence of what was going on in European-American relations at that time. The early 1970s were a period of major reshuffling in the relations between the Western countries. The cards were remixed and the rules of the game were reformulated.

These changes become very clear when one shifts one's emphasis away from the usual concentration on the "high politics" of defense and grand strategy to the supposed "low politics" of monetary relations and technology. Structural change in those two fields, and the way it was handled in Europe and the U.S., was decisive for the shifting power relations of the 1970s and beyond. Money and technology are not merely to be considered as of secondary importance, that is, as epiphenomena that reflected what went on at the high political level[6]; on the contrary, the effects of decisions in these fields often led to major political reorientations, such as the Europeanization of French and British foreign policies in the late 1960s or the dissolution of transatlantic cooperation at the same time. Different methods in the way monetary and technological issues were handled and intensified cooperation in these fields might have led to a qualitatively different relationship between the United States and the economically reemerging Europe. There might even have been a direct trade-off between the two realms, as Washington struggled with a dollar deficit and the Europeans worried about their technological dependence. In 1966, for example, the Italian foreign minister Fanfani presented the idea of a technological Marshall Plan in which European payments for American advanced technology would have wiped out a substantial part of the American balance of payments deficit.[7] However, neither transatlantic monetary nor technological cooperation advanced after 1966; things in fact moved in exactly the opposite direction.

The closing of the gold-window by Nixon in August 1971 signaled the end of the so-called Bretton Woods monetary system. Already in the mid-1960s, the system had balanced on the verge of collapse. European and American views on monetary affairs diverged increasingly, and when, at the European summit in The Hague at the end of 1969, the EC-countries decided to embark on the road to a common currency, this was a clear sign that they strove for more independence from the dollar, and that the transatlantic monetary system was about to be abolished. How and why did Americans and Europeans allow the system to disintegrate?

The publication of Jean-Jacques Servan-Schreiber's best-seller *Le Défi américain* (Paris 1967) was another event that stands as a symbol for a fundamental change in transatlantic relations. Servan-Schreiber urged European politicians to react vigorously to American technological superiority; otherwise Europe would soon be completely dependent on the U.S. in the most advanced fields of modern technology. He proposed that the Europeans join their national programs in an attempt to match American preeminence. However, was it not more rational for European nations to collaborate with the powerful partner across the Atlantic and benefit from technological spinoff? And yet, at the end of the 1960s, all European countries exhibited a clear preference for European programmes.

What had happened to Kennedy's vision of transatlantic interdependence? I argue that the lost chances in monetary and technological relations resulted from conscious policy decisions that signaled the end of a relationship based on cooperation and the beginning of a new one based on competition. This had major consequences beyond the 1970s. One of the most important of those was a new impetus to European integration. The American challenge in the monetary and technological field helped to reinforce Europe's identity. Or in other words, the assertive American policy in the late 1960s, culminating in the Nixon-Kissinger period, had the same kind of effect on the European unification process as the hegemonic U.S. policy in the early 1950s.[8]

THE EROSION OF THE TRANSATLANTIC PARTNERSHIP

Changing Patterns of Transatlantic Monetary Policy

The central features of the postwar monetary order in the Western world, usually called the Bretton Woods system, are well known: the core role of the dollar to whose value the other currencies participating in the system were pegged; the dollar-gold link that provided a guarantee of the dollar's value and was coupled with the promise that other nations could cash in their surplus dollars for $35/ounce at the U.S. treasury; and institutionalised cooperation among the major industrial economies to keep exchange rates stable and shield their domestic economies from the impact of unexpected movements in financial markets.[9] Less well known is the strongly political character of this system. It was based on an unintended "bargain" between Europe and the U.S.[10] In the 1950s the U.S. profited from the reserve role of the dollar insofar as it allowed the Americans to finance their huge Cold War effort without having to worry about their external balance; Europe, for its part, acquired the resources it needed to rebuild its industries in the postwar period. The resulting American balance of payments deficits were no problem as long as the Europeans had an economic interest in accumulating surplus dollars. This situation changed in the late 1950s and a serious problem emerged. If the Europeans transferred back to the U.S. treasury the surplus dollars that accrued to them (due to an undiminished American military presence in Europe, growing investments by U.S. industries in the Common Market, and a diminishing American trade surplus), the American dollar-gold exchange guarantee, and with it confidence in the dollar as the world's core currency, would soon be undermined. A real reversal of American deficits, however, would have required from the U.S. government such unpalatable policies as a retrenchment of the military effort in Europe, limitations on U.S. investments or restrictive trade policies. Only very few politicians in Europe wanted to provoke such reactions. They still agreed with the basic thrust of American economic and security policies. Therefore, they acceded to American requests to prolong the "bargain" by continuing to hold surplus dollars. This cooperation, however, rested on two conditions: that the Americans, as issuer of the reserve currency, would manage their domestic economy and their external commitments in a way that would not undermine the dollar's value, and that there would continue to be a large degree of agreement on basic economic and political goals among the partners on both sides of the Atlantic.

The American commitment to get their balance of payments under control required difficult negotiations with their partners and costly interventions in currency markets. However, the advantages of the system were considered large enough to offset the inconvenience of regular consultation. On the burden and benefits of having a reserve currency, Secretary of Treasury Dillon wrote to Kennedy:

> To date, foreign countries and their nationals acquired nearly $20 billion in dollar accounts. This is, in effect, a demand loan to us of $20 billion which has allowed us to pursue policies over the years that would have been utterly impossible had not the dollar been a key currency.[11]

In a discussion with the president, Undersecretary of the Treasury Robert V. Roosa was even more explicit when he emphasised that the role of the dollar made

> it possible for us to, year in and year out, and apart from situations that get completely out of whack such as we've had year in and year out, to finance every deficit we may run very readily, because you have the world accustomed to holding dollars. When you run behind for a year you don't have to negotiate a credit, they just hold dollars.[12]

In addition, the U.S. government also shared with the Europeans a major interest in preserving the dollar-consuming security commitment in Europe, though certainly not for eternity and in a size it considered excessive. However, as long as the Europeans supported the dollar there would be no immediate need to change this situation. This was the background of those numerous multilateral initiatives that were taken by the major industrial countries (including France) in the early 1960s to shore up the system.[13] Proposals by the European Commission (1962) or by French finance minister Giscard d'Estaing for a European currency (1964) were either ignored or dismissed as completely unrealistic.[14] Both the German and the French government made no secret of their disapproval for such plans, and Giscard even lost his post in 1966. Thus, the working of the international monetary system still rested on a basic political understanding among the countries of the transatlantic alliance.

However, the policy of "peripheral defenses" for the dollar, which was devised by the Kennedy administration, did not resolve the problem.[15] In the mid-1960s, it became increasingly difficult to keep the balance of payments deficits under control. The first reason for this was Vietnam. In February 1965, President Johnson ordered the bombing of North Vietnam. In July of the same year he decided that an additional contingent of fifty-thousand men would be sent to South East Asia. The war was Americanised and continued to absorb more and more of the government's attention in the years that followed. America's European allies reacted with alarm to this development. They had great doubts about the theory that the new Cold War border was in Southeast Asia and feared that the conflict diverted American energies away from Europe, which to them still was the principal theatre of the East-West conflict.[16] Therefore, they were rather dismissive when the Americans called for direct help on the battlefield, especially since the war proved to be extremely unpopular, not only with the European governments but also with the electorate. Even the country that publicly supported the Vietnam War most emphatically did not react to a strong call by the Johnson government for direct help. Asked by LBJ in January 1966 what contribution Germany had made, Secretary of Defense Robert McNamara grumbled: "Not a damn thing except a hospital ship,"—although the Americans had made strong efforts to get at least a token contingent of combat troops.[17]

The U.S. government soon realised that direct European involvement was out of the question. However, that led them to insist with growing vigour on cooperation in international monetary policy. The war effort had led to a sharp increase in military expenditure abroad (which had always been a major factor in American balance of payments deficits).[18] Even more detrimental to the external balance was Johnson's unwillingness to increase taxes in order to neutralise rising public expenditure in connection with the war and the Great Society programs. Thus, inflation started to undermine the dollar. Paul Volcker, Nixon's Undersecretary of the Treasury for Monetary Affairs, later wrote that Vietnam "was the period when inflation really gained momentum in the United States and threatened to spread to Europe too, and if we weren't willing to finance the war properly, then maybe we shouldn't have fought it at all."[19] Another serious problem for the monetary system was the seed of discord the war planted in the Atlantic Alliance at a crucial moment. Confronted with Europe's unwillingness to extend direct support in Vietnam, the U.S. government in private and Congress in public increasingly questioned the continuation of America's troop commitment in Europe.[20] The basic, common political understanding among Europeans and Americans was coming unstuck.

Furthermore, there was the "de Gaulle problem." In February 1965, the French president, in his campaign against American domination, had thrown down the gauntlet in the monetary field. He denounced the transatlantic monetary system as an unfair deal, which allowed America to finance its external commitments and buy up European industries by simply printing dollars. Therefore, he invited all industrial countries to follow France and exchange all of their dollars for gold in order to bring the system down.[21] Nobody followed his example, but the impression that America was not doing enough to bring its own house in order, thus endangering the international monetary system, was widespread in Europe.

In 1965, the Americans realised that it was not possible to save the postwar international monetary structure by small piecemeal steps, especially because they knew that Vietnam was wrecking U.S. external balances for the foreseeable future to a degree that better remained hidden to the public.[22] A comprehensive reform was necessary. A major political issue relating to this reform was how such a new system would accommodate the call of a resurgent Europe for a greater voice in the creation and management of international reserves. This would have been an extremely contested issue even in times of a perfectly working alliance. The growing distrust about future U.S. policy in Vietnam and the suspicion voiced in many quarters that Washington was financing the war by printing dollars made that task even more difficult. Secretary of the Treasury Henry Fowler had the ingenious idea of proposing a standstill agreement as long as the Vietnam conflict was going on:

> I propose that we give serious consideration to asking the key dollar-holding nations . . . to pledge *not to convert dollars they presently hold* and *not to convert any additional dollars* [emphasis in original] that may accrue to them as long as the Vietnam struggle continues. . . .We are bearing virtually the entire burden of the Vietnam conflict. We view this as commitment on behalf of all free nations. We do not ask others to see it this way, but we do ask that they not act in a manner that will prevent us from meeting our commitments and/or destroy the international financial institutions that are such a vital part of the world we are attempting to defend.[23]

This meant that Europe would have to continue extending credit to the U.S., and would have to forego its principal element of control over America's management of its reserve currency. Instead, it was asked to trust to an unbinding promise that the Americans would manage to control their deficits in a way that avoided a breakdown of the system. There is no evidence that a formal proposal along these lines was made in early 1966, but the Americans left no doubt that this was the policy they expected their allies to follow.

Indeed, hardly eight months later, a core country had to decide whether it would sign such a temporary limitation of its monetary authority. In the context of negotiations about the cost of American troops in Germany, the U.S. side proposed that the Federal Republic sign a pledge to not exchange dollars for gold. Since the early 1960s, it had been one of the most important mechanisms of monetary help for the U.S. that Bonn, in the so-called offset agreements, bought American weapons to offset the foreign exchange losses occasioned by the U.S. military presence in the FRG.[24] When the German government decided in 1966 that it no longer needed to buy American weapons, this practice ran into enormous difficulties. Relentless pressure by LBJ and McNamara to continue "offset," and the serious threat of American troop withdrawal, played a considerable role in chancellor Erhard's fall from power in October 1966. The trilateral negotiations at the beginning of 1967 (including the United Kingdom, which also had a major balance of payments problem linked politically to the British troop presence in Germany) essentially concerned the question of whether the transatlantic bargain in which the Americans provided military security and the Germans monetary support would be reaffirmed once more. Due to the overriding importance of American military protection, the German government pressed Bundesbank president Karl Blessing to agree to what the Americans were asking for; he reluctantly went along with government policy, and in the so-called Blessing letter, the Bundesbank pledged to continue supporting the dollar.[25]

This episode of brinkmanship without any doubt created deep resentment in Germany, as later remarks by Blessing show. Blessing stated that he should have started cashing in dollars for gold at that time, until the U.S. Treasury had been driven to desperation.[26] The ministers in the German cabinet were unanimous in their criticism of Washington's monetary policy; however, they also agreed that the French policy was not viable.[27] Therefore, they stuck to the transatlantic bargain in the hope that a quiet reform of the monetary system might still be in the cards.[28] Frustrated by American policy as well as by the rigidity of the French position, the Germans developed an increasing penchant for unilateral action in the monetary field. Frustration with the U.S. also ran high in other European countries, but, apart from France, cooperation with the Americans was still the preferred option.[29] The British were completely wedded to the defense of the pound as a reserve currency and this caused an increasing dependence on American monetary support.[30] The smaller industrial states were closely linked either to the U.S. or to England in security or economic terms, and in any case were too weak to advocate an alternative monetary system.

Despite the increasingly tense situation in international financial markets from late 1967 onward, the Johnson administration did not start a vigorous and acceptable program for international monetary reform.[31] Waiting out the Vietnam War and the corresponding inflation was the strategy, always in the hope that the Europeans would continue to play the game. During the trilateral negotiations, presidential advisor Francis Bator outlined the thrust of the American policy at the end of the Johnson administration:

> There is no hope for any sort of new 100 percent military offset deal with the Germans. However, we may be able to get them to agree to financial steps which would be far more valuable. Specifically: -that they will not use their dollars, old or new, to buy gold; -that they will join us in pushing the other Europeans, ex-France, to agree to the same sort of rules; -to support us against France in negotiations on longer-range monetary reform; -to neutralise the military imbalance by buying and holding securities which would count against our balance of payments deficit. If we can also get the Italians, Dutch and the Belgians, as well as the UK, Canada, Japan, to play by such rules we will have negotiated the world onto a dollar standard. It will mean recognition of the fact that, for the time being, the U.S. must necessarily play banker of the world.[32]

The consequence of such a step was that

> we will no longer need to worry about reasonable balance of payments deficits. This arrangement will not give us an unlimited printing press. But as long as we run our economy as responsibly as in the past few years, it will permit us to live with moderate deficits indefinitely.[33]

The actual transformation of the system to a pure dollar standard happened in March 1968 when, after a heavy wave of gold speculation, the major industrial countries decided to split up the gold market in an official and a private market. Belgium, Germany, Britain, Italy, the Netherlands, and Switzerland agreed to no longer demand gold from the U.S. The transatlantic system, however, was on the brink of collapse because Europe was increasingly relegated to a policy of merely reacting to what the U.S. was doing; Europe was unable to play a major role in the comanagement of the system, a role that corresponded to its economic weight. The hopes of saving the system concentrated on the talks on liquidity reform that had been initiated in 1965. They were to result in the so-called Special Drawing Rights, a form of reserve currency that was to relieve the pressure on the dollar.[34] However, Washington refused to accord Europe a veto right on the new reserve medium, fearing that this would give France the ability to block any American initiative.[35] Essentially, the U.S. was not ready to give up the role of the banker of the world, as long as the Europeans had no means to force them to do so. When the SDR agreement was finally signed in 1968, the result amounted to much less than a real overhaul of the system.

Thus in 1968, the transatlantic monetary bargain was in deep trouble and the Europeans began to look for alternatives. Certainly, their internal divisions, and particularly the uncompromising position of France, had played a big role in the failure of reform. Still, the major responsibility lay with the U.S. Less by deliberate action than by neglect and due to the inflexibility caused by the Vietnam War, the Johnson administration had allowed the system to disintegrate almost to a point of no return. The year 1969, however, seemed to open the prospect of a fresh start. A new president, Nixon, was installed in January; in April, the main adversary of the transatlantic monetary system, de Gaulle, left the stage. The core question now was how the reform of the monetary system (or the transition to a new system) would be managed: in a cooperative manner or in a way that would set both sides on a collision course?

A Transatlantic Technological Community?

The Grand Design of a European-American transatlantic community contained the notion of progressiveness, which in the 1960s was clearly associated with the field of high technology. It is therefore quite striking how limited the actual extent of technological cooperation between Europe and America was during the decade and beyond. What were the reasons?

Probably the most sensitive issue in transatlantic relations at the end of the 1950s was the problem of European participation in American nuclear planning and its access to advanced U.S. nuclear weapons. The debate concerned not only questions of national power and international security. It was also a contest for access to the most prestigious technology of the time. In the second half of the century, nuclear technology was seen as the key for the wealth of nations. America's top position in every aspect of this technology was a core element of its preeminence in international political life. As a result, Washington's partners depended on American decisions relating to one of the most vital sectors for their national wealth. No wonder that this situation caused deep apprehensions, even during the honeymoon years of the alliance. The attempt by countries such as Britain, France, Germany, or Italy to forge deals with the U.S. in order to close this yawning technological gap was at the core of the nuclear debate in the alliance.[36]

During Eisenhower's presidency, the government encouraged nuclear cooperation with the allies. Collaboration with the United Kingdom was in any case well developed, though beset with misunderstandings on both sides.[37] The British attempt to preserve their nuclear autonomy led, however, to increasing dependence on American technology, particularly regarding launchers. Nuclear sharing with France, Germany, and the smaller members of the alliance was a much more contested issue, although the Eisenhower administration was ready, in principle, to move forward in this area, too.[38]

Doubts in the State Department about the wisdom of a policy supporting several independent nuclear capabilities, particularly if this meant German access to atomic weapons, led to the proposal of a nuclear force assigned to NATO. Negotiations about what would later be called the Multilateral Force (MLF) were begun in 1960; the U.S. goal was ultimately to give a united Europe a nuclear force under its own control. The American readiness to share know-how and resources also included the civil uses of nuclear energy. Eisenhower's Atoms for Peace program of 1953 was an ambitious proposal for the controlled dissemination of know-how regarding the peaceful uses of nuclear energy.[39] In 1958, the U.S. signed an agreement with EURATOM (the newly founded European organisation for collaboration in nuclear research), which ensured the supply of American enriched uranium for European reactors. However, there was a little snag to this deal: most of those reactors were built under American licence and depended on American supply of uranium. For this reason France, which developed its own line of reactors based on natural uranium, saw no use in this agreement and soon came to consider EURATOM a failure.[40] This was an early instance of the mix of political rivalry, commercial interest, and industrial competition that was to plague transatlantic technological cooperation all through the 1960s.

With the advent of the Kennedy administration, a decisive policy change occurred: the readiness, in principle, of the U.S. to share civil and military nuclear technology was reversed. The risks of nuclear proliferation, especially to Germany, which propagated an anti-status-quo policy toward the Eastern bloc, were deemed too high. Initially, Kennedy and McNamara were not sure about the wisdom of a strict nonproliferation policy because of its corrosive effect on the alliance[41] and because the sale of hardware might bring in considerable economic benefit, for example balance of payments gains.[42] In effect, the above-mentioned offset agreements with Germany were to a large extent a deal trading German monetary help for the sale of U.S. advanced military technology. Nuclear weapons were excluded despite discreet German requests.[43] Finally, however, in 1964, nonproliferation became official government policy.[44] What was ruled out included "exchanges of information and technology between the governments, sale of equipment, joint research and development activities, and exchanges between industrial and commercial organisations."[45] The shift in policy that took place in 1961 had a very negative effect on cooperation in a number of other fields, as the U.S. ambassador in Paris, Gavin, explained in a letter to Kennedy:

> France will spend at least $700 million to build a gaseous diffusion plant which will produce enriched uranium by 1965. We sell enriched uranium to the United Kingdom. We have failed to give France any assistance in building a nuclear submarine despite secretary Dulles' offer to do so to de Gaulle in 1958. We are asking France to help us in redressing our balance of payments by making more

military purchases in the United States, but we will not sell the very items France wants because they are associated with modern weapons systems."[46]

Gavin cited the danger that this pattern of non-cooperation might spill over to the whole economic field. The subsequent American decision to refuse the sale of an advanced computer system, which might have helped France's nuclear program, made the new American policy very obvious.[47] Though this policy was directed mainly against France, the other members of the alliance received no better treatment. In early 1965, a government committee, chaired by former Deputy Secretary of Defense Gilpatric, recommended in a classified report to tie the strings attached to all exports related to nuclear technology even tighter.[48] The MLF receded more and more into the background and was kept alive only by the need to assuage Germany. The long-term objective was to force even the British out of the nuclear business, or at least to provide a NATO cover for their atomic arsenal.

Soon the Americans started negotiations with the Soviet Union to implement this restrictive policy on a global level. The nuclear test ban treaty of August 1963 was the first step. However, far more important was the Non-proliferation Treaty (NPT) of 1968. Non-nuclear members of the alliance realised that this treaty was destined to keep them permanently out of the nuclear weapons business. But apart from the military-political aspects of the possession of nuclear weapons, another serious issue was technology. Would the NPT also inhibit the spread of nuclear technology in the civil field? Would it endanger, at some later point, the continuation of the 1958 agreement between EURATOM and the United States that presently ran until 1975?[49] This turned out to be one of the major worries of countries such as Germany and Italy, which were completely dependent on American deliveries of enriched uranium. Very quickly, these countries started to look for alternatives.

Thus, in this key technological area, the NATO allies had turned away from real collaboration during the 1960s. This situation was to spill over into other fields. An important case in point is the development of advanced military technology. The priority the Pentagon under McNamara accorded to the sale of military equipment for balance of payments reasons impeded every possibility of large-scale technological cooperation between the U.S. and Europe. The huge project of the F-104G *Starfighter*, the principal fighter of the alliance built from 1959 on under American licence by a group of European countries, found no successor in the 1960s.[50] On the contrary, the American policy was to "move promptly to make sure that European countries place orders now for U.S. manufactured equipment, rather than make plans to meet their needs from their own production or from other foreign sources."[51] The sales offensive was mainly directed toward Germany, the most important arms market of the 1960s. In effect, German armed forces became increasingly dependent on U.S. weapons. The need to continue the offset agreements sharply curtailed German funds for shared weapons developments with other partners.[52] Despite the enormous amounts involved in these deals, no successful joint German-American project was agreed to. The only significant project, the joint development of a main battle tank for the 1970s (agreed to in 1964), was stopped in 1970 due to the mutual lack of funds and interest.[53] This was no exception: there were no major American collaboration projects with other allies either. The commercial interest of the arms industry and the Pentagon, as well as the lack of political initiative in the U.S. government, were the major factors in the conspicuous absence of American proposals.

Apart from nuclear weapons, space technology was the most prestigious field of scientific exploits in the 1960s. Again, collaboration between European and American programs was extremely sketchy. Although the Europeans had set up a European Space Research Organisation (ESRO) in 1962,[54] it was the Soviet Union to which, in September 1963 in a speech before the UN General Assembly, Kennedy proposed a joint effort in space research— with few practical consequences.[55] In meetings between LBJ and the German chancellor in 1965 and 1966, the desirability of joint projects in space research was given prominent mention; however, this clearly derived from American hopes to explore new ways of offsetting the foreign exchange cost of American troops in Europe, and thus the idea was not pursued when it became clear that the prospects of commercial and monetary benefit for the U.S. were small.[56] The close links between the nuclear and the space program limited the available options anyway.[57] American restrictions on the export of key technologies meant that offers by the Johnson administration to expand its cooperation with ELDO (European Launcher Development Organisation) were received rather coolly in Europe.[58]

These examples are representative of the general trend. In 1966, during several OECD meetings, the Europeans took up the question of the widening technological gap between America and Europe. Their delegates lamented the restrictive American policy with regard to technological exports and expressed the hope that this policy would be revised so that a kind of transatlantic technological community might develop. Italy took a much-publicised initiative at NATO and proposed a technological Marshall Plan.[59] However, these attempts came to naught. The American view was that only if the Europeans were "prepared [to] make progress in economic integration, Kennedy round and on monetary reform," could progress be made in their obtaining new technology.[60] This policy was reaffirmed at the top level of the State Department: "a technological subsidy would, I think, be doubtful wisdom, since it might serve to perpetuate bad European practices. Moreover, a substantial part of our favourable trade balance with the world depends on our technological superiority and we should not give it away for nothing."[61] In a 1967 memorandum for the National Security Council this position was reaffirmed:

> We cannot afford to see our international strength reduced further through continued deficits. . . . Correction of this balance of payments gap between North America and Western Europe is of much greater importance than a reduction of the "technological gap" which would work in the reverse direction, enlarging the existing imbalance between the two areas. . . . Thus, we should not encourage the strengthening of Europe, and especially that of the EEC, until the EEC demonstrates that it can carry out the responsibilities of a surplus area wisely and co-operatively.[62]

The strains in the transatlantic monetary system spilt over to the area of technological cooperation impeding progress in this field.

An additional problem was the different relationship between state and industry in U.S. and European society. The decade-long struggle about the organisation of *Intelsat*, a worldwide regulatory regime for telecommunication by satellites, is a good example. Founded on American initiative in 1964, *Intelsat* was managed in its first years by a private American company (Comsat), created specifically for this purpose by the U.S. government. However, the Europeans were apprehensive that *Intelsat* would make the creation of European satellites very difficult because it was so closely linked with industrial interests. In fact, *Intelsat* orders for the construction of satellites and their components went almost exclusively to American firms. This, of course, tended to enlarge the already existing technological gap in this field.[63] The Europeans demanded that Comsat be replaced by an intergovernmental body in which Europeans and Americans had equal voting rights. The Americans, however, refused to accede to this request. This reflected the American approach to the management of high technology in which government agencies (usually the Pentagon) provided initiative as well as start-up funds, and later on became the main clients. However, the development, control, and marketing of high-technology products was left to private firms, whereas in Europe the links between the government and (often state-owned) firms were much closer, particularly in high-tech sectors. American firms were not eager to strengthen potential competitors by collaborating with them.

Thus, a mix of competitive strategies, commercial considerations, the American balance of payments situation, and finally the feeling that the U.S. did not have much to gain from extended cooperation with small countries, was responsible for the lack of American interest in the development of a technological community with the Europeans. Kennedy, in his Philadelphia speech, had spoken of a United Europe as a possible partner of the U.S. In the technological field, a united Europe seemed rather remote as long as France and Britain pursued an expensive strategy of privileging national programs.

However, already in the mid-1960s the tide was turning against national autonomy—but also against cooperation with the United States. Faced by America's unresponsiveness and by the escalating cost of their national champions in high technology, one European country after the other turned to an alternative solution to the technological problem: European cooperation, directed explicitly against American superiority.

THE AMERICAN CHALLENGE AND
THE REAFFIRMATION OF EUROPE

The Hague Summit 1969 and the
Plan for a European Monetary Union

A sigh of relief was audible all through Europe when Richard Nixon took over from LBJ. It was expected that the new president would end the fatal involvement in Vietnam and restore Europe to its former central place in American diplomacy. In fact, the start of the new administration was auspicious. Right after his inauguration, Nixon announced that he intended to improve relations with Europe. He mentioned in particular technological questions.[64] In February 1969, he toured European capitals with the message that the new administration would fight against congressional initiatives for a reduction of the American military commitment in Europe. He also announced that he was ready to talk with the Europeans about their complaints in the monetary area.[65]

However, these positive signs were illusory. As it turned out, with the departure of the Johnson administration, the still undecided contest within the U.S. government between advocates of the transatlantic community and those who opted for a more unilateral policy was won by the latter. A major diplomatic effort to restore the privileged partnership with Europe was not part of the new administration's strategic concept. Nixon's core objective was to regain for America its freedom of action in the pursuit of its national interests instead of getting entangled in a more interdependent transatlantic community. The United States would cease to assume unnecessary responsibilities, pursue great power diplomacy and leave it to regional powers to sort out regional problems.[66] Europe, in particular, should concentrate on its own internal problems. This part of Kissinger's "Year of Europe" speech was particularly galling for the Europeans.[67] It explains why Germany's *Ostpolitik*—in its essence a reformulation of Germany's national goals and an attempt to gain freedom of maneuver for the Federal Republic—was regarded very sceptically by Washington. East-West diplomacy was the prerogative of the U.S. Other countries were "welcome to participate" in the East-West dialogue, but they should not play the role of initiators.[68] Already in November

1969, one month after Brandt had been elected chancellor, the American government was telling the Germans that "things are happening too fast" and that there was widespread disquiet in Washington regarding the activities of the new government.[69]

For Nixon, Europe was but one element in a global balance of power, and not necessarily a privileged partner. If American interests conflicted with those of Europe, America would use its full weight instead of embarking on long, tortuous negotiations with an often discordant chorus of Europeans. The Nixon administration also did not receive with enthusiasm the reaffirmation of the European community, which was to be so strongly accentuated in the second half of 1969. The immediate worry was that Europe would develop into a protectionist bloc, comprising not only the Six but, by concluding a series of preferential agreements with African and Asian countries, extending beyond the borders of Europe.[70] Certainly, the Europeans were still important allies insofar as they were vital to counterbalance the Soviets (after Nixon's China trip this function was reduced too). Beyond East-West politics, the Europeans were simply regarded as rivals. The Nixon doctrine's emphasis on the future unwillingness of America to shoulder "every burden" spilt over to the monetary and technological field. Since Kennedy's times, American governments and the Congress portrayed the support of the monetary system as a burden they were assuming for the benefit of the Western world. The consequence of the new policy was that this support was to be stopped and that, in case the Europeans had a problem with the resulting dollar glut, it was their responsibility to develop remedies. Similarly, if they had a problem with their technological inferiority, it was their task to reform their industrial structures in order to become competitive.

The new policy was nowhere more visible than in the monetary field, a former crown jewel of transatlantic cooperation. The core objective was to regain national autonomy in monetary policy, by flagrant unilateral action if necessary.[71] Nixon was not interested in multilateral negotiations in the framework of the Bretton Woods institutions. His Secretary of Treasury Connally was fundamentally of the opinion that "foreigners are out to screw us. Our job is to screw them first."[72] A recently declassified 1971 letter of Connally to Nixon shows the basic outlook. He warned that "there is a strong element of thinking within Europe that would take advantage of weakness or clumsiness on our part to promote the Common Market not as a partner but as a rival economic bloc, competing vigorously with the dollar and reducing or shutting out, as best it can, U.S. economic influence from a considerable portion of the world."[73] At the same time, he exhorted Nixon to put pressure on chancellor Brandt during his forthcoming visit; Brandt was to be told "that the continuation of Germany's present policy of holding dollars and not buying gold is absolutely fundamental to U.S.-FRG relations."[74] This recommendation was particularly delicate insofar as the U.S. was already preparing for a step that would result in a drastic reduction in the value of the European dollar reserves:

> If things come to the pass of a U.S. suspension of gold sales and purchases, we should do all we can—both substantively and cosmetically—to make it appear that other governments have forced the action on us. We want to portray suspension as a last resort and to present a public image of a cool-headed government responding to ill-conceived, self-defeating actions of others.[75]

Things came to that pass three months later, when, on 15 August 1971, Nixon, without any consultation with the allies, closed the dollar-gold-window and imposed a 10 percent surtax on all U.S. imports. The transatlantic monetary system was dead, and this caused growing rifts in the alliance and a rapid loss in the control of states over financial markets. This was not inevitable; it happened because of the absence of the political will on the part of the core country either to preserve the system or to manage a cooperative transition to a new international financial structure. It also happened because of the inability of Europe during the 1960s to reach a common stance, which might have forced the U.S. to reconsider its policy.[76]

At the end of the decade, the Europeans embarked on the long road toward European monetary integration. During the Hague Summit Meeting in December 1969, the EC member countries announced their intention to create a common European currency.[77] At the same meeting, they invited the United Kingdom to join the community. By accepting the invitation, London also accepted the goal of monetary union. The Hague declaration was a sensational and unexpected leap forward in the history of European integration. It has to be recalled that in 1967 and 1968, the UK still stuck to the world role of sterling, France showed no signs of abandoning its policy of monetary autonomy, and Germany was torn between the continued defense of the dollar-gold system and a more nationalist monetary policy. The explanation for the rapid reorientation is found in the American monetary challenge. By taking an attitude of benign neglect toward the dollar glut, the U.S. was reneging on the essential condition of the transatlantic bargain and permitted a freeing of financial markets, which turned out to be extremely disruptive to European domestic economies. It also undermined any attempt to pursue a policy of national monetary autonomy in Europe. The increasing mobility of capital and the absence of a political will and activity on a worldwide level to control the corresponding effects made autonomous policies increasingly costly for the Europeans.

The most spectacular expression of the futility of national monetary autonomy was the Bonn monetary conference of 1968. Prior to the meeting, massive speculative capital had fled from Britain and France to Germany. Faced by a drastic loss of their reserves, which had been used to defend the exchange value of their currencies, both France and Britain massively demanded a revaluation of the DM. Prime Minister Wilson called in the German ambassador, Herbert Blankenhorn, in the middle of the night to impress on him the need for an immediate action by the FRG.[78] The French were no less outspoken. In May 1968, student and worker unrest had undermined the French currency. In November, French reserves were reduced to about 50 percent of their value before the crisis.[79] Most of the speculative money went to Germany, which, according to France, for no legitimate reason stuck to an undervalued currency. On 9 November 1968, Prime Minister Couve de Murville, in a letter to Chancellor Kiesinger, warned the German government of the grave consequences of continued inactivity.[80]

Despite this pressure and the fact that the U.S. joined the chorus of the demanders at the Bonn conference, the FRG was not willing to take the requested step. By speculating on the necessity of French franc devaluation, Finance Minister Strauss even ignited new speculation against the battered French currency. The pride of de Gaulle rendered it impossible for him to accept defeat, and, after the conference, he refused to devalue. However, this heroic act could hardly hide the fact that the monetary conference had clearly demonstrated the failure of de Gaulle's policy. The idea of national autonomy had been severely undermined, and the reverberations of the austerity measures, which were adopted to enable France to sustain the franc, had a huge impact on many areas of French policy. This also included France's ambitious technological programs.

In 1969 the French balance of payments remained at the mercy of the Bonn government, which was pursuing an increasingly unilateral monetary policy. The French realised that they had not only been unable to dethrone the dollar, but ended up in a situation in which they were at the mercy of German decisions (or nondecisions), at least as long as both countries pursued a policy of monetary autonomy. In addition, the monetary turmoil threatened to destroy the Common Agricultural Policy, one of the core objectives of France's European policy. This realisation paved the way for the acceptance of the European solution, which became government policy after de Gaulle stepped back in April 1969. It was pushed in particular by Valéry Giscard d'Estaing, who became finance minister in the new French government of Georges Pompidou.[81] The question was whether the Germans would finally abandon the transatlantic system and their new unilateral strategy and agree to the Europeanization of their stable currency.

Once more, the Bonn monetary conference played a central role in this context. It made very clear that a monetary policy based mainly on narrow considerations of the Federal Republic's national interests would lead to an increasing alienation of its most important partners. Furthermore, successive speculative waves in 1969 had shown that the pursuit of an anti-inflationary policy under conditions of increased capital mobility and rapidly decreasing political control of financial markets was extremely difficult. And finally, the

French devaluation of August 1969 and the German revaluation two months later threatened to lead to the disintegration of one of the most important pillars of German foreign policy, the EC. Although the Bundesbank and large parts of the governmental bureaucracy still hoped for a reform of the transatlantic system, the political leadership considered the chances for such a reform increasingly sceptically, particularly in view of the passivity of the Nixon team in international monetary policy.

The key figure in this context is Willy Brandt. His most important project was *Ostpolitik*. The concept was based on a long-range perspective leading to the reduction of the huge influence of the superpowers in Europe.[82] However, the goal was not German unilateralism. A strengthening of European institutions, which would be widened to include Britain, was an essential complement to *Ostpolitik*. The new government in France and its proposal for a summit of the EC heads of government in late 1969 opened a realistic chance for a huge step forward in this field before formal talks of the Brandt government with the Eastern countries had even started. Trading British EC membership for large concessions to France in the agricultural domain assured the success of the summit and ended the long stagnation of the EC during the previous years. However, Brandt also was looking for a project that would provide Europe with a positive incentive for deeper integration. Virtually days before the Hague Summit began, Brandt seized on the idea of a European monetary union that also found the approval of Pompidou.[83] Under the chairmanship of the prime minister of Luxembourg, Pierre Werner, a high-level committee began to work on the steps that were necessary to achieve this ambitious project. It presented its final report already one year later. In the form of the Werner Plan, the EC countries disassociated themselves from the reform of the transatlantic system as the final goal of their international monetary policy. The difficulties that lay ahead on the way toward a European currency were certainly underestimated at the time; however, the idea was there, and although thirty years passed until it was implemented, monetary union was to remain the ultimate objective of European monetary policy.

It was no accident that the final declaration of the Hague summit also contained a paragraph on technological cooperation, although it did not have the symbolic and political significance of the monetary project. Disillusionment with the Americans and the huge costs of the attempt to develop national capabilities in high technology forced the Europeans to seriously consider the European road.

Towards a European High-Tech Community?

We have seen how initiatives for a closer and more systematic collaboration of European countries with the United States failed. However, by the late

1960s, it also became clear that in most fields of advanced technology, single European states had no chance of competing successfully with America. This quickly developed into a major political topic. On 5 July 1966, the former German defense minister Franz-Josef Strauß wrote a long letter to Chancellor Erhard in which he decried the extent of American investment in advanced sectors of European industry. He was also critical of the fact that the Federal Republic was buying most of its modern weaponry in America, thus undermining any chance for successful European cooperation in this field. According to Strauß, American technological superiority in all important sectors, backed by a cheap dollar that allowed U.S. firms to buy up European industries, threatened "to turn Europe into an intellectual and scientific vacuum."[84] It was no surprise that one year later, Strauß also wrote the foreword to the German edition of Servan-Schreiber's best-seller *Le Défi américain*, in which Servan-Schreiber made a passionate call for European collaboration in the face of American technological and managerial superiority. Otherwise, Europe would decline to the status of an American colony. Servan-Schreiber's major example was the fate of the European computer industry, which was about to be completely dominated by the Americans.[85] The book was a huge success and European governments, which had been thinking along the same lines, quickly took up the call.

As early as 1964, the French government commissioned a report that came to similar conclusions.[86] France proposed the creation of an intergovernmental European body that was to explore possibilities for technological cooperation. The EC council set up a high-level working group, the Maréchal group. The German foreign ministry noted with satisfaction that with this initiative Europe had embarked on a new field of common activity.[87] However, it soon turned out that ultimately de Gaulle's France clearly preferred national strategies for the most promising technologies. Another problem that impeded all progress in this committee was that the conflict between France and the other five member states about UK membership in the EC spilt over into the work of the committee. Britain still had the most advanced technological sector of all European countries and it was hard to imagine how Europe could confront the American challenge without its potential. However, de Gaulle did not bend. He suspected that proposals to include Britain in European technological projects were just strategies to get it into the EC by the backdoor, and that the British would ultimately prefer American offers if those were forthcoming.[88] In February 1968, the Dutch blocked further deliberations in the Maréchal group, which had achieved almost no results.[89]

The British for their part had given clear signs that they were interested in European cooperation. In November 1966, Prime Minister Harold Wilson proposed "to create a new technological community to pool with Europe the enormous technological inventiveness of Britain and other European countries, to enable Europe on a competitive basis to become more self-reliant and neither dependent on imports nor dominated from outside, but basing itself on the creation of competitive indigenous European industries."[90] He repeated this proposal, which was enthusiastically backed by the smaller European countries, frequently in the following months, echoing Servan-Schreiber:

> [T]here is no future for Europe, or for Britain, if we allow American industry, and American business so to dominate the strategic growth industries of our individual countries, that they, and not we, are able to determine the pace and direction of Europe's industrial advance. . . . [T]his is the road not to partnership but to an industrial helotry.[91]

Until then Britain had pursued a policy that privileged national technological independence and, if this was not possible, collaboration with the Americans (a strategy followed by almost all European governments until 1968).[92] The few projects it had undertaken with European countries such as the construction of the supersonic aircraft *Concorde* and the fighter *Jaguar* with France had been rather frustrating experiences. A series of defeats on world markets for British products, which were in competition with American goods, led to a reorientation of this policy. Instances in which the United States refused to sell the UK advanced technology for commercial reasons cast additional doubt on the special relationship.[93] Furthermore, a long series of failures with national developments of high technology tools led the UK to abandon the strategy of national autarchy. In 1965, the government approved the Plowden report on the British aircraft industry, which recommended that Britain should abandon its attempt to pursue an independent aeronautic program and that it should instead collaborate with the rest of Europe in this area.[94] The major reason for the new openness toward Europe, however, was that the UK considered its technological expertise a major bargaining chip in its campaign to enter the European communities.[95] This strategy failed. Yet, even after de Gaulle had made clear in late 1967 that he was not prepared to admit Britain into the community, the idea of intensified technological cooperation with the rest of the EC was pursued.[96] A series of important projects were initiated. Among the most significant of those were the planned construction of a gas centrifuge for the production of enriched uranium and the development of a Multiple Role Combat Aircraft (*MRCA*).

The former project was a consequence of European doubts regarding the long-term supply of European civil nuclear plants with enriched uranium from the U.S. Already in April 1967, the German government had approached London for a solution to this problem. Would the British government be interested in the construction of a European enrichment plant?[97] Germany was particularly keen on such a project because first, the development of a domestic enrichment capacity was too expensive; second, the

French road had led to nothing because the enrichment plant at Pierrelatte was too closely involved with the Force de Frappe; and, most importantly, the complete dependence on U.S. deliveries had to be reduced.[98] In July 1968, the UK proposed a trilateral working group for the development of a uranium enrichment plant that should also include the Netherlands.[99] In November 1969, the three countries reached an agreement. Negotiations regarding the participation of Italy and Belgium started. All participants considered the project as "of an economic, technological and political importance . . . comparable to EURATOM."[100] France was initially very critical of these proposals. When de Gaulle was in Washington for Eisenhower's funeral in 1969, he explicitly referred to the project in his talks with Nixon and warned that it might help Germany get closer to the nuclear club.[101] This attitude changed only with the reorientation of French policy after the general had left the stage.

A similar pattern developed regarding the second project, the *MRCA*. In 1968, a group of European countries (reduced in the end to Britain, Germany, and Italy) agreed to jointly develop a European fighter as replacement for the *Starfighter*.[102] The project was extremely ambitious and plagued by conflicts about the final configuration as well as unexpected cost explosion. Nonetheless, the governments stuck to it until completion. Once more, the French made it clear that they did not approve of these projects, mainly because they were developing a similar aircraft that they hoped to sell to other European countries.[103]

The French mistrust of Britain, however, was not unfounded, because Britain's commitment to joint European projects remained ambiguous. In April 1968, for example, the United Kingdom suspended payments for ELDO, founded in the early 1960s with the aim of developing a launcher for European satellites.[104] This was a hard blow for the European space effort because Britain had been the most important contributor. The whole project entered a deep crisis. After the lunar landing in 1969, the Americans invited the Europeans to participate in the development of a reusable space transportation system (the later space shuttle) and a permanent station in space. However, they refused to guarantee the availability of American launching facilities for satellites that were not operated within the framework of Intelsat.[105] Again, commercial interest impeded transatlantic cooperation from the very start. This wedded the Europeans together, and they carried on with their own launcher development. In the mid-1970s, Britain, which, due to close connections of British firms to ELDO, had never been completely excluded, officially rejoined the effort. In 1979, the first European rocket, *Ariane*, was launched into the orbit, and it became a serious competitor for the American space shuttle. The development of a European jetliner, *Airbus,* also showed Britain's initial ambiguity. In 1967, it had signed an agreement with France and the FRG for the development of an alternative to the almost complete

U.S. dominance on civil aircraft markets. As early as 1970, Britain cancelled its participation. Once more, despite many doubts as to the commercial viability of the aircraft, France and Germany laboured on, carrying the project to final success (together with Britain, which reentered in 1979).[106]

All of these projects share three characteristics. First, they were explicitly directed against U.S. dominance. Second, they demonstrated the great difficulty of reconciling notions of national autonomy with the necessity of collective projects, particularly in the first years. In 1968 and early 1969, the *MRCA*, *Airbus,* and ELDO were all in deep crisis, and it was only due to the reaffirmation of European cooperation in 1969 and 1970 that they survived despite those great difficulties. In 1970, technological cooperation had become an issue that was discussed regularly at the level of heads of state in Europe. Third, all of these projects were, in the end, successful. Thus, the late 1960s and early 1970s was a decisive period for European collaboration. It was not only those intergovernmental projects that were given a new vigour. Collaboration on community level also received renewed impetus. The Maréchal group was reactivated and, in November 1971, a program for Cooperation in Science and Technology (COST) was adopted, which was to coordinate joint European projects and eventually transcend the narrow confines of the EC.

On the whole, the course of technological and monetary cooperation in the transatlantic alliance exhibited a similar pattern. European countries had three basic options—transatlantic cooperation, national autonomy, and Europeanization—whereas the United States had the choice between the first two possibilities. The analysis has shown a clear trend in American policy toward increasing autonomy in the period studied here. The Europeans, for their part, moved away from a policy of favoring transatlantic and national solutions toward a marked preference for European collaboration.

THE PRICE OF DISUNITY

In 1973, in an edited volume on the foreign policy of the Nixon administration, Robert Osgood predicted a process which, as this chapter has shown, had already been completed: "If the United States abandons its role, it will probably be by neglect rather than design; and it will result in the erosion of the present structure of relationships, not in the construction of another."[107] What has been argued here is that in the field of *monetary policy*, a framework of transatlantic cooperation consisting of a series of tacit rules and common assumptions about how mutual problems were to be tackled came unstuck. Regarding *technology,* after timid efforts during the Eisenhower period, such a framework did not even develop and no major initiatives were undertaken in the 1960s and early 1970s, despite the fact that it was a time of enormous technological advance. Whereas during the 1960s the Europeans gradually came to appreciate the role technological and monetary collaboration might play in fostering a closer relationship between their countries and in enhancing competitiveness as well as their domestic economic welfare, the United States decided it would be better off pursuing a more independent policy, renouncing—not in theory, but in practice—the concept of a close transatlantic partnership. The reasons were manifold. The most important one was that the United States, battered by Vietnam and its balance of payments deficits, perceived itself to be in a kind of decline, and saw in the preservation of its national autonomy, to the largest degree possible, the best way to reverse this trend. Certainly, dealing with a disunited Europe was a difficult problem for American diplomacy. Privileged relations with single European countries such as they existed with Britain and as they were wished by General de Gaulle were extremely divisive for the alliance. However, a more determined effort, particularly after de Gaulle had left, might have prevented the mutual disenchantment of the early 1970s.

Thus, around 1969, in monetary as well as in technological matters, a transatlantic outlook was replaced by a Europe-centered view in most European countries. The result of the American challenge was highlighted by the decisions of the European summit in The Hague in December 1969. European, not transatlantic, cooperation was given top priority in the future. Of course, this was a muddy process with countless setbacks and numerous attempts during the 1970s to assert once more the autonomy of national governments or to strike new bargains with the United States, which still had a lot to offer—most importantly military security. In a short-term perspective, the Europeanization of the late 1960s and early 1970s even may seem a failure, particularly regarding the fate of the plans for monetary union. However, the ultimate objective of European cooperation remained paramount for a huge part of the political establishment (with the exception of the UK) and in the public imagination. What happened was a marked change in the ideological preferences of the European countries regarding international cooperation, even if the actual results of this change were to emerge only much later. In this sense, the years 1965 to 1973 were decisive for the future course of Europe, and the American challenge did play a very considerable role in this process. It is probably instructive to speculate on what would have happened had the United States been more willing to pursue real collaboration with Europe in the 1960s. Perhaps the European Union as we now know it would not have come into existence.

NOTES

1. John F. Kennedy, *Public Papers* (PP) (Washington: GPO, 1962), 538.
2. Text of the speech, in *Department of State Bulletin* (May 14, 1973), 593–598. For the European reaction, see Ronald E. Powaski, *The Entangling Alliance: The*

U.S. and European Security, 1950–1993 (Westport: Greenwood Press, 1994), 102–104.

3. Christian Hacke, *Die Ära Nixon-Kissinger* (Stuttgart: Klett-Cotta, 1983), 178–179.

4. J. Robert Schaetzel, *The Unhinged Alliance* (New York: Harper & Row, 1975).

5. "Western Europe had to remain an ally because its safety and prosperity provided the United States with essential trump cards in dealing with the USSR, but even this suggested that an end-in-itself had become a tool." Stanley Hoffmann, "Uneven Allies," in *Critical Choices for Americans VIII: Western Europe,* ed. David Landes (Lexington, Mass.: Heath, 1977), 64.

6. See for example Seymour M. Hersh, *The Price of Power* (New York: Summit Books, 1985); Seyom Brown, *The Crises of Power* (New York: Columbia University Press, 1979); Robert S. Litwak, *Détente and the Nixon Doctrine* (Cambridge, Mass.: Cambridge University Press), 1984.

7. Meyer-Lindenberg memorandum, "Italian initiative regarding international cooperation in the technological field," September 29, 1966, German Foreign Office Archives (Politisches Archiv—Auswärtiges Amt; henceforth cited as "PA-AA"), I A 6/83, Berlin.

8. On the latter argument, see the article by Marc Trachtenberg and Chris Gehrz in this volume.

9. In fact, the monetary system of the postwar period differed in important aspects, particularly regarding the core role of the dollar, from what had been agreed at Bretton Woods. See Ronald I. McKinnon, "The Rules of the Game: International Money in Historical Perspective," *Journal of Economic Literature* (March 1993), 1–44.

10. On the notion of a bargain, see also Benjamin Cohen, "The Revolution in Atlantic Economic Relations: A Bargain Comes Unstuck," in *The U.S. and Western Europe,* ed. Wolfram Hanrieder (Cambridge, Mass.: Winthrop, 1974), 116–118. A very good discussion of these links is Harold van B. Cleveland, *The Atlantic Idea and its European Rivals* (New York: McGraw-Hill,1966), 72–87.

11. Memorandum of 11 February 1963, U.S. Department of State, *Foreign Relations of the United States* (FRUS) 1961–63, 9: 164.

12. Meeting on international monetary relations, August 20, 1962, tape no.14, John F. Kennedy Library (JFKL).

13. See the article by Francis Gavin and Erin Mahan in this volume.

14. Kenneth Dyson and Kevin Featherstone, *The Road to Maastricht: Negotiating Economic and Monetary Union* (Oxford: Oxford University Press, 1999), 101–102, 274–276.

15. On this policy, by one of its principal architects, see Robert Roosa, *The Dollar and World Liquidity* (New York: Random House, 1967).

16. Alfred Grosser, *The Western Alliance: European-American Relations since 1945* (London: Macmillan, 1980), 237–243.

17. For the U.S. request, see U.S. Aide-Memoire to the FRG, July 6, 1964, George McGhee Papers, 1988 add., box 1, Georgetown University Library, Washington, D.C., and Johnson-McNamara telephone conversation, January 17, 1966, FRUS 1964–68, 2: 80.

18. For the figures, see Cora E. Shepler and Leonard G. Campbell, "United States Defense Expenditure Abroad," *Survey of Current Business* (December 1969), 44.

19. Paul Volcker and Toyoo Gyoohten, *Changing Fortunes* (New York: Time Books, 1992), 62.

20. Phil Williams, *The Senate and U.S. Troops in Europe* (London: Macmillan, 1985).

21. Charles De Gaulle, *Discours et Messages,* vol. 4 (Paris: Plon, 1970), 332.

22. Fowler to Johnson, May 10, 1966, FRUS 1964–68, 8: 269–70.

23. Ibid., 274–275.

24. For a detailed history of these agreements, see Hubert Zimmermann, *Money and Security: Monetary Policy and Troops in Germany's Relations to the U.S. and the United Kingdom, 1955–71* (Cambridge, Mass.: Cambridge University Press, 2002).

25. Memorandum of Political Director Harkort, March 6, 1967, PA-AA, B 150/1967.

26. Leo Brawand, *Wohin steuert die deutsche Wirtschaft?* (Munich: Desch, 1971), 61.

27. Excerpt from Notes on a Meeting of the German cabinet, March 27, 1969, PA-AA, IIIA1/611. In early 1967, the German government discussed the possibility of supporting de Gaulle's call for a change in the price of gold as expressed in dollars and very guardedly informed the French that they were not dead set against consideration of such a step. The Blessing letter prevented this policy from being further explored. See Economics Minister Schiller to Chancellor Kiesinger, January 12, 1967, PA-AA, IIIA1/180.

28. German Foreign Office memorandum on international monetary policy, February 5, 1969, PA-AA, IIIA5/610.

29. Finance Minister Dahlgrün to Foreign Minister Schröder, Results of a Meeting of EC-Finance Ministers on June 20–21, 1966, July 7, 1966, ibid.

30. Hubert Zimmermann, "The Sour Fruits of Victory: Sterling and Security in Anglo-German Relations during the 1950s and 1960s," *Contemporary European History* 9, no. 2 (2000), 225–243.

31. Robert M. Collins, "The Economic Crisis of 1968 and the Waning of the American Century," *American Historical Review* 101 (April 1996), 396–422.

32. Bator to President Johnson, U.S. Position in the Trilateral Negotiations, February 23, 1967, Francis Bator Papers, box 4, Lyndon B. Johnson Library (LBJL), Austin, Texas.

33. Bator to President, 8.3.1967, National Security Files (NSF), NSC Histories: Trilaterals, box 50, LBJL.

34. On these negotiations, see Stephen D. Cohen, *International Monetary Reform 1964–1969* (New York: Praeger, 1970).

35. Washington embassy to the Foreign Office, June 27, 1967, PA-AA, B 150/1967.

36. On this well-covered topic, see Beatrice Heuser, *NATO, Britain, France and the FRG: Nuclear Strategies and Forces for Europe* (London: Macmillan, 1998) and Marc Trachtenberg, *History and Strategy* (Princeton: Princeton University Press, 1991).

37. In 1958, both countries signed an agreement for "Cooperation on the Uses of Atomic Energy for Mutual Defense," Command Paper 537 (London: HMSO 1958).

38. This whole story is extensively analysed by Marc Trachtenberg, *A Constructed Peace* (Princeton: Princeton University Press, 1999), particularly chapters 5 and 6.

39. Joseph Manzione, "Amusing and Amazing and Practical and Military: The Legacy of Scientific Internationalism in American Foreign Policy, 1945–1963," *Diplomatic History* 24, no.1 (2000), 47–49.

40. Robert Gilpin, *France in the Age of the Scientific State* (Princeton, N.J.: Princeton University Press, 1968), 406.

41. The famous Nassau meeting in December 1962 resulted in an offer of U.S. nuclear help to both the UK and France. For the key documents, see FRUS 1961–63, vol. 13. However, due to deep doubts within the American administration about this policy and de Gaulle's press conference of January 14, 1963, in which he openly challenged the U.S., this option was not carried through.

42. See for example the discussion among Kennedy, McNamara, Rusk, and Bundy on April 16, 1962, in FRUS 1961–63, 13: 377–80.

43. For German interest in advanced rocket technology and nuclear warheads, see H. Zimmermann, "F. J. Strauß und der deutsch-amerikanische Währungskonflikt," *Vierteljahreshefte für Zeitgeschichte* 47, no. 1 (1999), 63–67.

44. Trachtenberg, *Constructed Peace*, 307–308.

45. National Security Action Memorandum (NSAM) 294, "U.S. Nuclear and Strategic Delivery System Assistance to France," April 20, 1964, *Declassified Documents Reference System* (DDRS), 1999, document 2312.

46. Gavin to Kennedy, March 9, 1962, FRUS 1961–63, 13: 687. Gavin was promptly rebuffed by the Department of State. See Ball to Gavin, March 14, 1962, ibid., 688.

47. On this and other episodes illustrating the restrictive policy of the American government vis-à-vis France, see Edward A. Kolodziej, *French International Policy under De Gaulle and Pompidou: The Politics of Grandeur* (Ithaca: Cornell University Press, 1974), 79–82.

48. *New York Times*, 12 February 1965. This policy was emphasised in a programmatic article by the director of the Arms Control and Disarmament Agency who argued for a "more widespread, and stricter, application of controls to the traffic in fissionable material and to the technology which may be useful either for peaceful or military purposes." See William C. Foster, "New Directions in Arms Control," *Foreign Affairs* 43 (July 1965), 592.

49. On these doubts, see a memorandum by Political Director Ruete, "NPT: Supply of fissionable material to EURATOM," April 24, 1968, *Akten zur Auswärtigen Politik der Bundesrepublik Deutschland* (AAPD) 1968, 1: 508–509.

50. The missile systems "Hawk" (1959–1965) and "Sidewinder" (1960–1965) were also built in Europe under license from the Americans. See Hanno O. Seydel and Hans-Georg Kanno, "Die Rüstung," in *Westeuropäische Verteidigungskooperation*, eds. Karl Carstens and Dieter Mahncke (Munich: Oldenbourg, 1972), 163.

51. Dillon to Kennedy, May 13, 1963, President's Office Files, box 90, JFKL.

52. Memorandum of Political Director Ruete, 15 September 1964, PA-AA, B 150/1964. This was explicitly in U.S. interest. See DOS/DOD Message to Bonn embassy, July 15, 1963, State Department Central Files for 1963, DEF 19 US-WGER, Record Group (RG) 59, U.S. National Archives (USNA), College Park, Maryland.

53. Seydel and Kanno, "Rüstung," 205.

54. For an archive-based history of the European space effort, see John Krige and Arturo Russo, *Europe in Space, 1960–1973* (Nordwijk: ESA, 1994).

55. Eugene Skolnikoff, *Science, Technology, and American Foreign Policy* (Cambridge: Cambridge University Press, 1967), 23–41. For documents on the history of this initiative, see FRUS 1964–68, 34: docs. 21–62.

56. Conversation between Chancellor Erhard and President Johnson, December 20, 1965, AAPD 1965, 2: 1925–1927; Treasury background paper on the trilateral talks, November 5, 1966, NSF, NSC Histories, box 51, LBJL.

57. Memorandum on space cooperation, March 23, 1966, FRUS 1964–68, XXXIV: esp. 85 n. 3.

58. Lorenza Sebesta, "The Availability of American Launchers and Europe's Decision 'To Go It Alone'," *ESA History Study Reports* 18 (1996), 21.

59. Meyer-Lindenberg memorandum, September 29, 1966, and German NATO representative to Foreign Office, December 7, 1966, both in PA-AA, I A 6/83. For an analysis of this initiative, see Lorenza Sebesta, "Un Nuovo Strumento Politico per gli Anni 60: Il Technological Gap nelle Relazioni Euro-Americane," *Nuova Civiltà delle Macchine* 17, no. 3 (1999), 11–23.

60. Embassy in France to Department of State, January 14, 1966, FRUS 1964–8, 34: 2.

61. Ball to Rusk, 6 June 1966, ibid., 3.

62. Memorandum on U.S.–European Relations, May 23, 1967, NSF, NSC Meetings, box 2, LBJL.

63. Werner Ungerer, "Satellitenprobleme und Intelsat-Verhandlungen," *Außenpolitik* 21, no. 2 (1970), 78–79.

64. Pauls (Ambassador in Washington) to Foreign Office, February 6, 1969, AAPD 1969, 1: 157.

65. Conversation between Nixon and Kiesinger, 26 February 1969, ibid., 286.

66. This was the essence of the so-called Nixon doctrine, announced by the president at a news conference on Guam on July 25, 1969. See PP Nixon 1969, 549.

67. Kissinger himself later doubted the wisdom of this assertion. See Henry Kissinger, *Years of Upheaval* (London: Weidenfeld & Nicolson, 1982), 151–156.

68. Henry Kissinger, "The Year of Europe," *Department of State Bulletin* (May 14, 1973), 598.

69. Memorandum of Political Director Ruete, November 27, 1969, AAPD 1969, 2: 1339.

70. Washington embassy to Foreign Office, "U.S. position on future development of the EC," November 25, 1969, PA-AA, I A 2/1440.

71. Henry R. Nau, *The Myth of America's Decline* (Oxford: Oxford University Press, 1990), 160–164.

72. Harold James, *International Monetary Cooperation since Bretton Woods* (Washington: IMF, 1986), 209–210.

73. The letter is dated 8 June 1971; DDRS 1999, doc. 385.

74. Connally Memorandum for the President, June 12, 1971, ibid., doc. 378.

75. Arthur F. Burns to Nixon, May 19, 1971, ibid., doc. 2317.

76. One of the most active participants in the monetary negotiations of these years, Bundesbank Vice President Emminger, said in a speech he gave in Basel on June 16, 1973: "There can be no doubt that had all the major countries pursued appropriate policies and fully lived up to the rules of the game the system or for that matter, any system—would have functioned well." Otmar Emminger, *Verteidigung der DM* (Frankfurt: Knapp Verlag, 1980), 228.

77. *Bulletin des Presse- und Informationsamts der Bundesregierung* 148, December 4, 1969, 1262–1263.

78. Ambassador Blankenhorn (London) to Brandt, November 20, 1968, AAPD 1968, 2: 1498–1500.

79. Kolodziej, *French International Policy*, 206–207.

80. AAPD 1969, 1: doc. 13, n. 9.

81. Ambassador von Braun (Paris) to Foreign Office, "Future French Monetary Policy," July 24, 1969, PA-AA, III A 1/612.

82. Memorandum of Political Director Bahr, June 27, 1968, AAPD 1968, 2: 796–814.

83. The genesis of this step is difficult to reconstruct. Andreas Wilkens suggests that a proposal by Jean Monnet in November 1969 caused this sudden initiative. See his "Westpolitik, Ostpolitik, and the Project of Economic and Monetary Union," *Journal of European Integration History* 5, no.1 (1999), 81. The Economics Ministry at that time had already presented plans for a monetary union in stages, which was to become the German negotiating position. See PA-AA, Joint Memorandum by AA/Ministry of Economics: Preparatory Meeting for Hague Summit, November 14, 1969.

84. PA-AA, II A 7/1191.

85. Jean-Jacques Servan-Schreiber, *Le Défi américain* (Paris: Denoel, 1967), chapter 14. Written in a similar vein, and also very influential, was the analysis by Christopher Layton, *European Advanced Technology: A Programme for Integration* (London: Allen & Unwin, 1969).

86. "Recherche Scientifique et Indépendance", *Le Progrès Scientifique*, September 1, 1964.

87. Foreign Office memorandum, November 3, 1967, AAPD 1968, 1: 277, n.19.

88. De Gaulle-Kiesinger conversation, March 13, 1969, AAPD 1969, 1: 371.

89. Document 135, AAPD 1968, 1: 486, n. 10.

90. See "Into Europe with Industry's Help," in *The Times* (London), November 15, 1966.

91. Speech in the Guildhall, London, November 13, 1967, PREM 13/1851, Public Record Office (PRO), Kew.

92. Henry R. Nau, "Collective Responses to R&D problems in Western Europe: 1955–1958 and 1968–1973," *International Organisation* 29, no. 3 (1975), 632–636. See also conversation of Brandt with the Italian Foreign Minister Fanfani, January 5, 1967, AAPD 1967, 1: 39–40.

93. Gilpin, *France*, 53.

94. Report of the Committee of Inquiry into the Aircraft Industry, Cmnd. 2853 (London: HMSO, 1965).

95. Burke-Trend to Wilson, 27 February 1968, PREM 13/1851, PRO; Susanna Schrafstetter, *Die dritte Atommacht* (Munich: Oldenbourg, 1999), 200–202.

96. Conversation of Foreign Minister Brandt with the British Ambassador Frank Roberts, December 28, 1967, AAPD 1967, 3: 1713.

97. Conversation of Brandt with British Foreign Minister Brown, April 13, 1967, AAPD 1967, 2: 584.

98. Memorandum of Political Director Frank, April 28, 1967, PA-AA, I A 6/72.

99. Memorandum of Ministerialdirigent von Staden, 12 July 1968, AAPD 1968, 2: 868.

100. Reinhard Loosch, "Kernenergie und internationale Zusammenarbeit," *Aussenpolitik* 20, no.7 (1969), 395.

101. Henry Kissinger, *White House Years* (London: Weidenfeld & Nicolson, 1979), 384. French Foreign Minister Debré voiced the same suspicions to the German ambassador in Paris, von Braun. Von Braun to Brandt, April 24, 1969, AAPD 1969, 1: 515–516.

102. Behrends memorandum, December 23, 1969, AAPD 1969, 1: 1456.

103. Arnold (Ambassador to the Netherlands) to the Foreign Office, February 20, 1969, ibid., 238.

104. John Krige, Arturo Russo, and Lorenza Sebesta, "A Brief History of the ESA," *History of European Scientific and Technological Cooperation*, eds. John Krige and Luca Guzzetti (Luxembourg: EC Official Publications, 1997), 199–200.

105. Ibid., 202.

106. Memorandum by Undersecretary von Braun, August 15, 1970, AAPD 1970, 2: 1482–1483.

107. Robert E. Osgood et al., *Retreat from Empire? The First Nixon Administration*, (Baltimore/London: Johns Hopkins University Press, 1973), 18.

7

Georges Pompidou and U.S.–European Relations

Georges-Henri Soutou

In the late 1940s, the Western powers organized themselves into a political bloc; the policy of building a unified Europe also had its start in that same period. And from that point on, France looked in both directions: toward "Europe," but also toward America, the leading Western power. The France–United States–Western Europe triangle thus provided a kind of framework within which French foreign policy was worked out. The basic French aim at that time was to reestablish a certain position in the world—a position as one of the world's major powers, which had been lost when France was defeated by Germany in 1940. If France was to recover what it had, even in part, it needed both to assume the leadership of Western Europe and cultivate a strong relationship with the United States. Those two orientations, moreover, were bound up with each other dialectically, for French views would carry more weight with the Americans if France could present itself as speaking for Western Europe as a whole; and, conversely, the other Europeans would be more likely to accept French leadership if it could develop a special relationship with the United States.

France could thus take advantage of the fact that it occupied a pivotal position—that it stood at the point where the Atlantic world and the European world overlapped. That position would give France the leverage it needed to deal with the Americans on non-European questions: it would give some weight to its policy on those African, Middle Eastern, and Asian issues in which it was particularly interested. By taking advantage of that triangular structure—in effect, by balancing between the "Atlantic" and the "European" orientations—France would in more general terms be able to recover a certain freedom of action. France, in particular, would be able to avoid losing its autonomy in a too-tightly integrated Atlantic system.

This was the basic framework within which France's policy toward the United States was worked out, but that policy was also framed with an eye to certain more concrete problems. The French military forces needed to be modernized; France needed access to advanced technologies, both nuclear and non-nuclear. In these areas, it was invariably with America above all that the French sought to cooperate during the Fourth Republic, for the simple reason that U.S. military technology was so advanced.[1]

It is often assumed that this aspect of French policy was dramatically altered as soon as General Charles de Gaulle returned to power in 1958. Indeed, it is often assumed that de Gaulle, from the start, was not interested in cultivating good relations with the United States. But from 1958 to 1962, he too sought to cooperate with America, especially in the military area.[2] To be sure, from 1963 on, de Gaulle's policy proceeded along very different lines, but the policy of his successor as president, Georges Pompidou, represented a clear return to the tradition that had taken root in the immediate postwar period. The France–United States–Western Europe triangle was to play an absolutely fundamental role in Pompidou's approach to international issues: the kind of thinking associated with that concept was to lie at the very heart of his foreign policy.

This sort of comparison is a natural point of departure for an analysis of Pompidou's policy as president. Indeed, during the period of his presidency, Pompidou's policy, and especially his American policy, was constantly compared to de Gaulle's. There were those, even within the government, always keeping a sharp eye out for how well the new president's policies measured up, in orthodox Gaullist terms.[3] And foreign policy was a particularly sensitive area: for that reason alone, new approaches had to be introduced with great care. And Pompidou himself was deeply Gaullist in terms of his basic approach to foreign policy, no doubt more than was often thought at the time. It is sometimes hard, therefore, to see what was distinctive about his policy—what exactly distinguished it from de Gaulle's. What, then, was de Gaulle's policy, especially in the final years of his presidency, and how was Pompidou's approach different?

The question of relations with America was fundamental in this regard. It is thus important to note the degree to which, starting in 1963, de Gaulle had turned against the idea of cooperation with America. To begin with, there was the famous January 14, 1963, press conference at which he had announced that France was vetoing Britain's entry into the Common Market, a decision framed in anti-American terms. And then there was the quarrel over the Multilateral Force in 1964. But the most important event here was France's departure, not from the alliance with America, but from the NATO military organization in 1966. All these actions indicated that de Gaulle's policy had taken a strong turn away from America. They were rooted in his view that on all levels—economically, politically, and militarily—Europe had to develop independently of the United States and not in cooperation with her, as the leaders of the Fourth Republic had wanted.[4] And it is striking how far he was willing to take that policy. During his visit to Moscow in June 1966, de Gaulle told the Soviet leaders that he accepted the principle of a European security conference without American participation. His objective, it seemed, was to construct a new security system on the basis of a Franco-Soviet entente and without Washington—a goal in line with the General's overall international conceptions at that time.[5]

The same basic aims were also reflected in de Gaulle's military policy. On January 24, 1967, he issued a "Personal and Secret Directive" for the prime minister and the minister of defense—a very important document that laid out the framework for military programming for the 1970s. Previously, as he pointed out in this document, French defense policy had been worked out "in the framework of the Atlantic Alliance," but henceforth it would be defined with a view to the "ubiquitousness, instantaneity, and totality" of the danger. There was no longer to be any question of a privileged alignment with the United States.[6] Those basic assumptions implied that the French nuclear force should be able to retaliate against any power, including both Russia and America, and indeed the so-called all azimuths targeting strategy was announced by General Ailleret, armed forces chief of staff, in an article in the *Revue de Défense Nationale* in December 1967. De Gaulle himself, in a January 27, 1968, speech to the *Centre des Hautes Etudes Militaires,* confirmed that that would be the strategy.[7] This clearly marked the end of any trace of Franco-American strategic and nuclear collaboration, of the sort de Gaulle had had in mind at various times in the 1958–1962 period.

How was Pompidou's policy different? Before becoming president in 1969, he had served as de Gaulle's prime minister from 1962 to 1968, and he had without question been a Gaullist in international affairs. Like de Gaulle, he had opposed the 1962 Anglo-American Nassau accords as well as the U.S.-sponsored plan for a Multilateral Force.[8] And like de Gaulle, he wanted a "European Europe," a Europe independent of the United States, and he was concerned about the prospect of a U.S.–Soviet rapprochement at Europe's expense. As he told the American journalist C. L. Sulzberger on January 23, 1968, there was a danger that an "American-Soviet condominium" would be imposed on Europe—a very Gaullist theme that he would come back to time and again as president.[9] But still, looking back even on that pre-presidential period, one can identify certain nuances, having to do especially with his attitude toward the United States, that distinguished his thinking from de Gaulle's. Indeed, he declared himself ready to consider much more positive relations with Washington, especially on economic questions, and in a conversation with Sulzberger on October 21, 1965, he took a far more moderate line on NATO issues than the one de Gaulle would take in 1966.[10]

Pompidou's fundamental policy can be characterized as a kind of prag-matic Gaullism—a "rationalized" Gaullism. His basic idea, during the period of his presidency, was to keep the spirit of Gaullism intact, but to develop it in a way that would free it from certain encumbrances that, in the new pres-ident's view, were essentially the product of the general's very strong and oc-casionally impulsive personality. As Pompidou saw it, if the basic Gaullist ap-proach was to endure, policy had to be rooted in reality: there could not be too great a gap between French policy and French power. "My goal," he wrote in June 1969, "is to try to base on solid realities—economic, social, and human realities—what has thus far rested only on the prestige of a single man."[11]

And that fundamental approach was in line with—and is, to a certain extent, to be understood in the context of—basic political realities at home. Pompi-dou, it is important to note, did not have the same historical stature as de Gaulle: in his case, normal domestic political considerations therefore played a greater role than they had when the general was in charge. To govern—indeed, to win election as president in the first place—Pompidou needed to hold together what was called the "presidential majority," a bloc that went well beyond the Gaullists and also included the Independent Republicans and the Centrists, two relatively moderate groups that did not share the anti-Americanism common in Gaullist circles. And so, given the political situation at home (especially after the Soviet invasion of Czechoslovakia in August 1968, which had turned public feeling against the USSR), a certain recentering of French policy was natural: a certain move toward Washington now made good domestic political sense.

Indeed, even before de Gaulle had left office in April 1969, but after Richard Nixon had become the U.S. president in January, there had been a sudden improvement in Franco-American relations. Nixon's visit to France late in February had gone well.[12] The general's basic line might not have changed, but still American diplomats in Paris had the impression that French attitudes had softened: disillusioned with the Soviets, the French now wanted to improve relations with the United States.[13] And indeed American policy was also beginning to shift. The new U.S. administration was willing in particular to take a fresh look at the key question of bilateral military co-operation with France. That issue, Nixon decided on April 15, was to be studied anew, without any a priori assumptions—that is, without any sense that American policy in this area was to be bound by assumptions that had taken root in the past.[14] And Nixon and the State Department were looking forward to a further improvement of relations following de Gaulle's depar-ture from office on April 28; they thought France and NATO would be able to work together better, at least on a practical level.[15] But Henry Kissinger, Nixon's national security advisor, was not so sure: he thought that with de Gaulle gone, the influence of the left on French foreign policy would grow.[16]

THE FIRST CONTACTS BETWEEN
POMPIDOU AND THE AMERICANS

Georges Pompidou took office as president in April 1969, and he soon made it clear that he wanted to put relations with the United States on a new footing. He met with Ambassador Shriver in July of that year, and the tone of his remarks was quite different from what de Gaulle's had been. The new president took it as self-evident that Europe needed the American strategic umbrella and that France in particular needed the Atlantic alliance. The French policy of military independence, he said, was not directed against the United States; it might in fact ease the American defense burden, and might also promote America's policy of détente with the East. An understanding was also possible in the economic area, especially in the agricultural area. Pompidou even suggested that the European Economic Community's—the EEC's—Common Agricultural Policy might be reconsidered, and that France might be willing to move toward a system where European agricultural prices were in line with those on the world market. Such a move, he said, would not just be to America's interest, but would be to France's interest as well. (It was, in fact, West Germany that had demanded high prices for wheat, and not Paris).[17] Pompidou, moreover, was not opposed in principle to American investment in France—another striking change from the previous period. A more liberal policy in this area, he suggested, could be put into effect as soon as the French electric and electronic industries were restructured.[18]

Another straw in the wind had to do with the German question. On November 6, Michel Jobert, secretary-general at the Elysée—that is, head of the president's office—told Shriver that Pompidou would be very happy to improve Franco-American relations because he feared a revival of German nationalism and wanted American support to counterbalance that threat.[19] In reality, Pompidou's German policy was much more complex than that, and it is doubtful that he viewed that issue so simplistically.[20] But the real point to note in this context is that Franco-American relations were changing—that the French were reaching out to the United States. American officials were struck by the change in atmosphere and were pleased by the way things were developing.[21]

It should also be noted in passing—the subject cannot be discussed in any detail here—that under Pompidou, the French provided considerable diplomatic assistance to the Americans in connection with the Vietnam War, particularly in its final phase in 1972. They were noticeably more cooperative in this area during the period of the Pompidou presidency than they had been when his predecessor was in charge. This again indicates that attitudes had changed considerably.[22] Or to give one final example: in 1970, Pompidou appointed Alexandre de Marenches director of the SDECE, the French secret service. Marenches's friendship for America was well known and he worked closely with the CIA and other Western services.[23]

But not all was sweetness and light, and the two sides did not see eye-to-eye on a whole series of issues—issues that we are going to encounter over and over again. First of all, there were problems having to do with monetary questions, especially the Eurodollar problem and the American balance of payments deficit. These posed specific problems in connection with plans for a European monetary union. And then there were problems having to do with the U.S.–Soviet negotiations on strategic weapons—the Strategic Arms Limitation Talks (or the SALT talks, as they were called). An agreement in this area, the French feared, might weaken the American nuclear guarantee. Those talks, moreover, might lead Washington and Moscow to view third nuclear powers as sources of instability, to be controlled in case of crisis. Another issue had to do with the proposal made by the Atlantic alliance in late 1969 for a conference on "mutual and balanced force reduction" (MBFR) in Europe. The Americans favored the proposal, but the French were against the idea. Aside from the fact that France was opposed in principle to all "bloc to bloc" negotiations (a standard Gaullist reflex), Pompidou was also afraid that an agreement in this area might actually worsen the conventional balance and lead to a kind of neutralization of Europe. On the other hand, Paris favored the idea of a conference on security in Europe (an old Soviet proposal renewed in March 1969), partly because the French felt the desire for détente on the part of most European countries could not be opposed forever, and partly because they thought it might allow countries like Poland or Romania to recover a small margin for maneuver. The American reaction to that proposal was much more reserved.

But whatever their differences, Paris was inclined to talk quite seriously with Washington about all of these issues.[24] And one should also note that French reservations about American policy on these matters had to do essentially with those points that threatened to weaken the unity of the West vis-à-vis the USSR, which was certainly a new theme. Pompidou, moreover, made it clear that in his view it was "natural" that the United States should participate in a conference on security in Europe. He noted explicitly, in a letter to Nixon—and this phrase is very important—that America was not "foreign to European problems."[25] This, of course, marked quite a change from the sort of position de Gaulle had stood for.

This shift away from the de Gaulle policy—this thaw in Franco-American relations—was, right from the start, most striking in the area of defense. Almost immediately, and at the highest political level, the French expressed the desire to renew bilateral contacts with Washington on military issues in general, and especially on weapons development.[26] This caught the attention of Nixon and Kissinger and set off a whole process of reflection in Washington.[27] On February 23, 1970, just before Pompidou was scheduled to visit Washington, Kissinger summed up for Nixon the conclusions that had been reached. All questions of a "theological" nature relating to Atlantic integration were to be set aside; the special position of France in the alliance would be accepted; a process of rapprochement should begin and should focus on things that could be done on the practical level. If the French were interested, areas of cooperation might include joint planning or coordinated targeting for the two countries' strategic forces. The same sort of planning for tactical nuclear forces, given that France would soon have such forces, was also possible. Cooperation on the development and production of nuclear weapons and missiles was a more complicated issue, if only because for legal reasons Congress would have to be involved. But if the French requested it, the Americans could indicate that they were willing to consider something of the sort, in certain specific areas.[28] But this was basically Kissinger's view: it was clear that other elements within the administration—the Defense Department, for example—were reluctant to move ahead so rapidly in that direction.[29]

POMPIDOU'S FEBRUARY 1970
VISIT TO THE UNITED STATES

It is well known that Georges Pompidou's visit to the United States in February 1970 was marked by major anti-French demonstrations in Chicago; the protesters had been angered by the French decision to sell arms to Libya.[30] But there had been warning signs, and it seems that this particular problem was rooted in the fact that French officials had not understood that in the United States, the municipal authorities were responsible for security and public order, and that preparations for the trip therefore needed to be made on the local level.[31] The files also show that, while the consuls in New York and San Francisco were very active in this area, the consul in Chicago apparently did less. Pompidou, moreover, clearly had not been aware of how strongly the American Jewish community felt about the sale of arms to Libya, nor did he do much to reach out to that community. And he refused to issue a general declaration that took a relatively balanced position on the Arab-Israeli question, even though one of his advisors had suggested that he might do so.[32] In fact, he told Jewish leaders in San Francisco on February 27 that a careful distinction had to be made between the question of Israel as a state and the question of Judaism as a religion; as he saw it, Israel's only chance of solving its security problems was if it came to see itself as a state among other states in the Middle East and not as a "religious community."[33] But at that time, this sort of language was bound to fall on deaf ears.

That sort of language, moreover, tended to give a misleading impression of what Pompidou's own Middle Eastern policy was. While pursuing and even developing the "Arab policy" of his predecessor, he in fact had softened French policy in this area. The total embargo on arms to Israel imposed on

January 1, 1969, was revoked on June 29, 1969. Instead, there would be a return to the selective embargo established in 1967; France would thus be able to furnish Israel with spare parts for weapons that had already been sold, which was in fact done.[34] Moreover, he accepted the idea—and this marked a major break with de Gaulle's policy—that the United States and the USSR could begin jointly to explore the possibility of a solution in the Middle East, a view that explicitly recognized America's role as Israel's protector.[35]

So the sense that there was a problem here was based in part on a misunderstanding. Some observers at the time thought that the Chicago incidents had turned Pompidou against the United States, and had a real effect on his later policy.[36] But in reality it does not seem that those incidents had a major impact: the course of Franco-American relations depended on structural, not accidental, factors. And it is a mistake to think that Pompidou's experiences during his American trip were entirely negative.

In fact, the new French leader's meetings with Nixon on February 24 and 26 went well. The two men agreed that international politics was becoming more multipolar in character, with America, Russia, Western Europe, China, and Japan all playing a role. They agreed also on the need to pursue a cautious policy vis-à-vis the USSR, on the importance of not isolating China, and on the need for the Germans to keep their partners in the West informed in detail about the progress of their *Ostpolitik*.[37] Nixon, moreover, recognized the French desire for independence.

By far the most important part of their discussion related to military matters. They agreed that secret bilateral talks between military officers from the two countries could take place—within the NATO framework, but outside the integrated structures—with a view toward preparing joint plans. In 1967, in the Ailleret-Lemnitzer accords, France and NATO had worked out certain arrangements in this area, but that agreement had applied only to the part of the French army stationed in Germany. Pompidou, however, was now inclined to extend that principle and work out a coordination of forces agreement that would cover all of France's military forces in Europe. He was also willing to revive the committee the two countries had established in 1962 to discuss cooperation in the area of conventional weapons. And he suggested that when its missile-launching submarines and tactical nuclear weapons became operational two or three years down the road, France might want to extend that cooperation to the nuclear area. The two men agreed that such discussions would not affect each country's freedom of decision in a crisis. They agreed, moreover, that confidential lines of communication were to be established: between Kissinger and Jobert on political issues, and between General Goodpaster, the NATO commander and U.S. commander in Europe, and General Fourquet, the French armed forces chief of staff, on military issues.[38] The damage that the relationship had suffered in the 1963–1968 period was in the process of being repaired. Nixon, moreover, had put France on a par with Britain, in terms both of its international status and of its relationship to the United States—a position the French had been trying to achieve for many years.

THE DEVELOPMENT OF FRANCO-AMERICAN RELATIONS IN 1970–1971

In 1970–1971, Paris and Washington agreed that, taken as a whole, Franco-American relations were developing favorably, especially on European issues.[39] They both felt it was important to pay close attention to the development of West German Chancellor Willy Brandt's *Ostpolitik,* not because they feared a revival of German danger, a fear they both considered outmoded, but rather because they were afraid that West Germany might give away too much to the USSR. As Kissinger told Charles Lucet, the French ambassador to Washington, on April 13, 1970, there was a danger that Brandt would give the Russians "essential things."[40] If there were to be an East-West agreement, Kissinger continued, "it would be made between the United States and the USSR, and not between the Germans and the USSR"—a point, however, that touched on a continuing French concern. The French government, for its part, did support the initial phase of *Ostpolitik,* the phase that led to the signing of treaties with the Eastern bloc countries recognizing the de facto division of Germany and the 1945 borders. But the French wondered about the Germans' ultimate goals; they were worried that their real aim was to bring about the reunification of Germany by creating a new European security system based on what was in effect a kind of German-Soviet entente. Pompidou might have been quite pleased to see the Germans accept—or appear to accept—the postwar status quo, but he was worried that eventually the *Ostpolitik* might develop into a far-reaching Russo-German rapprochement—something that would lead to German reunification, and that would have a profound effect on France's own security.

Ever since the 1950s, French policy had been based on the concept of "double security": with Germany divided, that country could pose no threat, and on the other hand the security of France vis-à-vis the USSR would be guaranteed by the alliance with the United States, and also by the integration of West Germany into Western Europe and into the West in general. In 1966, disappointed by the fact that the Franco-German treaty of January 1963 had led to little of real value, de Gaulle had begun to think in very different terms. His idea now—this was the period of his trip to Moscow—was that a new security system could be constructed, a system based essentially on a Franco-Soviet entente aimed at controlling German power, a system that would marginalize the United States. But in this area, Pompidou opted for a more traditional approach to these great issues, and his geopolitical vision of the future of Germany, the USSR, and Europe was more compatible with good Franco-American relations.[41]

Indeed, during his trip to the USSR in October 1970, Pompidou resisted Soviet leader Leonid Brezhnev's attempts to get him to in effect repeat what de Gaulle had said in Moscow in 1966 about France "favoring a gradual elimination of American influence in Europe." Europe certainly should be able to "get out from under the influence of the United States" and "be fully European," but the influence of America on the Continent resulted from the Soviet military threat and from the need to counter Soviet power with American military power and indeed with the military power of the whole Atlantic alliance. Only a genuine détente could change that situation, but it was mainly up to the USSR to bring that about. There could be no question of replacing what Pompidou refused to call "American domination" with "Soviet domination."[42]

On this fundamental issue of the Paris-Washington-Moscow triangular relationship, Pompidou's position was thus quite different from what de Gaulle's had been, even if he too wanted a "European Europe." He outlined the rationale for that new policy in a December 1, 1970, conversation with Sulzberger. "The basis of my thinking" on that issue, Pompidou said, was that France was bound to move "closer to the United States as U.S. superiority over Russia diminishes. My foreign policy, therefore, is less anti-American in its expression than de Gaulle's, because he strongly felt American superiority over the Soviet Union and other countries and believed he had to oppose this."[43]

It is also to be noted—and this too was new—that Pompidou wanted to talk seriously with the Americans about specific areas of tension in Europe, and in particular about the Soviet threat to Romania and to Yugoslavia, something the Western powers were very much concerned with in 1971.[44] The Soviets were aware of that, and suspected the French of deviating from de Gaulle's policy of "independence."[45]

On the military level, things were also developing favorably. On March 10, 1970, following Pompidou's trip to America, and on Kissinger's advice, Nixon approved a whole series of measures. General Goodpaster, first of all, was authorized to explore with General Fourquet all practical ways of improving cooperation with the French armed forces. In particular, the two generals could consider what arrangements were possible in the area of tactical nuclear weapons, and what sort of cooperation might be possible on naval questions. They would also discuss how plans for the use of strategic nuclear forces might be coordinated, taking care, on this issue, to respect the French decision to reject the principle of alliance-wide military "integration," and with the proviso that any arrangements they worked out would ultimately have to be approved by the two presidents. The Franco-American committee on conventional weapons, set up in 1962 but dormant since 1966, would be reactivated; the possibility of assisting the French with their missile program would be studied; a 1964 decision of the Johnson administration (NSAM 294), which ruled out all aid to the French relating to nuclear weapons and missiles, would be put aside for the time being.[46]

Not everyone in Washington was as willing as Nixon and Kissinger were to resume military collaboration with the French. Secretary of Defense Melvin Laird, for example, ostensibly supported the idea of missile assistance, but he was in fact not very eager to change policy in this area. In an April 1970 memorandum, he emphasized possible difficulties with Congress and possible repercussions on the SALT negotiations with the Soviets. And he too thought that whatever exchanges did take place should not "provide any significant technical impetus to French capabilities"—at least not at first. But if that were the case, the French would scarcely find an American offer of assistance particularly attractive! He wanted the French, moreover, to give America certain things in return for whatever they did get. They would, for example, have to take part in the study of strategy in the coming decade that NATO had begun.[47] But this sort of condition would be hard for the French to accept. It was clear that they were determined to stay out of the "integrated" NATO system, the system they had officially left in 1966; they therefore were unwilling to participate in exercises of this sort, exercises which, they were afraid, might pull them back into the "integrated" system through the back door. As Pompidou noted on April 24, Paris was willing to discuss these issues of strategy bilaterally with the Americans, just not within the multilateral NATO framework.[48] There is no better illustration of the ongoing French concern for a special relationship with Washington, the same sort of relationship the British had—indeed, for a relationship with the Americans that would allow France to play a pivotal and strategically central role in the Western world as a whole.

Kissinger chose to go ahead without paying much attention to what Laird had said. On April 24, 1970, he decided to send John Foster to Paris. Foster, the Assistant Secretary of Defense in charge of weapons development, was told to take account of Laird's concerns concerning secrecy, Congress, and the SALT talks, but it was also emphasized that the president wanted to help the French. Foster, moreover, was to make it clear that American assistance would not depend on a rapprochement between France and NATO.[49] Kissinger and Nixon were not going to let "theological" issues relating to NATO stand in their way.

In the summer of 1970, things were moving ahead quite nicely. General Goodpaster had had his first discussions with General Fourquet; there had been progress on military cooperation in central Europe in the event of war, even if the French were not yet ready to talk about their (future) tactical nuclear weapons; and Assistant Secretary Foster had begun to talk privately with Jean Blancard, a high French defense official in charge of weapons development and procurement, about what the French would like in terms of missile cooperation. At the same time, and in all sorts of areas, the exchange of scientific information was proceeding at an increasing pace; there was in fact more cooperation with France in this area than with any other country.[50]

But, as Kissinger's assistant Helmut Sonnenfeldt pointed out to him on August 3, 1970, all of those issues had been dealt with on an ad hoc basis; now things had to be systematized. There had to be a doctrine approved by the president. A coordinating committee had to be set up in Washington to supervise the exchanges with the French. A series of basic judgments had to be made: should the U.S. government support the French nuclear program, and thus reverse the decision the Johnson administration had made in 1964? What effect would a decision to support the French in this area have on the SALT talks? Sonnenfeldt's discussion of this issue implied that he was in favor of supporting the French program, if only because if there were no nuclear coordination with France, the result in the event of an armed conflict in Europe might well be catastrophic for the alliance as a whole. French nuclear forces, moreover, in his judgment would not really be large enough to stand in the way of a SALT agreement. Clearly the best thing, in Sonnenfeldt's view, would be for a program of American nuclear assistance to be worked out within the framework of a common Anglo-Franco-American nuclear strategy, as British leaders now suggested.[51]

In the months that followed, National Security Council, Pentagon, and State Department officials continued to consider these issues. These discussions took place within an ad hoc committee responsible for preparing a National Security Study Memorandum (what was to become NSSM 100) on military relations with France. It was not very easy to work out a new policy. The military authorities were against making any concessions for France unless it rejoined the integrated NATO organization, at least in practice. And it was also understood that Congress would be reluctant to accept a fundamental change of policy. Some officials were also worried about how other allies—West Germany above all—might react if a special bilateral relationship with France took shape in this area.[52] Given all these concerns, Kissinger therefore had to intervene repeatedly to keep things moving.[53]

Finally, in late March, the committee agreed on certain recommendations of rather limited scope, which were then approved by the president (in National Security Decision Memoranda, or NSDM's, 103 and 104). There would be a certain relaxation of the rules governing the export of supercomputers essential for the development of nuclear weapons. As for missiles, the French might be helped to improve the reliability of their existing systems, but the Americans would not help them develop systems that would allow those weapons to be targeted more accurately. (The French had been interested in getting help in that area). On warhead design proper, the Americans would limit themselves to resuming the talks, broken off in 1963, dealing with the procedures and systems for preventing accidents and guarding against unauthorized use.[54]

A memorandum was then handed over to the French on May 5, 1971, proposing discussions relating to missile technology, nuclear weapons safety, and high-powered computers.[55] That led to a meeting between Foster and Blancard in Paris on May 12 on the missile question. Blancard agreed completely that the exchanges should deal solely with the reliability of the existing systems. His main concern, in fact, was to make sure that the systems then under development, which apparently were having certain problems, would function correctly. He was not at that point interested in asking the Americans for help in developing a more advanced generation of missiles. The two men met again on June 15, and at that second meeting, Foster gave Blancard a draft of an agreement for cooperation on missiles and nuclear weapons safety.[56] On July 22, Blancard was authorized to sign that agreement and begin discussions in those two areas. It is important to note that this accord went far beyond what had initially been decided upon in Washington. It provided that arrangements could be made relating to missile guidance and accuracy and to the hardening of warheads (so that they could survive attack from a nuclear-based, antiballistic missile defense system, such as the Soviet Galosh ABM system)—a major development, even if the arrangements in those areas would be subject to special restrictions.[57] One thus has the impression that some U.S. officials wanted to go a bit beyond what was generally acceptable within the government. There were more discussions between Blancard and Foster, in Washington this time, in November. On the 12th, Foster formally proposed that the two sides begin discussions on nuclear weapons safety.

The Paris authorities, for their part, were quite interested in getting information from the Americans that would allow them to improve their missile systems—and to gain time and save money in the process. But independence was still a fundamental French concern, and for them as for the Americans, there were limits beyond which they would not go. The feeling on the French side was that in no case should the talks allow the Americans to get a clear sense of either the operational value of the French missiles or a clear understanding of the French system for strategic command and control. Moreover, under no circumstances should the Americans be in a position to intimate to the Soviets that these technical arrangements gave the United States any sort of control over the French nuclear force. So each side held back, albeit for somewhat different reasons.[58] But within those limits there were still many areas in which a considerable degree of cooperation was possible. The Goodpaster-Fourquet discussions about coordinating French military plans with those of NATO could proceed. The Ailleret-Lemnitzer accords of 1967 could be brought up to date (and another meeting for that purpose took place on January 27, 1971). But none of this meant that the French forces were to be placed under NATO command: French independence was not being compromised, and in a crisis France would remain free to act as it chose. Finally, the French were inclined to limit many of these arrangements, for the time being, to the French forces in Germany, and preferred not to extend them right away to the whole French army in Europe—something that would have raised various problems relating to the French short-range Pluton missile and the use of tactical nuclear weapons more generally before the French were ready to discuss them.[59]

So by the end of 1970, relations between the two countries were better than they had been in years. The only real problem in Franco-American relations was the international monetary question: in December, France again started buying gold, and again began to criticize American monetary and economic policy and complain about its negative impact on Europe.[60]

THE LIMITS OF MILITARY COOPERATION: HARDWARE YES, SOFTWARE NO!

The French were inclined to talk with the Americans about weaponry—about "hardware" (and even then with the reservations just noted)—rather than about the principles that would govern the actual use of nuclear weapons—that is, about "software." The basic 1966 decision to leave the integrated NATO system was not going to be reversed. To give but one example: after a serious and rather animated Defense Council discussion held at the Elysée Palace on February 26, 1971, a 1967 decision relating to the oil pipelines built by NATO on French territory was reaffirmed: in peacetime, those pipelines would continue to supply NATO forces in Germany; but if war broke out, France would be free to decide whether those pipelines would continue to be used in that way. This ostensibly technical issue raised the whole problem of the interpretation of Article V of the North Atlantic Treaty: Paris was in effect insisting on preserving its complete freedom of action, even for an act of assistance (making the pipelines available), which would not be a military action in the strict sense and would not mean that France would actually be taking part in the war. This was a very limited reading of Article V, and its legality was actually questioned by certain French diplomats. Pompidou was thus upholding the strictest possible interpretation of France's freedom of decision in the event of a crisis.[61] Beyond its general implications about France's relationship with NATO (the steadfast refusal of any automatic commitment of French forces), the pipeline question was a major source of irritation for Americans. They could no longer be sure that the pipelines, and indeed the entire French logistical system, would be available in the event of war. This to them was the most serious consequence of

France's withdrawal from NATO in 1966, and they hoped that the military rapprochement with Paris would allow this problem to be reconsidered sometime in the future.[62]

Not every major French official wanted to remain so aloof. Certain officials (like François de Rose, France's representative in the North Atlantic Council) were struck by the way American attitudes on strategic issues were changing. The Americans, in their view, were increasingly reluctant to contemplate the use not just of strategic but also of tactical nuclear weapons; they were also interested in reducing the American military presence in Europe and seeing the Europeans build up their own conventional capabilities. What this meant, as those officials analyzed the situation, was that the French authorities needed to talk with their American counterparts about the doctrine for the use of nuclear weapons, and especially for the use of France's own tactical nuclear weapons, such as the Pluton short-range missiles that were due to become operational in 1973; when they were deployed, a problem of coordination with NATO would naturally arise.[63] Pompidou categorically refused to consider anything of the sort: France had to make its "independence" abundantly clear; the prospect of talks with Washington on nuclear doctrine aroused his "greatest distrust."[64] He was afraid the Americans "would try to draw us into a discussion about our relations with them in the area of defense and nuclear weapons."[65] As for the Plutons, while the plan in 1970 had been to station them with the French forces in Germany (the fissionable core remaining stockpiled in France in normal times) by the beginning of 1971, the French were leaning toward the idea of keeping them in France. That would reduce problems with the Germans, who were worried about having their own territory targeted to an even greater extent than it already was, and who were particularly concerned about missiles with such a short (seventy-five mile) range. Keeping the Plutons in France would help preserve Paris's freedom of decision in the event of war, and would help the French government delay what it knew would be a difficult discussion with the Americans about doctrine for the use of those weapons.[66]

POMPIDOU AND THE ARMS CONTROL TALKS
WITH THE SOVIETS (SALT AND MBFR)

Despite the military rapprochement with Washington, the Gaullist dogma of national independence was still alive and well during the Pompidou period. But under Pompidou, that dogma took on a somewhat different coloration: Pompidou did not share some of de Gaulle's long-term goals, and for him "independence" was understood in a rather different way. This will become clear when we examine the French attitude toward the arms control talks with Moscow: SALT and MBFR. On these issues, Paris and Washington did not see eye-to-eye, and the gap between them actually widened, beginning especially in 1972. But Pompidou's point of view on these matters was only partially rooted in Gaullist principles. His main concern in fact was to maintain the strategic unity of the West vis-à-vis the USSR, which was not at all in line with de Gaulle's basic thinking.

As early as 1971, the French realized that the United States and the Soviet Union would probably soon reach an agreement limiting the size of their strategic forces, and that such an agreement might well affect France in some very basic ways. It might affect the political and military value of France's own nuclear force, and the French might also have to deal with American and Soviet pressure for the inclusion of French forces in the agreement.[67] So the French were concerned, and knew that they had to follow the SALT negotiations with great care.

With regard to the MBFR negotiations, their attitude was far more negative. They in fact rejected the very idea of such talks. Their fear was that an MBFR agreement would lead to a withdrawal of the American troops stationed in Europe, a constant fear in Paris during Pompidou period. It might also lead to a neutralization of central Europe, which in turn would allow the USSR to exert continuing pressure on Europe as a whole. Again, it is important to note that this was certainly not a "Gaullist" way of looking at things.[68] It was also feared that an MBFR agreement would rule out the possibility of a "European" defense of Europe, an option that Pompidou wanted to keep open.[69]

But Pompidou's greatest worry was that the Americans might be leaning toward a policy of disengagement; if that were true, an MBFR accord might well facilitate the implementation of such a policy—that is, it might lead to the withdrawal of foreign forces from both Germanies. The feeling was that this in turn might rapidly lead to the emergence of a politically free and re-unified, and indeed nuclearized, Germany; this set of concerns was also linked to the fear that reunification was the ultimate goal of West Germany's *Ostpolitik*.[70] As Pompidou saw the situation, if the West—the U.S. government above all—did not rein in the *Ostpolitik* and was not very careful in the arms control talks with the USSR, one of two things would happen. Either West Germany would end up falling under Soviet influence, or a reunified Germany, a nuclearized Germany, would again play a fully independent role in international affairs. Either result would be a disaster for France. Again, this had not been de Gaulle's view at all: Germany, in the general's view, could be kept in line by working with the Soviets, and indeed by establishing a new security system in Europe—a system based on a kind of Franco-Soviet entente, and one in which the Americans would play a marginal role.[71] Like most French political figures, both men were opposed to German reunification, but Pompidou approached the German question in a far more "Western" context and was more distrustful of the USSR than de Gaulle had been.

THE AZORES SUMMIT AND ITS
DISAPPOINTING AFTERMATH

Nixon and Pompidou met in the Azores in December 1971. The famous "Nixon shocks"—the announcement in July that the American president would soon visit Peking and the suspension of dollar convertibility on August 15—had come earlier that year. Paris had welcomed the U.S. decision on China; that move seemed to imply that the French had been right to recognize Peking in 1964, and it made obvious geopolitical sense.[72] But the U.S. decision to end convertibility—the U.S. decision, that is, to put an end to the Bretton Woods monetary system—was viewed in an entirely different light. And indeed the monetary issue was to be a major source of Franco-American discord in this period.

It was in fact to be one of three major areas of disagreement, the other two being the question of a conference on security in Europe (which Paris wanted but which Washington still opposed), and the MBFR issue (on which positions were reversed).[73] The complex discussions Pompidou, Nixon, and Kissinger had on December 13 and 14 will not be reviewed in detail here, but it is important to give some sense of what went on at the Azores meeting.[74] The French president had sought that summit, and he presented himself there as a sort of spokesman for Europe. His whole strategy at the Azores meeting, ostensibly accepted by Nixon and Kissinger, was to place the monetary problem in the broader context of the political solidarity of the West as a whole. "France," he told his American partners, "is a western country, for that reason, and for historical reasons as well, she is determined to maintain the alliance and remain friendly with the United States." The monetary issue was to be dealt with in that framework. And for Pompidou, a former banker who was resolved to modernize France and place it firmly in the world economy, the monetary issue was of fundamental importance in its own right. But the way he framed that issue typified the basic Pompidou approach to foreign policy: France wanted to develop the European Economic Community and sought to play a decisive role in the EEC, but that "European" orientation was to be balanced by the cultivation of a certain relationship with Washington, a relationship that would actually strengthen the French position in Europe. The goal was to put "theology" aside and strike a balance that made practical sense—not just a balance between Europe and America, but a balance in France's relationship with America. France would be neither satellite nor challenger—indeed it made little sense to try to compete with America, since if forced to choose, no one in Europe at that time would follow France.

On the political issues, the two leaders thus reached agreement rather easily. Détente with the USSR, they both felt, was necessary, but one had to proceed cautiously in this area, and the *Ostpolitik* also had to be pursued with great care; U.S. troops had to be kept in Europe, and congressional pressure for withdrawal needed to be resisted; the Sino-American rapprochement was to be pursued. In the monetary area, however, the talks were very difficult, but ended in compromise. The dollar would be devalued (since the French balance of trade with the United States showed a 50 percent deficit, that was an important concession for Paris), but there would be a return to a system of fixed exchange rates. Those fixed rates would be different from what they had been, but once set they would be defended. This point was essential for France. It was connected both to the problem of its internal economic equilibrium and to the very delicate problem of the relationship between the franc and the German mark. Moreover, in a secret agreement, the Americans promised eventually to restore the convertibility of the dollar, which was obviously essential if a new and solid fixed exchange rate system was to be put in place, a system in which the Americans would play a key role.

As it turned out, those U.S. commitments were honored only in part. The so-called Smithsonian Agreement of December 18, 1971, which was supposed to implement the Azores decisions, did set new exchange rates. (The dollar was devalued by 7.9 percent, the pound and the franc retained their old value and were, in fact, revalued by 8.57 percent with respect to the dollar, the mark was revalued by 13.58 percent and stopped floating, and the yen was revalued by 16.88 percent.) But the dollar remained nonconvertible and the Americans made no promise to defend the dollar at that new level. It followed that the maintenance of that new exchange rate depended on the willingness of the central banks outside of the United States to accumulate unlimited quantities of dollars. So the Smithsonian Agreement was very fragile. Floating the dollar was thus inevitable, for if the dollar was not convertible into gold, its devaluation with respect to gold no longer had any meaning.

Indeed, with the floating of the pound in 1972, the limited value of the Smithsonian Agreement became apparent. A new monetary crisis that erupted in February 1973 led to an additional 10 percent devaluation of the dollar. That in turn led on March 16 to the historic decision to allow the European currencies to float jointly against the dollar. The Bretton Woods system of fixed exchange rates—even "adjustable" fixed rates, as they were called for a time—had thus been effectively abandoned, even before it was officially abandoned at the Jamaica Conference in January 1976. The Americans had thus achieved a goal that at least some U.S. officials had been aiming for since 1971: freed of the constraints imposed by a system of fixed exchange rates, the United States could henceforth allow the dollar to move in accordance with America's commercial interests; at the same time, the United States would benefit from the fact that the dollar would continue to serve as a transnational currency, and that meant that the chronic U.S. payments deficit could continue, and that even U.S. capital exports did not have to be limited.[75] This represented a fundamental shift in the policy the Americans had followed since 1947: from this point on, the strictly national interests of the United States, in a very basic area, were now more important than America's responsibilities as leader of the Free World.[76]

The failure of the Azores Conference was a failure for the Pompidou concept of a Europe led by France that collaborates with America on an equal footing in a basically united Western world. Pompidou, who had been more accommodating on monetary matters than de Gaulle had been, was well aware of what had happened. He complained to Nixon on February 4, 1972, that the United States had not kept its promises: "When we met in the Azores," he wrote, "I of course understood that there was no longer any question of a return to full convertibility for your currency [into gold, which the French had previously sought]. But, as I indicated there, if you agreed to control capital movements, if you developed a system that would stabilize the foreign dollar balances, if you agreed to establish a system that would enable you to defend the value of your currency by buying dollars in exchange for other currencies, then for all practical purposes we would have full currency-to-currency convertibility." Nixon, Pompidou continued, had alluded in a message to Congress to a growing acceptance of flexible exchange rates, but that general attitude, the French president pointed out, "did not appear to be in line with the commitments you and I made" at the Azores meeting.[77] Washington had not taken any steps to control U.S. capital exports, a key issue for the French, who criticized the Americans for buying up European firms with dollars that were accepted abroad because of that currency's international role—dollars that were accepted in spite of the fact that the United States was running a payments deficit year after year, and were thus, in a sense, devoid of real exchange value. One important point to be noted here is that Pompidou did not demand a return to the gold standard, as de Gaulle had done in 1965—and that fact meant that compromise was not out of the question. But Nixon's rather vague February 16 reply showed that the U.S. government was not really interested in reaching one. Reviewing that exchange on March 28, 1973, in the light of what had subsequently transpired, Jean-René Bernard, who followed issues of international finance at the Elysée, noted: "these documents show that the Americans do not really think the monetary commitments they made at the Azores are to be taken seriously."[78] The deterioration of Franco-American relations that followed had a good deal to do with the fact that such beliefs had taken hold in Paris.

French officials were in fact fully aware of the fragility and temporary character of the Smithsonian Agreement. At a meeting on monetary issues held on February 7, 1972, finance minister Valéry Giscard d'Estaing outlined the situation. Either the Smithsonian Agreement would be implemented, or the crisis could serve as an occasion to take another step toward European economic and monetary union. Pompidou strongly expressed his preference for that latter solution, since choosing the first would be tantamount to "admitting that the United States was in charge of world economic and monetary policy." The Germans would also have to make the same choice: they would not be able to go against Europe despite their tendency to follow the United States.[79] Pompidou had thus crossed a certain threshold: in the final analysis, a European monetary agreement was more important than getting the Americans to accept a fixed exchange rate system. For the French, this was a complete conceptual about-face. An agreement of that sort could now be negotiated, and, as noted above, a very important agreement that provided for a common float of the European currencies against the dollar was actually signed the following year.

The monetary question was thus one of the key factors that led to the recasting of Pompidou's American policy in 1973. From that point on, the French sought less to play the role of intermediary between the United States and Europe. It was more important now to try to organize Europe—that is, to create a strong European counterweight to American preponderance within the Western world—and this marked a certain return of Gaullism. The U.S. embassy in Paris, for its part, noted the damage the monetary question had caused and sensed that French policy was coming to have a more "European" orientation.[80]

POLITICO-MILITARY RELATIONS IN 1972

The French may have been disappointed by the results of the Azores Summit, but in the military area, Franco-American relations continued to improve in 1972. Defense minister Michel Debré, for example, was struck by how forthcoming the Americans were in the Foster-Blancard talks. The U.S. government, he wrote Pompidou in March, was offering technical information of the utmost importance. "We are justified," he said, "in thinking that the American leaders intend to provide us with very valuable assistance—that is, that they consider it in their interest to support and improve the development of our nuclear force. They are asking us for absolutely nothing in return."[81] The Americans had clearly gone much further than what had been officially agreed upon in Washington.

On July 7 and 12, Debré had a series of conversations in Washington with Kissinger, Laird, and Nixon.[82] Those discussions developed along very positive lines; indeed, the Franco-American relationship in this area was marked by a certain intimacy. Debré asked for information about the Soviet radar system and Soviet ABM defenses; that information was essential if the French nuclear force was to be able to attack Soviet targets effectively. Kissinger promised to provide that information to him directly if the relevant government agencies proved unwilling to turn it over themselves. This, incidentally, again indicates that the president's advisor had moved well beyond the cautious policy that the administration as a whole had been able to agree upon. Laird, for his part, promised that the MacMahon law about atomic secrecy would be interpreted liberally after Nixon was reelected in November. As a result of these discussions, General Walters, the deputy director of the CIA, would meet with Debré in September to provide him with the information about the Soviet ABM defenses; this highly technical information was extremely confidential, and had been obtained by American intelligence agencies using very advanced methods.[83]

The SALT issue was, of course, more of a problem. The basic SALT agreements were signed in May 1972; the French were worried about how their country might be affected. On June 13, the French president wondered aloud, in a meeting with Soviet foreign minister Gromyko, whether the SALT agreements "did not correspond more or less to a kind of desire to establish a condominium over the rest of the world." This "condominium" theme would recur frequently later on.[84] Moreover, France ran the risk of being at least indirectly involved because of its own nuclear force. Nixon wrote to Pompidou on June 9 to tell him about his trip to Moscow, and in that letter he alluded to the SALT agreements. The Soviets had demanded the right, Nixon said, to increase the number of their nuclear submarines if France and Great Britain went beyond their programmed total of nine nuclear submarines (four British and five French; there was a strong interest in building a sixth French nuclear submarine so that at least two would always be at sea). Nixon had categorically rejected that demand, but it was clear that Moscow would bring it up again during the next phase of the negotiations and that Paris and Washington would have to reach a common view on the subject. Pompidou answered on July 1 in a way that made France's very cautious attitude on that point quite clear.[85]

Another point of great concern to France was the Soviet-sponsored idea of a treaty in which the United States and the USSR would each promise not to use nuclear weapons against the other. Obviously, the Americans were not inclined to accept something that was so totally at variance with basic NATO strategy, but they did not think they could respond in a purely negative way. Brezhnev and his détente policy—opposed, in their view, by elements within the Soviet leadership—were to be supported; a simple rejection would therefore not be a good idea.[86] That U.S. position worried the French quite a bit: the West, in their view, could not rule out the possibility that it might use nuclear weapons first. And there was another point in the draft treaty that they particularly disliked, the point about how America and Russia should cooperate in preventing situations from developing in which third parties might bring about a U.S.–Soviet nuclear confrontation. This might well apply to France, and it again raised the specter of a kind of U.S.–Soviet "condominium"—a theme that would become particularly important the following year.[87] Pompidou would express such concerns when Kissinger visited him on September 15, 1972; on that occasion Kissinger assured him that the United States would sign only a very general declaration aimed at ruling out the use of military force against any country.[88]

The French, of course, also remained opposed to the MBFR talks. They were quite concerned that the U.S. government, under pressure from Congress and public opinion, was increasingly inclined to contemplate a reduction in U.S. force levels in Europe.[89] Paris continued to refuse to take part in those talks, even indirectly.

In early 1973, even though bilateral French-American relations were good, the best they had been in a long time—this was reflected in the fact that anti-American rhetoric had disappeared both in official discourse and in the government-controlled media—there were still important differences of opinion on certain multilateral problems. There were, in particular, problems relating to the SALT and MBFR negotiations and to the preparations for the Conference on Security and Cooperation in Europe (CSCE): the French, as we have seen, were concerned about the SALT talks and disliked the whole idea of an MBFR agreement; on the other hand, they were more enthusiastic than the Americans about the CSCE. But the real area of conflict—the three issues that would dominate Franco-American relations in the 1973–1974 period—lay elsewhere. First, there was the monetary problem. And then there was a series of economic problems, relating specifically to the EEC's Common Agricultural Policy and the question of special economic arrangements between Europe and Africa. Such issues were rooted in a more general conflict between the particular economic structures the Europeans had put in place, and the American pressure for the dismantling of such structures in order to bring about a more liberal international trading system. Finally, and most importantly, there was the American goal of creating a framework within which the U.S. government could "deal with Western Europe as a whole on a basis which permits a comprehensive, closely linked discussion of the entire range of questions—security, political, monetary, trade, and investment—which comprise our interest in Europe."[90]

And it was precisely that idea—the idea of a more or less formal restructuring of the U.S.–European relationship on the basis of an American plan—that the French were to oppose so forcefully in 1973 and 1974. The United States, for its part, was quite determined in 1973 to resolve the international questions still on the agenda. The Americans intended to pursue the détente policy with the Soviets and lay the basis for a stable and durable U.S.–Soviet bilateral relationship, and they also intended to redefine their basic relationship with Europe. The French, the Americans hoped, might be induced to go along with that policy, but in no event would they be allowed to stand in its way.[91] The two sides were thus set on a collision course: from that point on, a clash with Paris was inevitable.

THE REYKJAVIK CONFERENCE (MAY 31–JUNE 1, 1973)

In the spring of 1973, developments proceeded as Washington had foreseen at the beginning of the year. On April 23, Kissinger had announced the "Year of Europe": during that year, U.S.–European relations were to be redefined around a new Atlantic Charter.[92] It should be noted at this point that Pompidou was indirectly the source of that initiative. Kissinger came up with the idea right after one of his meetings with Pompidou, and after the French president had suggested, in an interview with James Reston of the *New York Times*, that regular talks be held among the Western leaders "at the highest level." But Kissinger did not handle the "Year of Europe" initiative in a particularly skillful way, and that—combined with the fact that his real reasons for pressing that initiative were understood perfectly well in Paris—led to a major crisis with France.[93]

During this time, the Americans together with the Soviets were working out the agreement "for the prevention of nuclear war," which Brezhnev was due to sign in California on June 22. Furthermore, as Kissinger and the Soviets had agreed in September 1972, negotiations on security in Europe had begun in Helsinki on November 22, and the MBFR talks had begun in Vienna on January 30, 1973. In July, the ministers of foreign affairs were scheduled to meet in Helsinki to prepare for a CSCE. The international scene was thus quite active.

Georges Pompidou and the very Gaullist Michel Jobert, who had become minister of foreign affairs in April, were worried about what was going on. Were the Americans going to reach an agreement with the USSR at Europe's expense? On April 23, Kissinger gave a speech in which he had referred to Europe as a "regional entity" with limited interests. Was Washington out to dominate the Western world? Were the Americans trying to create a system in which Europe would fall in behind America's global policy, and indeed accommodate the Americans on economic issues (where Europe was in a relatively strong position vis-à-vis the United States) in exchange for the American security guarantee? Wasn't the plan for a new Atlantic Charter—for a restructuring of the U.S.–European relationship—just a kind of cover that would help America achieve its real goals? Jean-Bernard Raimond, Pompidou's diplomatic advisor, characterized that Kissinger speech as an "imperious text, one that fundamentally expresses the thirst for power of the United States"; it was reminiscent, he thought, of Kennedy's Philadelphia speech of July 4, 1962. The danger was that France's European partners might be tempted to go along with that American policy: "their preference was for an Atlantic world under American control."[94] Jacques Kosciusko-Morizet, the French ambassador in Washington, was worried about the agreement the Americans and the Soviets were negotiating on preventing nuclear war: with "the Americans seeking in effect to avoid any use of nuclear weapons, and with the Russians at the same time trying to denuclearize and neutralize Western Europe, by cutting it off from the United States and dismantling the system of the Atlantic alliance," the road that that agreement was opening up might well lead to disaster for Europe—and for France in particular.[95] Jean-Bernard Raimond shared those fears and, in early May, even went further. "Strengthening cooperation between the USSR and the United States," he told Pompidou, would threaten "the world political balance," and could result in "the political neutralization of third powers." He advised Pompidou to undertake a major policy initiative and approach France's European partners with the goal of opening up a serious discussion of these fundamental issues with the United States.[96]

The French were increasingly worried about the specter of a "U.S.–Soviet condominium" (a term that, as we have seen, Pompidou also used, but in his mind was directed at least as much against the USSR as against the United States), but that was not their only concern. There was also the monetary question; French officials objected to the U.S. government's refusal to submit to the slightest discipline in that area, and some of them continued to believe a return to the gold standard was possible. With regard to trade policy and the "Nixon Round" of trade negotiations, they noted Washington's opposition to the EEC's Common Agricultural Policy. In the area of energy policy—an area of growing tension even before the 1973 Yom Kippur War—they noted the U.S. government's wish (which Nixon's April 18 energy message had made clear) to form a bloc of oil-consuming nations to deal with the producers' cartel, something they viewed as very dangerous.[97] But the French authorities seemed divided among themselves as to what line to follow on these areas. The Washington embassy recommended negotiation and suggested possible compromises.[98] Others, like Olivier Wormser, governor-general of the Bank of France, thought it was necessary to remain firm: the United States itself, he thought, would someday return to the gold standard as the basis of the international monetary system.[99] As we have seen, Georges Pompidou did not share that illusion.

A new Pompidou-Nixon summit meeting was scheduled to take place in Reykjavik at the end of May, and to prepare for that meeting Kissinger and Pompidou met on May 18.[100] That meeting was very important: it was, in my view, the most open and most significant meeting that ever took place between Pompidou and an American leader. The French president in that May 18 meeting was quite accommodating. With regard to the "Year of Europe," he was not shocked by Kissinger's idea of Europe as a regional power (the region in question, however, would include the Mediterranean and Africa). He was not against the idea of bringing the Europeans and the Americans together to talk about all of the problems they faced, both economic and political—in other words, he was not against the idea of establishing a political framework within which U.S.–European economic problems could be dealt with. He was thus not opposed in principle to the notion of a "new Atlantic Charter." He was willing to talk about wheat at the Reykjavik meeting and was prepared to propose an entente among grain-exporting countries. The international monetary question would obviously have to be discussed, since things could not just be left as they were, but on this issue as well he clearly was prepared to approach the problem in a very pragmatic way. On one point he was firm: there could be no question of involving the United Kingdom as a third party in Franco-American military discussions. And he raised an excellent question concerning the impending U.S.–Soviet agreement on preventing nuclear war. The problem was not so much one of avoiding war, but rather preventing a series of moves the Soviets could make below the threshold of a war—the sort of move they had made against Czechoslovakia in 1968, the sort of action they might take against Yugoslavia when Tito died, or against China when Mao died. If the fear of war had held them back in the past, wasn't it possible that reducing that fear might lead them to move forward more actively in the future? "Brezhnev," he said, "is a pleasant man and a bon vivant, but he is not easy to stop when he moves forward." How did the Americans propose to halt "a camouflaged Soviet advance," one that took place without the actual use of force, like a stream that kept on moving? He thought the Americans did not realize the threat that the Soviet Union still posed to the West; he warned Kissinger against opting for the USSR over China.

Kissinger responded by unveiling the real strategy of the United States. There was absolutely no question, he said, of establishing a U.S.–Soviet condominium or of choosing Moscow over China. The U.S. goal instead was to support China—that is, to prevent the USSR from crushing China. If the Soviets were allowed to crush that country, they would go on to "Finlandize" Europe; the United States would then be isolated. But to prevent the Sino-American rapprochement, which was going to deepen in the years to come, from serving as a pretext for a Soviet attack on China, it was necessary to pursue a policy of détente with Moscow at the same time. The aim was to "gain time, to paralyze the USSR." The American strategy was "perhaps complex, but it was not stupid." The Americans, in pursuing that policy, were not giving way to the USSR. Their goal was "to catch her in a net." One should note at this point that the explanation of American policy Kissinger gave here was the same sort of explanation he gave the Chinese at the time.[101]

In this context, a strong Europe, Kissinger added, one in which a "pivotal role" would be played by France (and not Germany, which was too open to Soviet pressure), suited the United States. It was for this reason, he said, that the U.S. government was prepared to help the French develop their military capabilities. The Nixon administration, he pointed out, had never laid out its thinking so openly with a foreign leader. Pompidou replied by noting the importance of what Kissinger had said, and promised "to consider it carefully."

That these were Kissinger's real views seems quite clear, and internal White House documents show that he really did want to reach a great overarching agreement with the Europeans on political and economic issues—an agreement that would set up a system in which France would play a key role. Not only do these sources echo the same points about China and the USSR that Kissinger had made in his May 18 meeting with Pompidou, but they also show how important the European question was in the eyes of Americans, and how important it was in their view to develop the U.S.–European relationship in order to combat isolationist trends on both sides of the Atlantic. (One should note in this context that the U.S. administration was quite worried about an amendment introduced by Senator Mansfield to reduce American troop levels in Europe by 75,000 to 100,000 men).

As the Americans saw it, the first step toward a formal restructuring of the U.S.–European relationship would be the establishment of an informal high-level group composed of representatives from the United States, Great Britain, France, and West Germany, which would tackle all the major political and economic problems that the Western world faced. After his May 18 meeting with Pompidou, Kissinger thought that the French president—with the March elections behind him, with a new government composed of men loyal to him, and no longer so dependent on Gaullists of the orthodox school—was someone he could do business with. Pompidou might be a tough negotiator, but he was basically a pragmatist, and he would be willing to cooperate with the sort of policy the Americans had in mind, provided it was consistent with France's autonomy and would not prevent the emergence of a "European personality." French support might be more easily gained if the United States offered greater assistance in weapons development and in the high technology area in general (especially with regard to aircraft engines).[102]

Kissinger's May 18 visit thus led to a certain easing of relations, at least at the Elysée, where Edouard Balladur had replaced Michel Jobert as secretary-general. The impending U.S.–Soviet agreement was still a source of concern, since it might make it easier for the USSR to maneuver below the threshold of war—that is, it might make it easier for the Soviets to use all sorts of indirect methods, methods that took advantage of local Communist parties and revolutionary movements. But that agreement was no longer considered an expression of an American will to power; in fact, it did not seem to be in line with America's own interests. As for the "Year of Europe" and the "new Atlantic Charter," it was important to take care to avoid being pulled back into the integrated NATO system through such channels, but the French had no objection to the "declaration of principles" that Kissinger had proposed on April 23.[103]

The French foreign ministry—the Quai d'Orsay—especially when Michel Jobert was in charge there, seems to have taken a much harder line. And a certain segment of the press, and Gaullist elements who saw the evolution of U.S. policy as confirming standard Gaullist arguments about "American imperialism," also tended to take a relatively hard line on these questions.[104] So from the spring of 1973 on, Pompidou was getting rather contradictory advice about what attitude to adopt toward the Americans. People at the time felt quite strongly about all of these issues, so Pompidou had to be quite careful in expressing his own views; thus, it is hard at times to know for sure what his position really was, a problem complicated by the fact that he was very ill.

But the president seems to have been quite intrigued by what Kissinger had told him. He met with British Prime Minister Edward Heath on May 21; in that meeting, he appeared to want an agreement with the Americans, and he thought such an agreement was possible. Having heard what Kissinger had had to say, he was clearly not as pessimistic as some of his advisors. The key thing in his view was that America not allow itself to disengage from Europe, but there were limits to what he would agree to. Pompidou and Heath recognized that the U.S. contribution to the defense of Europe was indispensable, and they did not think that Mansfield's views would prevail. But still they did consider the possibility of cooperating on the next generation of their strategic nuclear systems, due to be deployed around 1985.[105] Pompidou, however, was very cautious on this issue. He did not take Anglo-French cooperation in this area as a given; he viewed it instead as a possibility that could be explored more carefully when the time came to decide on the next generation of weapons.[106]

The Reykjavik summit itself is generally presented as a failure, but that judgment seems rather one-sided; it in fact deserves a more nuanced assessment. To be sure, the two sides exchanged views on a whole range of international issues, and the discussion at Reykjavik went around in circles a bit. There was certainly no progress on monetary issues. Pompidou tried to reopen that question the following month. In a June 25 letter to Nixon, he insisted on the importance of the struggle against inflation and on the need to defend the new exchange rates set in March 1973. He thought it was essential that short-term capital movements be controlled. With regard to the gold problem, Pompidou thought the deadlock could be ended by allowing the central banks to buy or sell gold on the free market, which would have put an end once and for all to what had become the purely theoretical gold price of thirty-five dollars an ounce. (It should be noted at this point that from 1968 on, a two-tiered gold market had been in place; there was the open market, where gold was bought and sold at a price set by supply and demand, and a system limited to the central banks, who exchanged gold at the official rate of thirty-five dollars an ounce.) But implicit in Pompidou's proposal was the idea that gold would still play a special role in the international monetary system. To give gold a special role would benefit countries like France, who had large gold reserves, and gold producers like South Africa and the Soviet Union, but it would hurt those European countries who had kept their reserves in dollars. And there was no chance at all that Washington would accept such a plan: Nixon, in his August 6 reply, simply avoided the issue.[107] One should also note that Pompidou was now taking a somewhat harder line than he had taken at the Azores meeting, where the gold question had not been raised. Indeed, he was less flexible now than the French had previously been: in the 1967–1969 period, they had been willing to contemplate an international monetary system not based on gold, as long as that system had some real structure to it—as long as it provided for a certain degree of monetary discipline, as long as the dollar's role was brought into balance with the rest of the system.[108] This shift again marked a certain return to a harder version of Gaullism; we shall see further examples of this later on.

With regard to the proposal for a new Atlantic Charter, the way this issue was dealt with at Reykjavik should not be counted as either a success or a failure. Pompidou was much more reserved than he had been on May 18. In particular, he rejected the U.S. proposal for a four-power preparatory meeting.[109] He insisted in effect that the preparatory work be done initially in bilateral meetings, and not in a multilateral group that was too closely linked in his mind with NATO. But discussions did take place between Kissinger (who had become secretary of state in August) and Jobert; the French had thus not opted for a simple policy of obstructionism. It is also important to bear in mind in this connection that Pompidou had to keep the majority coalition together within France. To that end, he had to pursue a policy that was balanced in domestic political terms—and in particular had to take hardline Gaullist views into account to a greater degree that Kissinger had supposed.

On the other hand, with regard to the military issues, the summit was a real success. Pompidou stated to the press following the meetings that he favored a continuing American troop presence in Europe. This corresponded to a deep conviction on his part, but a public pronouncement of this sort was quite new for the Fifth Republic! Even more important was a highly secret agreement relating to nuclear weapons technology that was reached at the third meeting at Reykjavik, a meeting specifically devoted to military issues.[110] (One should note in passing that the fact that the agreement was kept secret no doubt contributed to the impression that the summit was a failure.) Pompidou and Nixon at that session agreed that the talks would be extended to include nuclear weapons technology as such. The Franco-American discussions up to that point had been limited to what were, in the final analysis, secondary issues, such as missile technology and Soviet ABM capabilities. But now cooperation would be extended to the holy of holies, the most fundamental area, the design of the nuclear warheads themselves. "I am happy to agree," Pompidou declared, "that our experts will go to Washington and that the exchanges will be speeded up." On the American side, Kissinger would be in charge of those talks.

It is quite clear that for the Americans, the offer they made in this area was designed in part to facilitate the acceptance by Paris of America's whole European program. And indeed that program had a number of features that were rather attractive from the French point of view. France, in the great Euro-Atlantic system Nixon and Kissinger envisioned, would enjoy the same special position as Britain.[111] And the Americans were also willing to guarantee that West Germany would not acquire nuclear weapons, a subject that worried Georges Pompidou a great deal. All of this, the French president understood, was of considerable value, but he was sure that the Americans would ask for something in return. The central question was what that price would be. "Naturally," he said, "given the progress we are making in the area of defense, our principle is to not sell our soul for a bowl of porridge, no matter how good it is."[112]

POMPIDOU REJECTS THE "BOWL OF PORRIDGE": THE COLLAPSE OF THE MILITARY TALKS

Robert Galley, the minister of defense, and Jean Blancard, in accordance with the Reykjavik agreement, went to the United States in late July and late August 1973 to discuss military cooperation.[113] Up to that point (as noted above), the talks had dealt only with existing French missiles and Soviet ABM defenses. Now the French proposed that the talks also deal with the missile systems still being developed and with the design of the nuclear warheads themselves. While recognizing that previous exchanges had provided the French with very valuable information—it helped them improve the reliability of their existing missiles and understand the vulnerability of their existing nuclear force to Soviet defenses—the French now wanted help with the development of a new generation of weapons: missiles with multiple independently targeted reentry vehicles (or MIRVs, as they were called), hardened thermonuclear warheads, and "clean" tactical nuclear weapons. "Many solutions are possible," Galley pointed out, "but finding them will take up endless amounts of time and money. It would be very valuable if French scientists and technical people could learn the best ways to develop strategic weapons and clean tactical weapons."

The Americans were reluctant to go along with these rather far-reaching requests. They were not willing for the time being to talk about advanced programs like the M4 missile that was planned for the 1980s. (This was an MIRVed missile carrying six hardened thermonuclear warheads.) They would discuss only the systems currently deployed and those due to be deployed in the near future (that is, in the 1970s). They questioned whether

France needed MIRVed weapons that could attack several widely dispersed targets, and thought simple MRVed missiles (that is, missiles with multiple warheads, but which could not be independently targeted) should suffice. Indeed, they did not hide the fact that they did not want at that point to complicate the SALT negotiations with Moscow: the assumption was that if it were revealed that America was helping France develop these very destabilizing weapons, the SALT talks would be affected. They insisted, moreover, that the French (like the British) conduct their testing at the Nevada test site. And they emphasized the need for an effective warning system: given the prospect that the Soviets would have an MIRVed force by the end of the 1970s, in the absence of such a system, the USSR might be able to destroy the entire French nuclear force in a single strike. But the only effective warning system in place at that time was the American system, so that point, along with the point about the Nevada test site, implied—unambiguously in the French view—that the Americans, in exchange for their technical assistance, and despite everything, really wanted to establish a certain control over the French nuclear force. And the assumption was that that policy had been framed with the SALT talks in mind.

Hence the military talks simply ended, at least for the period of Pompidou's presidency. On December 20, 1973, Kissinger proposed resumption to Pompidou, but the French president ignored the suggestion.[114] At the same time, the talks between the French armed forces chief of staff (now General Maurin) and the U.S. commander in Europe (General Goodpaster) moved into very low gear. The two generals were supposed to work out arrangements that would allow French and other allied forces to fight together in the event of a European war. The basic principle of conducting such talks had been approved by the French Defense Council, and arrangements of that sort had been very much in line with Pompidou's original policy. Yet on October 30, Pompidou decided to slow down those talks, at least until the situation brought on by the Yom Kippur War had become clearer. The negotiations would proceed at a very slow pace: first Maurin and Goodpaster would get together just to exchange information; political discussions would follow; a discussion of military cooperation at a more detailed, technical level might then "possibly" take place. The French were just as reserved when Admiral Moorer, chairman of the U.S. Joint Chiefs of Staff, came to France in December.[115]

The Pompidou line in the military area had thus hardened since the summer: there had been a certain return to "Gaullist orthodoxy." As proof, let me cite a very important document, Pompidou's "strategic testament." The existence of this document has long been known, but not its content. The text was written by Pompidou himself on February 1, 1974; copies went only to Prime Minister Pierre Messmer and to Minister of Defense Robert Galley.[116] To be sure, in this document certain extreme notions were dropped that had been included in the last document of this sort a French president had drafted, namely de Gaulle's "Instruction personnelle et secrète" of 1967—for example, the idea of an "all azimuths" defense, and the related point about the need for intercontinental missiles. But the document as a whole had a rather pessimistic tone. The U.S.–Soviet conflict would continue, Pompidou thought, but at the same time Washington and Moscow would deal with each other on a purely bilateral basis; the Europeans would not be involved. The Americans, he believed, might be impetuous and unpredictable, or American actions might be highly calculated; in either case, one was struck by the "imperious" character of American policy. There was, moreover, a certain tendency on the Americans' part to reduce their commitment to the defense of Europe. Then, of course, there was the monetary problem and the energy problem. All of that, taken together, made for "a permanent state of uncertainty and anxiety."

If that was the problem, what then was the solution? There could be no return to Atlantic integration: France's freedom of action had to be preserved, even if it was likely that in the event of war it would fight side-by-side with its NATO allies, all the more so given that the German attitude in case of crisis was quite uncertain. An Anglo-French nuclear force was no solution either, because Britain had no freedom of action vis-à-vis the United States, and because both Germany and the USSR would react negatively to an arrangement of that sort. The only remaining solution was to build up France's own deterrent force: six nuclear ballistic missile launching submarines should be produced, instead of the five that were planned. The stockpile of tactical nuclear weapons should also be built up: this was essential if France's deterrent threat was to be credible. (This corresponded to the doctrine of the "final warning" laid out in the 1972 Defense White Paper, providing for a tactical nuclear strike as a last warning before a strategic strike.) More generally, France's armed forces in Europe would have to be strengthened: the French combat corps would most likely be part of the alliance's reserve force, but when it was committed to battle, it had to be provided with nuclear support, the French having ruled out the idea of a purely conventional war in Europe. Once again, it is important to note that NATO had a different doctrine for the use of tactical nuclear weapons; military coordination in this area was quite difficult for that reason alone.

The document's conclusion reflected its basic Gaullist spirit—although again this was a kind of rationalized Gaullism. It also reflected the fact that talks with the Americans had ground to a halt—or at least that the brake had been pulled down hard on the policy those talks had come to represent. "We must pursue this effort alone and without compromises," Pompidou wrote, "until we are forced to deal with the problem of the alert [meaning the necessity of acquiring means to get a timely warning of an impending Soviet attack]. Although the allies and especially the Americans tend to inflate the importance of this problem for reasons that can be imagined, there must be no information given about our plans, and there must be no negotiations with anyone at all without my personal authorization."

THE FINAL PHASE:
THE PERIOD FROM THE SUMMER OF 1973 ON

The bilateral military relationship that had begun so promisingly had thus been brought to an end. The decision to do so had been made for reasons of general policy: Pompidou's February 1, 1974, "testament" makes this quite clear. What had happened? It should be recalled, first of all, that the Soviets and the Americans had signed an "agreement on the prevention of nuclear war" during Brezhnev's visit to the United States in June 1973. According to that agreement, the two signatories would not threaten one another or use force against one another, and they would consult with each other if there was a danger of nuclear war or if there was a risk that a conflict between two other powers might lead to nuclear war. It was this last point especially that caused concern in Paris. It is important to remember in this context that as late as September 15, 1972, Kissinger had assured Pompidou that the agreement proposed by Moscow would have only a very general scope; Washington was, in fact, aware of the "condominium" overtones of the Soviet proposal. But as it turned out, the Soviets had held out for a more precisely-worded text, and during a meeting with Brezhnev in Moscow in early May 1973, the Americans gave way and agreed that the two countries would act in concert and do everything they could to prevent the risk of a nuclear war developing from a conflict between third parties.[117] The text went well beyond what the Americans had originally had in mind, and the French disliked what it seemed to imply: Pompidou, as he wrote to Nixon on July 13, saw the danger of a "kind of tutelage" being imposed on Europe.[118] His suspicion that some sort of U.S.–Soviet condominium was taking shape, which had been partially allayed by his May 18 meeting with Kissinger, now welled up again. What gave particular force to that fear in Paris was the way all of these developments—the "prevention of nuclear war" agreement, the SALT talks and what they implied about the dilution of the American nuclear guarantee to Europe, the MBFR talks, which, it was feared, might end up giving the USSR an important right of oversight over central Europe—all seemed to fall into a pattern. "Everything was happening," the foreign minister wrote, "as though the Russians and Americans were in the process of defining the rules of a worldwide game in which they would be the only real players." "In this framework," he thought, "each superpower seems willing to grant the other the right to reorganize its own camp."[119] Certain distinctively Gaullist ways of looking at things had thus resurfaced in Paris.

But the developing U.S.–Soviet relationship was not the only problem here, and soon other issues were linked to it—especially the American plan for a "Common Declaration of Principles for the Atlantic Alliance." On this issue, the Americans miscalculated. They thought that the French, ever since Reykjavik, accepted the U.S. plan in principle—that they wished only to make sure that this business did not appear to be tied to NATO, but was instead dealt with in a series of bilateral discussions. Kissinger, moreover, in general tended to think that the French government's reserved attitude with regard to the June 22 agreement and to the proposed Atlantic Charter was for public consumption only, and did not reflect the actual thinking of the government.[120] But in Paris, the real issue posed by the Atlantic Declaration, as Jean-Bernard Raimond stressed in a July 4, 1973, memorandum for the president, was substantive and not just a question of procedure. Kissinger's draft declaration gave the United States the leading role in every area of policy. It implied a de facto return of France to NATO, and it would lead the EEC to give up any hope of "gradually establishing its own autonomy or of creating a political personality of its own vis-à-vis the United States." Kissinger's concern was to maintain American leadership in a period of profound change in international relations, but his planned declaration was not "acceptable." The French response should not, however, Raimond thought, be purely negative: "the maintenance of western solidarity is necessary for us." The solution might be for France to present a draft of its own as an alternative: the issue might well be negotiable. The State Department had in fact prepared another draft that was "quite reasonable," not as "bad" for France as Kissinger's. Kissinger's "excessive" text did not necessarily reflect a fixed American position.[121]

And on October 3, 1973, after meeting with Pompidou the previous day, Jobert did submit to the North Atlantic Council a French counterproposal for a Fifteen-Power Declaration.[122] The text reflected the French government's basic thinking on all of the key issues of the day. The importance of Atlantic solidarity and the continuing need for an American troop presence in Europe were reaffirmed, and so was the continuing need for an effective nuclear deterrent. (Here again the French were taking a stand against what they suspected was a tendency on the Americans' part to move toward denuclearization, something they feared the SALT talks especially might lead to.) The Jobert draft also called on America to not let Europe be exposed "to external political or military pressure that might destroy its freedom." This again reflected the French fear that the American commitment to the defense of Europe was weakening, and that the Americans were moving away from nuclear deterrence, a fear linked in the official mind at Paris with the June 22 U.S.–Soviet agreement. The Jobert text, moreover, explicitly recognized the importance of the European contribution to the defense of Europe—their conventional contribution and, in two cases, their nuclear contribution as well. Here the French had two goals. First they wanted to secure recognition of the value of their Force de Frappe—their nuclear strike force—for the alliance as a whole. They also wanted to give formal expression to the possibility that an essentially European defense system—a system with a distinctly European political personality—might take shape at some point in the future, a possibility Jobert would also discuss in his famous November 21, 1973, speech to the Western European Union.

The French counterproposal was a major success, a point that was obscured at the time by the crises of autumn 1973 and winter 1973–1974, and by the much publicized rivalry between Kissinger and Jobert (which Kissinger, to my mind, also overemphasizes in his memoirs). The Americans were, of course, well aware of the basically very Gaullist sort of thinking that lay behind what the French were doing in this area, but they understood that the French text was the most they could hope for and that it had "the immense advantage of coming from the leading NATO dissident." They decided at once to withdraw the Kissinger draft, which opened the way for Jobert's draft.[123]

The Declaration on Atlantic Relations that was finally adopted after Pompidou's death by the North Atlantic Council in Ottawa on June 19, 1974, was thus based essentially on a French text. Indeed, the first ten articles in that document were carried over almost verbatim from the Jobert draft. The French had managed the affair brilliantly. On the one hand, they had gotten rid of the objectionable Kissinger draft and at the same time they had used the occasion to get the alliance to formally accept some of their basic positions on nuclear deterrence, on détente, and on the "condominium" issue. And finally—and this is less well-known—they had reaffirmed the solidarity of the alliance at what happened to be a crucial time: beginning in June 1973, the German government (or at least Chancellor Brandt and Foreign Minister Scheel) had been considering the possibility of establishing a new European security system, a system which, they hoped, might open the way to German reunification; in that context, they had suggested to the French that a purely European defense system might be set up outside of NATO.[124] The Atlantic Declaration affair thus provides a very striking example of Georges Pompidou's rationalized Gaullism: a tough defense of French independence, but a fundamental solidarity with the United States in dealing both with the Soviet threat and also with the risk of a German drift toward neutralism.

The issue of a "new Atlantic Charter" had thus been resolved, but the same sort of problem soon cropped up in another area: the question of relations between the United States and the European Economic Community. During the summer of 1973, the Belgians and Germans, concerned about the Atlantic Charter negotiations (which at the time were being held up by the French), had proposed that another document be drafted at the same time, one dealing with relations between the United States and the EEC. Their thinking was that there were certain problems in U.S.–European relations that were not covered by the Alliance.[125] The Americans liked the idea. They might have had to drop their own rather demanding text, but they might now be able to get what they wanted through the back door—that is, by having France's Common Market partners put pressure on it in a purely European framework. The U.S. authorities wanted this document in particular to reaffirm the "centrality of trans-Atlantic relationships"; the document should also call on the Europeans to consult with the United States before any economic decision was made by the EEC.[126]

The French agreed that a U.S.–EEC declaration could be drafted, but only if a text on "European identity" was worked out at the same time. The goal here was to keep that latter issue from being diluted by too strong a dose of Atlanticism.[127] In fact, in the autumn of 1973, a new effort to "build Europe" seemed in Paris to be the only way to deal effectively with the uncertainties of the international situation—the only way, above all, to deal with the German situation, with all of its ambiguities.[128] At his September 27, 1973, press conference, Pompidou had proposed that the European heads of state and government meet on a regular basis to discuss the ways they might cooperate politically, probably adopting one of Jean Monnet's ideas. On October 31, following a council of ministers meeting devoted to that question, Pompidou sent Brandt a letter in which he laid out his thinking on this issue. The heads of state and government, he thought, should meet just by themselves, with no agenda, for very open discussions aimed at "harmonizing their views in the framework of political cooperation."[129] This French initiative led to the summit conference of the nine Common Market countries held in Copenhagen on December 15–16, 1973, a meeting that was the forerunner of the European Council of Heads of State and Government. On that occasion, a "Declaration on European Identity" was adopted. The text affirmed "the close ties" between the Nine and the United States and called for that relationship to become even closer. But at the same time, and in accordance with the French thesis, it also stated that the Nine formed a "distinct and original entity." The document laid out the main lines of European policy on various world problems, including détente, the Middle East, China, and underdevelopment. The language was very general, but the point was made that Europe was not just a regional power.

The October 1973 Yom Kippur War and the oil crisis that followed, as is well known, had a major impact on Franco-American relations. The French disagreed with America's Middle East policy and were against the American idea of organizing a group of oil-consuming countries. This issue cannot be dealt with in detail here, but it should be noted that for the French, Nixon's January 9, 1974, call for a conference in Washington on energy problems was viewed as, among other things, a way of reviving Kissinger's original plan for an Atlantic Declaration. For them, America's underlying goal here was to create "a United States/Europe/Japan community" under American control. But Pompidou's advisers at the Elysée were divided as to how to respond. Some thought Jobert should not go to Washington, others thought that he could but should do nothing more there than simply discuss the issue; in no event should the meeting actually set up an organization of oil-consuming countries. In the end, at a February 6 Council of Ministers meeting, Pompidou took Edouard Balladur's advice and opted for a relatively moderate course of action: Jobert would go to the Washington conference five days later, but only for a simple exchange of views. The government also announced, moreover, that its "decision should not be interpreted as implying that France agreed to the establishment, by a certain number of large industrialized countries, of an institutional framework for dealing with a whole range of political and economic issues."[130] It is true that, in the wake of the oil crisis, France was in a particularly weak position; on January 19, Paris had to leave the European monetary "snake" that had been set up the previous year and announced that the franc would be allowed to float for six months.[131] This was a major blow to France's European policy— the only policy, it seemed, which might allow France to deal not just with the growing problem with Washington, but with Bonn and Moscow as well.

In March 1974, the question of a U.S.–EEC declaration returned to center stage. Washington was on the march again, and pressed for a text that would reflect certain American views. The Nine, the U.S. government thought, should consult with the United States before making any important decision, and the two sides should work out an "organic consultative arrangement." Michel Jobert and the political director of the Quai d'Orsay, François Puaux, thought that that basic idea needed to be firmly rejected. At most, a very limited version of that notion—one that provided for consultation on a simple case-by-case basis—might be acceptable. They were prepared to take this line even if it led to a crisis. But at the Elysée, Gabriel Robin thought that while safeguards were necessary, a less negative attitude was called for. And that, it soon became clear, was also Pompidou's view: while France had to be "firm," he also could accept "the principle of consultation."[132] As it turned out, the plan for a U.S.–EEC declaration was put aside; it was decided that it was enough to include the substance of what had been agreed on in Article 11 of the Ottawa of June 22, 1974. This article called for "close consultation" between America and Europe: in their dealings with each other, events taking place in other parts of the world, and the linkage between security questions and economic questions, would each be taken into account. And that was all that remained of Kissinger's ambitious plan for a fundamental restructuring of the Atlantic alliance: in this toned down form, the idea was perfectly acceptable to Paris. In this area as well, final agreement was reached only after Pompidou's death, but he had cleared the way for compromise by accepting the principle of trans-Atlantic consultation and by resisting the temptation to escalate the conflict.

Nevertheless, despite this solution to the problem of the U.S.–European declaration, Franco-American relations had clearly deteriorated since the summer of 1973. But at the same time, the Elysée was growing increasingly concerned about the growth of Soviet power and influence. It was clear that relations with Moscow were deteriorating; Soviet pressure on France was growing; the fact was that the real partners of the USSR in the West were now the United States and West Germany.[133] And yet, because Pompidou was worried about West Germany and unhappy with America, the sort of language he used with the Soviets remained rooted in the old Gaullist formulas about independence and equidistance between the blocs. But this very fact suggested that French policy had reached a certain impasse—that France was now somewhat isolated.[134]

On October 30, 1973, the State Department noted that Paris and Washington had been moving apart; it was particularly critical of France's attitude during the Middle East crisis. It listed for Kissinger a whole series of "possible pressure points on France," but made it clear that the United States needed to be very careful if it tried to put pressure on that country—if only because U.S. pressure might be used to justify the French policy of independence in the eyes of France's European partners.[135] In June 1974, after Pompidou's death, the State Department reviewed the recent course of Franco-American relations. The way it summed up what had happened was by no means entirely off-base. It noted how relations had deteriorated since the beginning of 1973, how the French attitude had hardened, how neo-Gaullism was on the rise, and how French policy had come to have a stronger "European" flavor. Pompidou, it noted, had evidently come to the conclusion that those more strident French goals "could be reached only by adopting a more distant and sometimes hostile stance toward the U.S."[136]

CONCLUSION

When Georges Pompidou became president of France, he had a certain sense of what he wanted to accomplish. France, in his mind, was one point in a triangle; its relations with the other two points—Europe and America— were of fundamental importance, and each of those relationships was closely linked to the other. The goal was to carve out a special niche for France in that triangular structure—to allow France to play a central role, a pivotal role, in the Western world, and thus in the world as a whole. A sort of special relationship with the United States was thus of major importance, and Pompidou had sought to improve Franco-American relations. His goal, in fact, had been to put them on an entirely new footing.

In 1970–1971, a real Franco-American understanding of this sort—a far-reaching understanding on political, economic, and military issues—did not seem by any means out of the question. Nixon was in effect prepared to accept the pragmatic Gaullism of his partner; he was willing to view France as an important link between the United States and Europe. But the attempt to reach such an understanding was to fail—the December 1971 Azores Conference was the key turning point here—and it failed for essentially structural reasons.

To be sure, problems like the nuclear question and the monetary question were inherently complex, and their very complexity made compromise difficult. But the fundamental problem was political in nature. Pompidou was more "Gaullist" than was often thought at the time, and was not inclined to make the slightest concession when the principle of national independence was involved. Nor was he prepared to cooperate within the NATO framework except within very narrow limits, or to accept an international monetary agreement that gave America a privileged position but gave France nothing in return. As for Nixon and Kissinger, they certainly had a more positive attitude toward France than Kennedy and Johnson had had, but despite their proclaimed vision of a multipolar world in which Europe would play its role, they never in reality abandoned the notion of a U.S.-led Atlantic world.

But there were also causes having to do with the changing international situation. The crises of the autumn of 1973 played a certain role. And there was the more basic fact that with the end of the Vietnam War, with the changes produced by the Nixon shocks of 1971, with the SALT talks and improved U.S.–Soviet relations, the United States had less need for French help. It could now pursue a more unilateral policy both in Europe and in the world as a whole, and could afford to be less accommodating toward France. From that point on, U.S. policy toward the Soviet Union and China was far more important than anything else; as the global system was recast, America's allies had to be kept on a short leash; the political development of an economically powerful European Community also had to be kept under control. But Pompidou, at the same time, faced with the uncertainties of the international situation, and concerned in particular about Soviet, and German, policy, was drawn back to a more purely Gaullist conception of what French foreign policy should be.

But in spite of everything, Georges Pompidou never wanted a break with Washington. Even at the worst moments (the autumn of 1973 and the winter of 1973–1974), his instinct was to reach for compromise. In comparison with other French leaders—Michel Jobert, for instance—his inclination was to take a relatively moderate line. And his policy of rapprochement with Washington did bear fruit after his death. Nuclear cooperation was resumed by his successors; the Ottawa agreement was signed in June 1974; the Valentin-Ferber accords, the product of talks that had been going on since 1972, were signed on July 3, 1974. Those accords, signed by the commander of the French armed forces in Europe and the NATO commander for central

Europe, extended the 1967 Ailleret-Lemnitzer agreement to the entire French force in Europe, which had applied only to French forces in Germany.[137] Relations between France and NATO remained defined by these texts until the 1980s.

More generally speaking, one has the sense that the heart of Pompidou's policy, the goal of bringing the various key elements of French foreign policy—policy toward Washington, toward Moscow, toward Bonn, toward the Alliance, and toward Europe—into balance with each other, was not in any fundamental way repudiated by his successors. His basic vision of a rationalized Gaullism, but one that did not reject the idea of good relations with America on principle, one that sought to put that relationship on a bilateral, rather than on an "Atlantic," basis, remained at the core of French foreign policy for the rest of the Cold War period. Pompidou influenced even the style of French diplomacy in the 1970s and 1980s: his basic approach was carried over even into the sort of language that was typically used; it was embodied in the way French officials reflexively reacted to developments. His policy was nuanced; therefore, its impact might at times be hard to detect. But in fundamental terms, his influence was lasting.

NOTES

1. G.-H. Soutou, "La France et l'Alliance atlantique de 1949 à 1954," *Cahiers du Centre d'Etudes d'Histoire de la Défense*, 3 (1997).

2. See Georges-Henri Soutou, *L'Alliance incertaine: Les rapports politico-stratégiques franco-allemands, 1954–1996* (Paris: Fayard, 1996).

3. For Pompidou's foreign policy and his relations with the Americans, see Eric Roussel, *Georges Pompidou* (Paris: J. C. Lattès, 1994), and Association Georges Pompidou, *Georges Pompidou et l'Europe* (Brussels: Complexe, 1995), especially Pierre Mélandri's essay, "Une relation très spéciale: la France, les États-Unis et l'Année de l'Europe, 1973–1974." For Franco-American military cooperation in the Pompidou period, see Pierre Mélandri, "Aux origines de la coopération nucléaire franco-américaine," in *La France et l'Atome* (Brussels: Bruylant, 1994). The basic memoir sources are obviously of fundamental importance here: Henry Kissinger, *White House Years* (Boston: Little, Brown, 1979); Henry Kissinger, *Years of Upheaval* (Boston: Little Brown, 1982); Michel Jobert, *Mémoires d'avenir* (Paris: Grasset, 1974); and Michel Jobert *L'autre regard* (Paris: Grasset, 1976).

4. See Soutou, *L'Alliance incertaine.*

5. Ibid., and private archives.

6. Box 1040, fonds 5AG2, Archives nationales, Paris. This source will henceforth be cited in the form: 5AG2/1040.

7. Institut Charles de Gaulle, *L'aventure de la Bombe* (Paris: Plon, 1985), 210–211.

8. Alain Peyrefitte, *C'était de Gaulle*, vol. 1 (Paris: de Fallois/Fayard, 1994), 339; and Cyrus L. Sulzberger, *An Age of Mediocrity* (New York: Macmillan, 1993) 133 (a very useful source).

9. Sulzberger, *Age of Mediocrity*, 406.

10. Ibid., 216–217.

11. Philippe de Saint Robert, *Le secret des jours* (Paris: J. C. Lattès, 1995), 33.

12. See Kissinger, *White House Years*, 106–111.

13. American embassy in Paris to State Department, April 3, 1969; and Sonnenfeldt to Kissinger, April 8, National Security Council Files (NSCF), box 674, folder "France, vol. I," Nixon Presidential Materials (NPM), U.S. National Archives, College Park, Maryland. Henceforth cited in the form: NSCF/674/France vol. I.

14. Kissinger memorandum, April 15, 1969 (approved by the president); and note Secretary of State to Kissinger, April 22, 1969, NSCF/674/France vol. II.

15. Martin Hillenbrand (Assistant Secretary of State for European Affairs) memorandum for the president, April 29, 1969, Kissinger to Hillenbrand covering note, May 3, 1969, thanking Hillenbrand for the memorandum on Nixon's behalf, NSCF/674/France vol. II.

16. Kissinger to Nixon, April 28, 1969, NSCF/674/France vol. II.

17. Pompidou-Shriver meeting, July 23, 1969, 5AG2/1022.

18. Pompidou-Rogers meeting, December 8, 1969, 5AG2/1022.

19. Paris embassy to State Department, November 8, 1969, NSCF/676/France, vol. IV.

20. G.-H. Soutou, "L'attitude de Georges Pompidou face à l'Allemagne," in *Georges Pompidou et l'Europe*.

21. See, for example, the conversation between Secretary of State Rogers and André Fontaine of *Le Monde*, December 15, 1969, in NSCF/676/France vol. IV.

22. H. Froment-Meurice, *Vu du Quai: Mémoires 1945–1983* (Paris: Fayard, 1998), 321ff. Meeting of Kissinger with Maurice Schumann (French foreign minister), September 22, 1972, and note from Kissinger to Nixon concerning a conversation between General Walters and Pompidou, October 30, 1972, both in NSCF/679/France vol. X.

23. C. Ockrent, Comte de Marenches, *Dans le secret des princes* (Paris: Stock, 1986), 100ff.

24. Pompidou-Rogers meeting, December 8, 1969, 5AG2/1022 and Paris embassy to State Department, December 12, 1969, Subject-Numeric Files for 1967–69, box 2103, POL FR-US 1/1/69, Records of the Department of State, Record Group (RG) 59, U.S. National Archives, College Park, Maryland. That latter source will henceforth be cited in the following form: Subject-Numeric Files 1967–69/2103/RG 59. Notes of Jean-Bernard Raimond, diplomatic adviser at the Elysée, for the president of November 18, 1969, and January 21, 1970, 5AG2/1041.

25. Pompidou to Nixon, July 1, 1972, 5AG2/1021.

26. Pompidou-Shriver meeting, July 23, 1969, 5AG2/1022; and meeting of Schriver with Beaumarchais, political director at the Quai d'Orsay, July 29, 1969, Subject-Numeric Files 1967–69/2103/RG 59. Comments of Michel Jobert, Secretary General of the Elysée, in Paris embassy to State Department, November 8, 1969, NSCF/676/France vol. IV. Note from Michel Debré, Minister of Defense, for Pompidou in February 1970, 5AG2/1021.

27. Memorandum of conversation, June 27, 1969, NSCF/675/France vol. III.

28. Kissinger-Shriver-Sonnenfeldt meeting, June 27, 1969, NSCF/675/France vol. III.

29. One high Pentagon official, for example, thought that the French ought to be asked to reimburse the United States for the relocation costs France's departure from the NATO military organization had caused a few years earlier. He also thought the question of the use of French military facilities by the United States in an emergency should be brought up with Pompidou, and was reluctant to share advanced American computer technology with the French. David Packard (Deputy Secretary of Defense) memorandum for the president, February 12, 1970, NSCF/676/France vol. V.

30. For a full account of the trip, see Roussel, *Pompidou*, 349–367.

31. See the file for the trip, 5AG2/1022.

32. Annotations on a note of Jean-Louis Lucet of February 11, 1970, 5AG2/1022.

33. Quoted in Roussel, *Pompidou*, 362–364.

34. Annotation on a note of June 29, 1969, and the entire file, 5AG2/1040.

35. Conversation with Shriver, July 23, 1969.

36. See Roussel, *Pompidou*, 366–367.

37. In private conversations after the meeting, Nixon stated that he was very pleased. See Sulzberger, *Age of Mediocrity*, 614–615.

38. Roussel, *Pompidou*, 350ff.

39. Kissinger to Nixon, November 11, 1970, before Nixon's meeting with Pompidou at de Gaulle's funeral; and a memorandum from Kissinger for Nixon of January 25, 1971, NSCF/677/France vol. VII.

40. Lucet to Maurice Schumann, April 14, 1970, 5AG2/1021.

41. See Soutou, "L'attitude de Georges Pompidou face à l'Allemagne."

42. Pompidou-Brezhnev conversation, October 13, 1970, 5AG2/1018.

43. Sulzberger, *Age of Mediocrity*, 690.

44. Pompidou annotation on July 26, 1971, telegram, 5AG2/1041. For a complete dossier dealing with a possible Soviet intervention in Yugoslavia (dated February 21, 1972), see 5AG2/1040.

45. See, for example, the conversation between Soviet ambassador to Paris Zorin and Michel Debré, Minister of Defense, January 16, 1971, 5AG2/1018.

46. NSCF/676/France vol. V.

47. Laird to Kissinger, April 2, 1970, enclosing draft memorandum for the president on "Possible Assistance to French Ballistic Missile Program," NSCF/676/France vol. VI.

48. 5AG2/1041.

49. Sonnenfeldt to Kissinger, June 23, 1970, NSCF/677/France vol. VI.

50. Sonnenfeldt to Kissinger, December 11, 1970, NSCF/677/France vol. VII.

51. NSCF/677/France vol. VI.

52. Kissinger to Nixon, January 25, 1971, NSCF/677/France vol. VII.

53. Sonnenfeldt to Kissinger, January 9, 1971, NSCF/677/France vol. VII.

54. Kissinger to Nixon, March 25, 1971, NSCF/677/France vol. VII, and Kissinger to the Secretaries of State and Defense, April 15, 1971, NSCF/678/France vol. VIII.

55. Michel Debré, Minister of Defense, to Pompidou, early 1972, 5AG2/1040.

56. Packard to Kissinger, May 25, 1971, NSCF/678/France vol. VIII.

57. Debré to Pompidou, early 1972, cited in n. 55.

58. 5AG2/1040.

59. Debré to Pompidou, early 1972, cited in n. 55.

60. Bergsten to Kissinger, on French gold purchases, December 10, 1970, and a series of documents relating to the visit to Washington of Hervé Alphand, Secretary General of the Quai d'Orsay, in particular to his meetings with Kissinger, December 10 and 11, 1970, all in NSCF/677/France vol. VII.

61. See the entire file in 5AG2/1041.

62. Sonnenfeldt to Kissinger, August 3, 1970, NSCF/677/France vol. VI.

63. François de Rose notes, February 1 and September 22, 1971, 5AG2/1041.

64. Pompidou annotation on the note on the September 22, 1971, de Rose note, 5AG2/1041.

65. Annotation on a note from Jean-Bernard Raimond of January 28, 1971, 5AG2/1041.

66. Note from Pompidou's private staff, February 22, 1971, 5AG2/1041.

67. Annotation of Georges Pompidou of May 13, 1971, 5AG2/1041.

68. Jean-Bernard Raimond to Pompidou, October 8, 1971, 5AG2/1018.

69. Jean-Louis Lucet to Pompidou, January 12, 1973, 5AG2/1041.

70. Pompidou-Brezhnev meeting, October 29, 1971, 5AG2/1018; and a remark Pompidou privately made to the journalist André Fontaine, quoted in Roussel, *Pompidou*, 394.

71. G.-H. Soutou, *L'Alliance incertaine*, 301–305.

72. Note of Henri Froment-Meurice, director for Asia at the Quai d'Orsay, of July 19, 1971, 5AG2/1021.

73. Raimond to Pompidou on December 7, 1941, 5AG2/1022.

74. For the minutes, see 5AG2/1022. For another copy, see Roussel, *Pompidou*, 464ff. For the American minutes, see William Burr, ed., *The Kissinger Transcripts*, (New York: The New Press, 1998), 33ff.

75. On these issues, the best account is that of J. Denizet, *Le Dollar* (Paris: Fayard 1985).

76. See Robert Litwak, *Détente and the Nixon Doctrine* (Cambridge University Press, 1984), 136–137; William Bundy, *A Tangled Web: The Making of Foreign Policy in the Nixon Presidency*, (London: Tauris, 1998), 261–269; Denizet, *Le Dollar*, 109–125.

77. 5AG2/1021

78. 5AG2/1021

79. 5AG2/1011.

80. Paris embassy to Secretary of State, September 20, 1972, POL FR-US 1-10-72, Subject-Numeric Files 1970–73/2278/RG 59.

81. 5AG2/1040.

82. Debré-Kissinger meeting, July 11, 1972, NSCF/678/France vol. IX; Debré to Pompidou, July 13, 1972, 5AG2/1040.

83. Sonnenfeldt to Kissinger, September 7, 1972, NSCF, Henry A. Kissinger Office Files (HAK Office Files), box 24.

84. An account of the meeting is in 5AG2/1018.

85. 5AG2/1021.

86. Conversation of Kissinger with the French ambassador of September 7, 1972; and a note of September 3, NSCF/HAK Office Files/24.

87. Raimond to Pompidou, September 12, 1972, 5AG2/1021.

88. Roussel, *Pompidou*, 524–528.

89. Debré-Kissinger meeting, July 7, 1972, cited in n. 82 above; Pompidou annotation, December 28, 1972, 5AG2/1041.

90. Paris embassy to Secretary of State, January 1, 1973 (an important general overview), POL FR-US 1-10-73, Subject-Numeric Files 1970-73/2278/RG 59.

91. Ibid. The January 1 document was very clear on that subject.

92. On the problematic of the "Year of Europe" as an issue in Franco-American relations, see Mélandri, "Une relation très spéciale."

93. Bundy, *A Tangled Web,* 415–419.

94. Note of May 3, 1973, for Pompidou, 5AG2/1021.

95. Kosciusko-Morizet to Jobert, May 4, 1973, 5AG2/1021.

96. Raimond to Pompidou, May 10, 1973, 5AG2/1021.

97. File sent by Kosciusko-Morizet to Jobert on May 11, 5AG2/1023.

98. Ibid.

99. Olivier Wormser note, May 10 (returning to the gold standard would be no more difficult for Washington than going to see Mao!), 5AG2/1023.

100. 5AG2/1022.

101. See, for example, the notes of Kissinger's meeting with Mao on November 12, 1973, in Burr, *Kissinger Transcripts,* 179–199.

102. Kissinger memorandum for Nixon, "Meeting with President Pompidou: Iceland," n.d., but written in late May 1973, NSCF/949/Pompidou-Nixon meeting.

103. Two notes from Raimond for Pompidou of May 18 and 29, 1973, 5AG2/1021.

104. For a typical example, see Saint Robert, *Le secret des jours.*

105. Roussel, *Pompidou,* pp. 548–549.

106. Pompidou to Heath, June 29, 1973, 5AG2/1040.

107. 5AG2/1021.

108. See my comments in Raymond Aron, *Les articles de politique internationale dans Le Figaro de 1947 à 1977,* vol. III, *Les Crises (février 1965 à avril 1977),* presentation and notes by G.-H. Soutou (Paris: Editions de Fallois, 1997), 29–31.

109. The minutes can be found in 5AG2/1023. See Roussel, *Pompidou,* 549–571.

110. This was the 10 A.M. session on June 1; the notes are in 5AG2/1023.

111. See Kissinger's pre-Reykjavik memorandum for Nixon, cited in n. 102 above.

112. Third session, June 1, 10 o'clock, cited in n. 110.

113. Minutes of two meetings with Kissinger, Secretary of Defense Schlesinger, and General Walters, July 27 and August 31, 5AG2/1040.

114. Minutes in 5AG2/1023, and published by Roussel, *Pompidou,* 611. On this whole affair, see Mélandri, "Aux origines de la coopération nucléaire franco-américaine." Mélandri wonders whether despite this deadlock, the two sides continued to exchange information in deep secrecy, even during President Pompidou's time. The French and American documents now available lead me to think that the exchanges about nuclear missiles and warheads did in fact stop, and that this was related to the general deterioration of Franco-American relations from the summer of 1973 on.

115. Two notes from General Thenoz, head of the private staff at the Elysée, of October 30 and December 5, 1973, with the president's annotations, 5AG2/1040.

116. 5AG2/1040.

117. Kissinger, *Years of Upheaval,* 274–286.

118. 5AG2/1021.

119. Note from the Minister of Foreign Affairs, June 20, 1973, 5AG2/1019.

120. Kissinger to Nixon, June 29, 1973, NSCF/679/France vol. XI.

121. 5AG2/1021.

122. 5AG2/1021.

123. Sonnenfeldt to Kissinger, October 3, 1973, NSCF/679/France vol. XI.

124. Soutou, "L'attitude de Georges Pompidou face à l'Allemagne." I cannot discuss the details of the German position at the time, which was very complicated and even contradictory—a position rooted in Atlanticism but at the same time tempted by neutralism. But these contradictions themselves worried Paris a great deal.

125. Kissinger, *Years of Upheaval,* 183ff.

126. Walter Stoessel to Kissinger, October 5, 1973, POL FR-US 1-10-73, Subject-Numeric Files 1970-73/2278/RG 59.

127. Sonnenfeldt to Kissinger, September 20, 1973, NSCF/679/France vol. XI.

128. See Soutou, "L'attitude de Georges Pompidou face à l'Allemagne."

129. 5AG2/1009.

130. Note from Gabriel Robin (Jean-Bernard Raimond's successor) of January 10, 1974, for Balladur, with Balladur's annotations, and annexes, 5AG2/1021.

131. Jobert, *Memoires d'avenir,* 283–287.

132. Puaux notes of March 19 and 20, 1974, and Robin note of March 28, and annotations by Pompidou, 5AG2/1021.

133. Gabriel Robin notes of February 13 and March 6, 1974, 5AG2/1019.

134. The notes of his meetings with Brezhnev on this subject (in Pitsounda on March 12 and 13, 1974) are very revealing. They are to be found in 5AG2/1019.

135. George Springsteen to Kissinger, October 30, 1973, POL FR-US 1-10-73, Subject-Numeric Files 1970–73/2278/RG 59.

136. State Department Briefing Paper, "Issues and Talking Points: U.S.–French Relations, June 1974," Executive Secretariat, Briefing Books 1958–76, box 190, "Secretary's Trip to Moscow and Europe 25 June 1974–9 July, 10th of 10," RG 59, U.S. National Archives.

137. Frédéric Bozo, *La France et l'OTAN* (Paris: Masson, 1991), 117.

Index

About the Contributors

Francis J. Gavin is an assistant professor of public policy at the Lyndon B. Johnson School of Public Affairs at the University of Texas at Austin.

Christopher Gehrz recently received his Ph.D. from Yale University after completing his dissertation on "reeducation" in occupied western Germany after World War II.

Wolfram Kaiser is a professor of European studies at the University of Portsmouth in Britain and visiting professor at the College of Europe in Bruges, Belgium.

Erin R. Mahan, a historian at the U.S. Department of State, received her Ph.D. in History from the University of Virginia in May 2000.

Leopoldo Nuti is a professor of the history of international relations at the University of Rome 3.

Paul M. Pitman is a research fellow at the Miller Center of Public Affairs at the University of Virginia.

Georges-Henri Soutou is a professor of contemporary history at the University of Paris IV—Sorbonne.

Marc Trachtenberg is a professor of political science at the University of California at Los Angeles.

Hubert Zimmermann is an assistant professor at the Chair for International Relations, Ruhr-University, Bochum.